The Political awakening of
Africa.

edited by Rupert Emerson
and Martin Kilson.

THE GLOBAL HISTORY SERIES

Leften Stavrianos, *Northwestern University*
General Editor

This series aims to present history in global perspective, going beyond national or regional limitations, and dealing with overriding trends and forces. The various collections of original materials span the globe, ranging from prehistoric times to the present, and include anthropology, economics, political science, and religion, as well as history.

The editors of this volume, Rupert Emerson and Martin Kilson, have both traveled extensively in Africa and carried on research there. Dr. Emerson received his doctorate from the London School of Economics, and is currently Professor of Government at Harvard University and President of the African Studies Association. He is the author of numerous books and articles, including *From Empire to Nation*. Dr. Kilson, who holds a doctorate from Harvard University, is Lecturer in Government at Harvard, and currently Visiting Professor at the Institute of African Studies, University of Ghana. Dr. Kilson has published extensively in various journals; his most recent book, *Political Change in a West African State*, will be released this fall.

THE POLITICAL AWAKENING

OF AFRICA

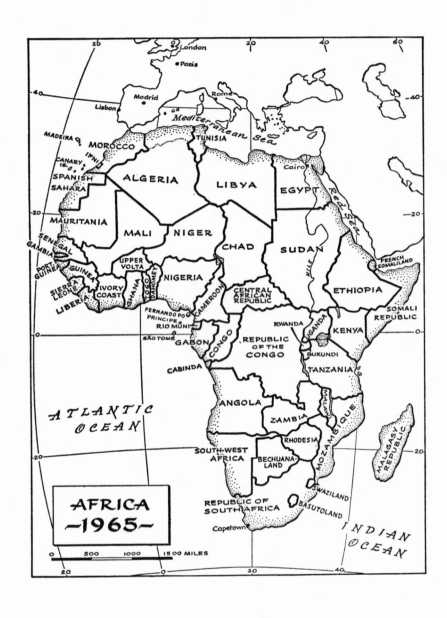

AFRICA
-1965-

THE POLITICAL AWAKENING

OF AFRICA

EDITED BY RUPERT EMERSON
AND MARTIN KILSON

GREENWOOD PRESS, PUBLISHERS
WESTPORT, CONNECTICUT

Library of Congress Cataloging in Publication Data
Main entry under title:

The Political awakening of Africa.

    Reprint. Originally published: Englewood Cliffs,
N.J. : Prentice-Hall, 1965. (The Global history series ;
S-124) (A Spectrum book)
    Bibliography: p.
    1. Africa--Politics and government--1960-   --Ad-
dresses, essays, lectures. I. Emerson, Rupert,
1899-   . II. Kilson, Martin. III. Series: Global
history series ; S-124.
[DT30.5.P64 1981]   320.96   81-4166
ISBN 0-313-23013-7 (lib. bdg.)   AACR2

Reprinted in 1981 by Greenwood Press
A division of Congressional Information Service, Inc.
88 Post Road West, Westport, Connecticut 06881

Printed in the United States of America

10 9 8 7 6 5 4 3 2 1

PREFACE

This book attempts to let the African leaders and intellectuals speak for themselves by limiting the editor's role to the selection of passages to be reproduced, with the addition of introductory notes to identify the author and describe the specific context of what he wrote or spoke. On rare occasions we have taken the liberty of correcting what were obviously typographical errors in the original texts without going through the procedure of adding a clumsy and supercilious "sic." Considerations of space have, of course, made it necessary to cut material which might otherwise have been included, but we have attempted to be scrupulous in making sure that what appears here is a fair and representative sample of what the speaker or author actually intended. Only thus could we convey the rich variety of modern African thought, as well as its continuity over time.

Although the selections which follow have, inevitably, been chosen on somewhat arbitrary grounds, and others might have been reproduced which give different viewpoints, cover other ground, or more fully expound matters which are only hinted at here, we have endeavored, in organizing the book along both topical and historical lines, to embrace as many of the main currents of modern African thought as possible. As a general rule, we have avoided the more obvious and easily available sources, such as books or articles recently published in this country, and have turned instead to materials to which the ordinary reader and student would find it difficult to gain access.

We have seen the African awakening as a revolution which is still under way. We hope that this book conveys an authentic sense of how the Africans themselves have viewed and dealt with the problems and potentialities of the new era into which they are now entering.

We should like to express our gratitude to Laurie Vermilyea and Jonie Reischauer who cheerfully bore the burden of typing the manuscript for this book.

R. E.
M. K.

CONTENTS

THE POLITICAL AWAKENING

OF AFRICA

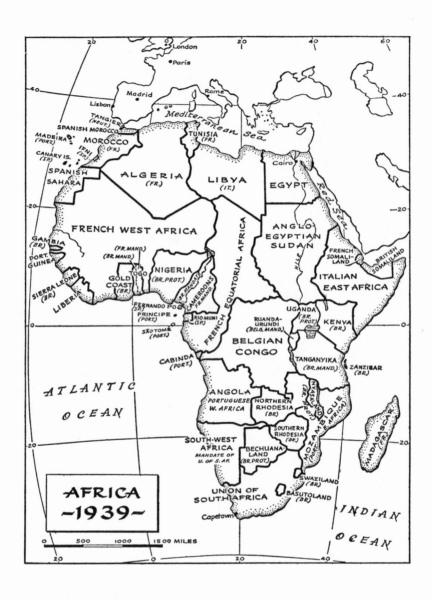

AFRICA
~1939~

INTRODUCTION / THE AWAKENING OF AFRICA

The awakening of Africa?

Which awakening, and when did it happen? What were the forces and circumstances which caused it?

Africa has had many awakenings. The white man may still take it for granted that the only awakening of consequence is that which derived from European contact with Africa, bringing the continent into touch with the "modern" world shaped by the developments of the last centuries in Europe. That is, indeed, the subject dealt with in this book, but it must never be forgotten that this is only the most recent of the awakenings, following others and with more still to come. Undoubtedly it was an event of major importance, both for Africa and for the world at large, and its effects will be felt for many generations to come, no less in Africa than elsewhere in the world. The fabric of African life and thought in all its aspects is undergoing revolutions of various kinds, comparable to those which have swept and are sweeping other countries, but there is at the same time an insistent upsurge of confidence that Africans have an identity of their own which they must cherish and preserve.

However great the significance of the contemporary awakening, the overwhelming trend in recent years has been to press the knowledge of African history backward in time and to see the European encroachment as only one phase in a long and ancient history which exists in its own right. The white man's conceit that African history started when the Europeans "discovered" the continent and began to take it into account has come to be abandoned as an obvious absurdity. As colonialism has come to an end, so have the beliefs which nurtured and justified it. The drive to establish the claim of Africa to have a distinctive history of its own is, in fact, one of the striking and inevitable elements of the awakening of recent times.

The emergence of nationalism has everywhere been accompanied by the search for a history that will lend dignity and validity to a newly asserted demand for a separate existence among the peoples of the world.

1

In the case of Africa this need has been even more keenly felt than elsewhere because of the long cherished assumption that Africa was the dark continent, and that its past consisted only of primitive tribalism until the white man brought light, learning, and civilization. The spread of racist thinking in the nineteenth century, influenced by Darwinian or pseudo-Darwinian conceptions, lent credence to this kind of view. If Africa had no culture worthy of taking its place among the other cultures of mankind, and no history other than that of barbarism and slavery, then it was inevitable that the awakening of this inferior black race be seen only as a growing awareness of what Europe had to offer, and its advance measured only in terms of development along the lines laid down by the white man.

What has been happening in the last years, as the accompaniment of the movement toward independence, is the rediscovery or, if you will, the creation of a potent, if indefinable, essence of Africanism which has given strength and meaning to people who were asserting their right to live their own lives.

This awakening of Africa—in the sense of the adaptation of traditional and indigenous Africa to the pressures of the white man's modernity—has come with a rush, but it started belatedly. The Africans were the last of the great peoples to feel the winds of European change blowing through their countries. The hazards of geography, climate, and health combined to isolate most of the continent from more than casual coastal contact with the Europeans until the latter part of the last century. Even that contact was for long largely limited to the devastating experience of the slave trade, as Arab incursions on the east coast and into eastern Sudan were also primarily slave-raiding expeditions. Both the slave trade and more legitimate commerce were carried on by Europeans through the coastal peoples, who served as middlemen, raiding or trading with the peoples of the interior.

The heart of the continent was revealed to world view only following the great explorations of the nineteenth century, which opened up the hidden recesses of its obscurity and disclosed its vast lakes and the sources and courses of its rivers. The renewed burst of imperialism in the last two or three decades of the nineteenth century—the Berlin Conference of 1884-1885 can be taken as the conventional watershed—was marked by the "scramble for Africa," which for the first time brought Europeans in any number into the interior and into touch with its people. Only in the extreme south of the continent, where the Dutch had stopped on their way to the Indies, and, much later, in Algeria, had white men established themselves other than precariously on the fringes. Europe's penetration into Africa was slow to get into motion compared with European intercourse with the Americas and Asia, but once it was under way virtually the entire continent was in a few years partitioned among the colonial powers. If colonialism took over speedily, the sweep into independence of almost all the African colonies has come even more rapidly in the course of the last decade. The example of freedom for the Asian colonies following close on the heels of World War II set a precedent which Africa was quick to adopt for itself. The four independent African countries which existed in 1950—Ethiopia, Egypt, Liberia, and South Africa—had multiplied to thirty-seven by 1965, with more still to come.

OTHER AFRICAN AWAKENINGS

If the present reading of the anthropological record is sustained, the greatest awakening which the continent has undergone is the birth of man in Africa in his transition from the anthropoid ape. The discoveries and reconstructions of L. S. B. Leakey, Kenya-born British archeologist and anthropologist, and those working with him in East Africa have been of central importance in substantiating the African claim to have been man's starting point.

Beyond this, Negro Africa went through most of the early stages of human and cultural evolution experienced by other areas of the world. According to George Murdock of Yale University, the Neolithic Revolution, entailing the transformation from hunting and fishing to settled agriculture, may have been indigenous to Negro Africa (circa 4500 B.C.), rather than a result of cultural diffusion.[1] If so, Africa would rank with western Asia, South Asia, and Middle America as one of the originators of this basic transformation in agricultural organization and method which constituted a major stride en route to civilization.

Whether it reached the Neolithic through indigenous change or diffusion, much of Negro Africa remained at this stage until modern times, while western Asia, South Asia, East Asia, Middle America, and Europe evolved more technologically elaborate societies. This fact, as will be seen from several of the selections in this volume, has greatly influenced modern African social and political thought, especially the response to the white supremacists' claim that the Negro African was biologically incapable of advancing beyond the Neolithic. No reliable scientific evidence exists for this claim, and, what is more, it is seldom recognized that non-Negro peoples in other areas of major population settlement equally remained in the Neolithic until modern times. This is so for the Indians of North America, the peoples of the island communities in Melanesia and Polynesia, and the indigenous peoples of Australia and New Zealand. The latter did not possess the ingredients of Neolithic culture until modern times.

There is little doubt that stages in the technological evolution of human society, beyond those of the Neolithic Revolution, entered Negro Africa through cultural diffusion. This is true for those crucial ingredients

[1] George P. Murdock, *Africa* (New York: McGraw-Hill Book Company, 1960). For a different view, cf. J. Desmond Clark, "The Spread of Food Production in Sub-Saharan Africa," *The Journal of African History*, Vol. III No. 2 (1962), pp. 219 ff.

of what V. Gordon Childe called the first Urban Revolution—namely, writing, the wheel, harnessing animal motor power, copper and bronze metallurgy, and so on. The Iron Age, too, entered Negro Africa through diffusion, first appearing among the Meroe in the Eastern Sudan some several hundred years before Christ.

The indisputable high point of cultural achievement in Africa was, of course, the extraordinary civilization which Egypt built in the Nile valley, beginning several millennia before Christ and creating one of the peaks of human accomplishment. What is more obscure is the nature of the relationship between ancient Egypt and the Africans to the south of it. Considerable evidence has been gathered together which leaves no doubt that there were many links and inter-connections between the Egyptians and the peoples to the south, but no detailed and acceptable account or estimate of the degree of intercourse and its results is now available. Contemporary African scholars and leaders, seeking to reconstruct the African past, generally tend to take pride in the mark which Egypt left on the world, and to assume that Negro Africa had some share in it, at least as its partial heir and perhaps as a partner in its creation. The less restrained enthusiast plunges in head over heels to proclaim that the Egyptians were in fact black Africans and that the white man has deliberately distorted the historical record in order to conceal the color and race of the makers of Egypt's glory.

Recently, a significant redressing of the balance appears in the breach with the earlier view which held that, since the Africans were a primitive people from whom nothing of consequence could be expected, any evidences of advanced civilizations or cultures in Africa south of the Sahara must be attributed to other peoples. With the passing of the need to justify slavery and colonialism by demonstrating how low in the scale of humanity Africans stood, the more plausible position has become a general acceptance of the fact that archeological remains found within the vast area normally inhabited by the Africans must be assumed to be the product of their ancestors unless there is solid reason to attribute them to some people stemming from remote countries. Thus the Meroitic civilization of the upper Nile, greatly influenced by its Egyptian contacts, is now taken to be that of an African people, as are the impressive stone ruins of Zimbabwe in southern Rhodesia.

The relationship with ancient Egypt, whatever its precise nature, and with such intermediaries as may have plied between the Egyptians and the Africans, is one important element among the influences which have been brought to bear on Africa, but it is only one. There is much evidence of extensive east coast intercourse with China, and the Arabs were also regular sea-faring visitors to that coast. Constant contact has been maintained across the Sahara with the Islamic peoples of North Africa who have strongly influenced the development of West Africa.

Paul Bohannan, perhaps overstressing the degree and significance of African intimacy with other peoples and parts of the world in order to compensate for the past inclination to write the continent off as having been almost wholly isolated, has summed the matter up in the following terms:

> Africa has, in short, been almost at the hub of the meeting of cultures from the Near East, from Europe, from India, and from Indonesia. All have been implanted on African cultures. The myth of African isolation is disappearing before our eyes. . . .[2]

In Africa, as elsewhere in the world, one of the great spurs to an awakening, a setting off on new paths with a new vitality, is the stimulation of contact with other peoples and other cultures. Such contact, which undoubtedly has been one of the regularly recurrent features of the African scene, joins with changes which have taken place autonomously in the continent to dispel the notion that a single and unvarying "traditional" Africa has been in existence since time immemorial. What does to a considerable degree distinguish sub-Saharan Negro Africa from most of the rest of the world is that the African written record is far smaller, where it is available at all, and that the archeological survivals of various kinds are less numerous and frequently more difficult to interpret. In consequence, it is necessary to rely more heavily than elsewhere on the occasional writings of alien chroniclers and travelers, on oral tradition, and on the miscellaneous haul accumulated by the archeologist. Not until European colonialism was well established at the close of the last century could a reasonably full and consecutive written record be found, and even then it tends inevitably to record what the European rather than the African found of moment. It is, of course, also true that in Africa, as elsewhere in the world, European scholars and administrators gathered and made generally available a large amount of anthropological and historical material which might otherwise have been lost.

In the political realm with which this book is primarily concerned, the succession of empires which dominated substantial portions of the western Sudan and West Africa should be acknowledged as so many moments of awakening in Africa. The earliest of these empires flourished before the end of the first millennium of the Christian era, and they continued to rise and decline, replacing each other in prominence, until the European take-over. Two of them, Ghana and Mali have had their names appropriated by new states of the present day to emphasize the continuity with earlier African power and majesty. A more recent development, representing an awakening to Islamic orthodoxy and puritanism similar to that which was taking place in other parts of the Islamic world, was the Fulani *jihad,* or holy war, of the early nineteenth century led by Othman

[2] Paul Bohannan, *Africa and Africans* (Garden City, N.Y.: The Natural History Press, 1964), p. 97.

dan Fodio and culminating in the establishment of Fulani rule in the Hausa states of northern Nigeria. Thomas Hodgkin, in an interesting passage, compares what he calls "the two major empire building movements which marked the beginning and the end of the century—the Fulani and the British," and finds them to have, in the intellectual renaissance deriving from them, as well as in political results, more in common than is usually realized.[3]

Over the centuries states and empires throughout Africa rose and fell, and the combination of internal and external forces brought into being the highly variegated continent with which Europeans began to come into contact from the time of the Portuguese voyages in the fifteenth century—voyages carrying Portugal around the Cape of Good Hope, up the east coast, and to India.

THE PRESENT AWAKENING

The forcing of the imprint of Europe upon Africa in any decisive fashion was, however, long delayed. The arm's-length dealing characteristic of the relationships between Europeans and Africans meant that contact could only rarely achieve any degree of intimacy—except the degrading intimacy of slavery—prior to the last decade or two of the nineteenth century. Even the Portuguese, despite their several centuries of involvement with Africa, penetrated into the interior only casually and occasionally, and such penetration as did take place was largely a product of the slave trade which, it has been said, converted Angola in the seventeenth and eighteenth centuries "into a howling wilderness." [4]

The nineteenth century was one of transition for Africa. The great explorations were under way, missionary activity was markedly expanded, the slave trade was replaced by more legitimate commerce, and the end of the century brought virtually the entire continent under European imperial control. The distinguished African historian, K. Onwuka Dike, now Vice Chancellor of the University of Ibadan, has written of the middle decades of the century as constituting an epoch of change and revolution for West Africa. He has pointed out, however, that the impact on Africa was much less than might have been expected because the chiefs on the seaboard, safeguarding their own power and carrying on a profitable middle-man trade, succeeded for a surprising length of time in barring the European traders from direct access to their hinterland. His summary conclusion is that:

> the buying and selling of commodities is almost always accompanied by the contact of cultures, the exchange of ideas, the mingling of peoples, and has led not infrequently to political complications and wars. Trade with the

[3] Thomas Hodgkin, *Nigerian Perspectives* (London: Oxford University Press, 1960), p. 51.
[4] Roland Oliver and J. D. Fage, *A Short History of Africa* (Baltimore: Penguin Books, Inc., 1962), p. 128.

Arabs, by way of Saharan caravans, brought medieval West Africa into touch with the world of Islam, and with Islam came Arab culture and civilisation. Nothing comparable to this occurred on the coasts of Guinea.[5]

With three or four exceptions of no great magnitude, any extensive contact of cultures and mingling of peoples had to wait until the imperial powers determined that arm's-length coastal commerce was not adequate and that there must be a full colonial take-over, imposed by treaty, trickery, and force. As the century progressed, all the factors which led to the colonial partition of Africa were gathering, but even after 1880 Europe's colonial holdings were for the most part limited to ill-defined coastal strips. Once the powers took the decision to act, the partition was swift and ruthless.

At a few points on the west coast contact was sufficiently intensive prior to the burst of colonialism to allow of at least a tentative start toward the new-style awakening which did not come to full expression until after World War II. Only a relatively small handful of Africans were significantly involved, but they played a highly important role in the spread of European ways and conceptions elsewhere on the west coast and beyond. In this respect two territories—Liberia and Sierra Leone—stand out in a unique way because of their function as stations for the return of freed slaves whose knowledge, both of English and of the shape which the modern world was assuming, separated them from the native peoples among whom they were placed, and enabled them to contribute to the processes of adaptation. Two territories of a somewhat more routinely colonial variety also deserve mention. Senegal, the original inhabitants of whose four communes had the unique distinction of being full French citizens, was an old, established French base of operations utilized in the latter nineteenth century as a jumping-off point for exploration and colonial acquisition in the western Sudan. The Gold Coast played a somewhat similar role for the British and started on the path toward modernization well before neighboring territories.

The advances made in the nineteenth century, as defined in terms of adaptation to the new European civilization, might almost be seen as a prelude to a prelude. As has been said, the full flowering of Africa's awakening did not take place until after World War II, and even the two decades between the great wars were little more than a period of preparation behind the scenes for what was about to come. In the nineteenth century a few striking figures can be singled out, of whom Edward Wilmot Blyden was presumably the most distinguished as statesman and writer; at the same time, the Fanti Confederacy and the Aborigines Rights Protection Society are clear evidence that new political forces were gathering. The first stirrings of a new kind of life and outlook can be discerned here, but not until many years later did Africa

---

[5] K. O. Dike, *Trade and Politics in the Niger Delta, 1830-1885* (Oxford: Clarendon Press, 1956), p. 5.

south of the Sahara produce anyone comparable to Mohammad Ali and his successors in Egypt who openly acknowledged the most advanced countries of Europe as their models.

Both the drastic shock of subjection to alien colonial rule and a longer exposure to European influences of all kinds were necessary before any considerable awakening was possible. The tempo of enforced adaptation to the new civilization which was encroaching upon Africa was less rapid than it might otherwise have been because the imposition of European colonial regimes only rarely brought any rush to exploit and develop. European and American economic interests demonstrated no impatient zeal to establish themselves in Africa, and even at the end of the colonial era much of Africa remained undeveloped. Economic penetration was often slow and hesitant, making a minimal contribution to the well-being and development of the peoples concerned, and in some instances—for example, in Leopold's Congo or in the domains of the big French concessionaire companies—actually holding back progress.

The colonial governments were almost equally slow to do much more than maintain the basic necessities of law and order after the original take-over and after pacification, where necessary, had been completed. It was the general political assumption that the dependencies should pay for themselves and that the imperial power had no more than incidental responsibility for welfare measures of any kind. Education was left almost wholly in the hands of the missionaries, and while the accomplishment in this sphere was of immense importance for the next stages of advancement, the number of Africans who were given schooling remained tiny and grew with tragic slowness. The possession of Western education was almost always the indispensable precondition for taking significant part in the new African world that was coming into being, but no one in authority was prepared to act on the belief that Africans in the mass were entitled to be educated. In this, as in so many other spheres, a real departure from the policy of letting nature take its deliberate course did not come until after the Second World War. An important negative element in this picture was the almost unquestioned assumption that European colonial rule was there to stay for the indefinite future, perhaps to dominate the scene for centuries.

Although it is obviously impossible to sum up the attitudes and reactions of an immense and diverse continent in a single phrase, it is not far from the truth to say that on the whole the Africans, once their original resistance had been overcome, themselves accepted the assumption of the long continuance of colonial overlordship, and even perhaps of its beneficence. With very rare exceptions it was only after 1945, or even later, that the proposition was put forward that colonialism was an evil to be overthrown as speedily as possible. To understand the development of African political outlooks and institutions, we must realize that, by the time African nationalist demands had become widespread, European rulers were already well along the path to a readiness to comply with these demands and to co-operate in the achievement of a generally orderly and peaceful transition. The experience gained in bringing an end to colonial rule in Asia, both through agreement and on the battle-field, was persuasive in clearing Africa's path to independence. Generally it was the territories settled by whites which caused the greatest difficulty, as evidenced by the Algerian war, Kenya's Mau Mau, and the complica-tions in the Rhodesia-Nyasaland Federation, particularly in Southern Rhodesia, leaving aside the appalling problems of South Africa.

Recognizing again that conditions varied from territory to territory, the generalization may be hazarded that, until a fairly late stage in Africa's colonial history, the Africans took calmly the alien regimes which had been thrust upon them, accepting them as remote and incompre-hensible facts which for good or evil formed part of the world in which they lived. Explicit awareness of the colonial situation and mounting protest against it tended to be confined to the small minority educated along European lines, whether at home or abroad. They were not only the people who achieved at least some measure of familiarity with European ideas, techniques, and institutions but also the ones who were likely to find themselves in competition with the white men who had taken over all the commanding positions in the society. For the first generation or two, however, Western education did not normally lead to agitation and organization for independence. The social and political climate gave no encouragement to so radical an approach, and it is by no means implausible to believe that for most of the educated Africans, as for the masses, the fundamentals of the colonial relationship were ac-cepted as a given fact of life which they hardly thought of challenging.

Rather than seeking independence, these early nationalists (or prede-cessors of nationalists) sought acceptance as educated and civilized men by their white superiors. Optimistically seizing on the tenets of Christianity which the missionaries had brought them and on the democratic and egalitarian doctrines which they found in the schools and literature of the West, they politely presented their case for taking a part in the management of the new order which was being constructed in their own countries. Until they discovered that their polite moderation yielded few fruits their avowed political aspirations were temperate and mild. A single example chosen from the many which might be cited will perhaps give the flavor of those intermediate times. In his inaugural address delivered during the British West African Conference at Accra on March 11, 1920, Casely Hayford, the prominent Gold Coast leader, quoted with approval the comments of one of his friends who had been an original promoter of the Conference:

> This Conference is not founded as an anti-government movement but for the purpose of helping the Government in the work of civilisation that they are doing in our midst; sometimes they may make mistakes, but this must be

pointed out in a loyal and constitutional manner, knowing that after all we are all human beings and that the Government is working for our good, and we must do all we can to help them and let them know our minds, and that our intentions and aspirations are loyal and good.[6]

Casely Hayford himself, who regularly proclaimed the need to act constitutionally, testified to his attachment to the Empire in the following terms in a Legislative Council speech three years later:

Now one word more as to what happens to be the feeling not only of this country, but of all British West Africa, and that is that we feel that our loyalty and co-operation with His Majesty's Government is no mere matter of sentiment; for we feel and realise that our interests as a people are identical with those of the Empire, and we mean, as in the past, in the present and in the future, to stand by the Empire through thick and thin in every circumstance.[7]

The different colonial regimes contributed in different fashions to the African awakening and provided different kinds of outlets, where they provided any at all, for the new energies and ambitions which were being generated. In the large, the British and the French moved substantially further and faster than the Belgians, Portuguese, and Spanish, but all were slow in getting into action on any large-scale program of education, training, and experience for self-government and eventual independence.

Both the British and the French increasingly made provision for, or at least tolerated, the spread of Western education among the peoples for whom they were responsible and allowed a limited few to move on to higher education in the metropolitan center or elsewhere. The result was that a new middle class of Western educated men—teachers, journalists, professional men of various kinds—came into being, often drawn from the traditional chiefly families, which moved speedily toward political self-assertion. A few were taken into the colonial civil service and, in a slow and hesitant fashion, appointive and then elective councils were provided to give the Africans an opportunity to express their political grievances and desires. In general, save in Kenya and the Rhodesias where the white settlers were accorded privileged positions, the British gave somewhat larger scope to their African subjects in these respects than did the French, but neither made any drastic moves in the direction of self-government until after 1945. A characteristic difference between the two was that the British tended to assume that the proper destiny for the African was to move forward in his own country, building on his traditional foundations, whereas the French were always tempted to look to an ultimate indivisible Greater France in which all the diverse

[6] Magnus J. Sampson, *West African Leadership: Public Speeches delivered by The Honourable J. E. Casely Hayford, M.B.E., M.L.C.* (Ilfracome, N. Devon: Arthur H. Stockwell, Limited, n.d.), p. 59.
[7] *Ibid.*, p. 79.

peoples would have been assimilated to the superior French culture. The British provided local political institutions in which the Africans were represented while the French opened their governing bodies in Paris to African participation, although on a proportionately much more restricted basis than for white Frenchmen. It is probably also true that the British practised a substantially larger measure of racial discrimination, but there is much evidence that French Africa was very well aware of the gap which separated the white man from the black.

No other country possessing African dependencies made correspondingly effective moves to start its subjects on the path to management of their own affairs. The Belgian Congo presented a unique mixture of approaches, which might well have produced admirable results in another thirty or forty years, had the Belgians held to the course which they professed to have adopted. As it was, they carried through an impressive, if often unbalanced, economic development which was supplemented by paternalistic social welfare measures and by a broad spread of education at the primary level, the opening up of what promised to be an extensive system of secondary education, and the first beginnings of higher education. Working on the theory that access to the universities should be denied until mass education was well under way and the secondary schools were turning out a substantial middle class, the Belgians had provided almost nothing in the way of an upper elite which was trained to take charge of affairs when independence came along. Furthermore, the control of the government was centralized in Brussels and in the colonial administration, with neither the private Belgians in the Congo nor the Congolese given any access to power. Only in the last couple of years before the sudden swing to independence was provision made for even the most limited African elective participation at the lower governmental levels. Belgium looked to a postponement of African awakening for decades. In consequence the Congo was shockingly unprepared for the freedom which it so unexpectedly acquired.

Despite high-flown theories and pretensions, neither Spaniards nor Portuguese contributed much to the awakening. The Portuguese clung to the doctrine of assimilation even more rigorously than the French, firmly asserting that Portugal possessed no dependencies and that all the territories in Africa and elsewhere were integral parts of a single country. If Portugal drew racial lines less sharply than did the other colonial powers, she also did less in the way of economic development, education, and social welfare, and was prepared to extend virtually nothing by way of self-governing institutions.

The employment of Africans abroad as laborers or in military service during the First World War opened up some further contact with the outside world, and stimulated such economic development as was calculated to meet wartime shortages; but the colonial regimes held Africa firmly in their grip during the interwar decades. Until after the Second World War the initiative and the power to make decisions still rested with the colonial powers and, locally, with the colonial administrators. The peace imposed by colonialism gave at least the surface appearance of an almost unbroken calm, which was utilized, among other things, to deepen the channels of trade and intercourse between each dependency and its imperial center. The colonial system, however, provided a minimum of contact and communication between even neighboring African territories and not much more with the rest of the world.

The parochial confinement of each African territory within its own boundaries, and the limitation of access to ruling power made it inevitable that, as the political awakening began, interest was concentrated on wresting control of the particular territory from the imperial center. Although it was rarely if ever the case that the people of these territories had overcome their tribal diversity to the point of actually becoming consolidated nations, the politically active forces in each of the territories came to assume the title of a nationalist movement. The focus of such movements was, however, by no means always clear. Thus British West Africa, for example, for some time saw itself as having a single political identity, which only gradually broke down into its component parts, and Nigeria's continued unity could at no point be taken for granted. Among the French territories, the existence of the two big federations of West and Equatorial Africa made it uncertain at least until 1957 whether they or the dozen territories composing them constituted the "nations" which would take over the future.

A further element of uncertainty, big with portents for the future, derived from the fact that the conception of pan-Africanism was beginning to make an appearance, particularly through the activities of people of African descent on the other side of the Atlantic. For the African at home, restricted to his tribe or his territory, it was evidently a difficult feat to conceive of the continent, or of the African people, as a whole. For those of African descent in the Americas, however, it was more natural than not, having lost the knowledge of their place of origin in Africa, to see the black race confronting the white, and continental Africa, or at least Africa south of the Sahara, as a single entity. At the time of the Versailles Peace Conference there was some agitation on behalf of Africa, and the first of a series of Pan-African conferences was held in Paris. Such very different figures as W. E. B. Dubois and Marcus Garvey contributed to the sense that the entire mass of continental Africa had a proper political and cultural destiny of its own of which not only Africans but the world at large must take cognizance. As increasing numbers of African students came to carry on their higher education abroad, they likewise came to be imbued with the sense that Africa as a whole had a distinctive identity.

THE FULL AWAKENING

If the 1920s and '30s were the seedbed, and World War II with its immediate aftermath a period of forced growth, then the postwar years brought the full flowering of Africa's independent political life; from 1956 to 1960 came the crucial years of harvest, during which more than twenty African states achieved their sovereign independence and membership in the United Nations. In the two interwar decades there was a very significant increase in education, particularly in the numbers from the French and British territories educated in Europe and America. Despite the setback of the depression, a continued economic expansion brought new social elements into existence, and speeded the development of the African communities.

Although Morocco, Tunisia, and the Sudan had all come to independence by the mid-fifties, it was not until the transformation of the Gold Coast into independent Ghana in 1957 that the tidal wave of African freedom from colonialism really began to sweep over the continent. This political awakening continues to the present day, as the masses are gradually weaned from illiteracy and come to have political aspirations of their own. The African states have only just begun the evolution of the political style and institutions fitted to their history, their needs, and their desires. Both internally and in their relations with each other and with the rest of the world, the African states are engaged in the process of finding their own footing and working out a balance of forces suitable to their new condition.

The effects of World War II on Africa may be compared with the effects of World War I on India. In each instance the stage of social and political development fell just short of the point where the war would produce any immediate revolutionary consequences, except a concealed revolution whose overt expression would be delayed for some time. Not until a decade after the war in Africa did the full effects of the war become inescapably evident, but the inner changes which it stimulated were immense. The denunciations of racialism and the declarations of Allied leaders as to the virtues of freedom and the right of peoples to a freely chosen self-government could not help but be turned by the African nationalists to their own purposes. Presumably of even greater importance were the contacts with Western cultures established by African troops and civilians abroad, and by the presence in several African countries of American and other foreign armed forces. Furthermore, the drive to increase production of a number of products for Allied or African consumption also stimulated change and development.

As a result of wartime pressures as well as of changes in outlook at home, both Britain and France before the end of the war moved toward changed colonial policies. For the French the event which signaled the start of a new era was the convening early in 1944 by de Gaulle's provisional government of a conference in Brazzaville to lay out the policies to be followed by France. Although the conception of self-government for the French dependencies, even in the distant future, was outlawed, an impressive start was made toward an elimination of major abuses of the past and the attainment of a closer and more nearly equal association of the territories and their people with France. The British on their side accepted a larger measure of responsibility for the welfare and development of the peoples for whom they were responsible, and moved cautiously in the direction of greater participation by the people of the dependencies in their own government.

What was proposed and undertaken by both of these major imperial powers contained no suggestion at the outset that independence for African colonies could be discerned even on the horizon, but forces were released which moved irrevocably toward ending the colonial relationship. As soon as the British adopted the practice of including elected African members in the Legislative Council of a particular territory and, more definitively, as soon as the Africans constituted a majority, it became virtually impossible to check the demand for full self-government and independence, no matter what safeguards were written into the series of constitutions which swiftly succeeded each other in the march toward a greater relaxation and an ultimate abandonment of colonial control. The example of British Guiana demonstrates the possibility of pulling back—a possibility which can be realized only in the rarest of circumstances and only with much heart-searching.

A combination of forces was at work which soon proved irresistible. In the imperial centers several factors were involved, of which one of the more important was unquestionably the weariness, weakness, and exhaustion brought by two world wars in quick succession. But this was by no means the only cause of the change. At least since the turn of the century there had been growing opposition at home to colonialism and all its works. Pacifists, liberals, socialists, and others grew increasingly hostile to the old systems, and, whatever their equivocations may have been when they were in office, their ideas and programs looked to a new order of free relationships. The changing balance of forces and outlooks at home inevitably reflected itself in due course in the colonial sphere.

In Africa the corresponding forces were coming to increased prominence. However inadequate the colonial programs of education and development, their net result produced a substantial body of people no longer content to tolerate the existing colonial situation nor modestly to suggest that they might be accorded some participation in colonial political management. A new militancy was growing in several of the African dependencies, and its leaders were thrusting themselves ahead. Among them were such significant personalities as Jomo Kenyatta of

Kenya, Nnamdi Azikiwe of Nigeria, Kwame Nkrumah of Ghana, and, later, Dr. Hastings Kamuzu Banda of Malawi, all of whom returned from education abroad—the last three from American universities. Comparable figures in the French sphere were such men as Leopold Sedar Senghor of Senegal and Félix Houphouet-Boigny of the Ivory Coast. As the postwar years advanced, the growth of the labor movement opened up a new channel for access to political power and brought forward such men as Tom Mboya of Kenya and Sékou Touré of Guinea. Headline leaders such as these, no longer moderate in pressing their claims to take over from the colonial powers, were supplemented by a second and third rank of leadership who were usually products of local schools, drawn from the uprooted who had moved into the modern economy in agriculture, mining, or government employment, and from the unceasing tide which flooded the urban centers. Here were the top nationalists who laid out the plan of campaign, founded and ran the new political parties, and often worked through an unrestrainedly exuberant African press. Behind them stood the junior officers who carried the nationalist movement to the people, and then the rank and file drawn from those elements of the general populace which gave active support to the drive against colonialism.

These forces in the imperial centers and in the dependencies themselves derived important support from what was going on in the rest of the world.

First, the Russian Revolution had brought into being a power committed to the cause of anti-colonialism and eager, wherever possible, to annoy and undermine the imperialists whom it saw as its most implacable enemies. Victory in the Second World War established the U.S.S.R. as one of the two superpowers, and the addition of China to the revolutionary ranks in 1950 weighted the world balance further against colonialism.

Second, the United Nations was, at its inception, endowed with a far larger interest in the problems of colonialism than had been its predecessor, the League of Nations. Through the Mandate System the League had exercised a mild supervision over a small corner of the world's colonial domains, whereas the UN's Trusteeship System represented a marked tightening of international supervision over some of the same territories. A more significant contribution of the UN was its general concern with colonialism which found fullest expression in the resolution unanimously adopted by the General Assembly in 1960 (although with nine abstentions, including the United States, United Kingdom, and France), denouncing colonialism as contrary to the Charter and to fundamental human rights, and asserting the right of all peoples to self-determination. The immediate membership of the constantly multiplying African states in the UN gave them an international forum in which, through collaboration with Asian and other countries, they could largely dictate the nature and pace of the attack upon colonialism and press for aid in development.

Third, the end of colonialism in Asia brought independence to the many hundreds of millions of people in India, Pakistan, Indonesia, Indochina, the Philippines, and other dependencies. The attack upon colonialism, to which the United States also contributed, came to be so all-embracing that, once cracks began to appear in the solid colonial mass of Africa, the entire structure crumbled away with amazing speed.

It would be neither possible nor in order to attempt to recount here the detailed and often intricate story of the transition to independence of the bulk of the African colonies, of their subsequent successes and set-backs, of the movement toward pan-Africanism in its several guises, and of the recalcitrance of Portugal in refusing to concede the end of the colonial era. Many of these matters, as they were seen through African eyes, are dealt with in the selections which make up the heart of this book.

In conclusion, one single theme seems worth developing because of its unique and special relevance to the African scene. Paul Bohannan has written that when the duality of viewpoint inherent in colonialism—the traditional and the colonially imported—breaks down and the absentee sovereign is rejected, a desperate search for identity remains.[8] One of the most significant features of the heritage of colonialism in Africa is that the boundary lines which the imperial powers drew on the map of the continent have, with only insignificant exceptions, survived as the frontiers of the new states and, at least potentially, of the nations which are being shaped within them; but these boundaries are very recent creations, superimposed upon and cutting across the traditional ethnic alignment of Africans in their clans, tribes, and indigenous empires. To this confrontation of the indigenous-traditional and the alien-new must be added the very sizable gap which has grown up between the peoples brought into the modern world under differing colonial systems—particularly the contrast between those who were under the French and those who were under the British. In this connection, it is a striking point of difference that, whereas it was natural for the inhabitants of British dependencies to assume that their proper and destined goal was a full independence, presumably but not necessarily within the Commonwealth, it was, until the end of the 1950s, the general presumption among the Africans in French territories that their goal was equality with Frenchmen and a position of equality with France in a French community of some sort. Thus the demand for independence was a very late development in French Africa, coming to wide acceptance only after Sékou Touré led Guinea to a "No" vote in the de Gaulle referendum of 1958. It may be that the very close ties which most of the ex-French territories

[8] Bohannan, *op. cit.*, p. 30.

have maintained with France—denounced by others as a deplorable demonstration of neo-colonialism—are to be traced in part to this earlier assumption that freedom was to be sought not in Nkrumah's demand for independence but in Houphouet-Boigny's desire for continued intimacy with France.

The search for identity has led to the tribe, to the colonially defined state, and in some part to the former colonial power. It has led also to federations and unions of African states on some partial basis, of which a number have been tried out and still others proposed; but beyond these it led also to a Pan-African union of all the peoples of the continent.

Of such things as these was the African awakening composed.

I / REACTIONS TO COLONIALISM: SELF-IDENTITY IN AFRICAN DEVELOPMENT

INTRODUCTION

The selections in Part I of this volume indicate the variety of reactions by representatives of the African intelligentsia to colonialism as a social and cultural system. It is not always properly recognized that colonialism was something more than a system of political and economic control. It was no less than a system of social and cultural subordination of Africans to the standards of Europe and the prejudices of the colonial power. As such it represented, to one degree or another, a form of denial of African social and cultural systems.

Insofar as this denial was intimately associated with European theories or assumptions, often supported by the Christian church, regarding the biological or mental inferiority of Negroid, as compared to Caucasoid, peoples, it was natural, once a self-conscious African reaction to colonialism occurred, that it emphasize the distinctive features of African life and culture, as well as the resentment against the discrimination inherent in colonialism. As long as the myth of the human and cultural inferiority of Negro Africa remained unquestioned, the African could never reach that status of self-identity and self-esteem required for the protracted nationalist attack against colonial subordination. In this respect, the African response to colonialism differed from that in the Middle East and in Asia. European colonial domination of these areas was less likely to be rationalized in terms of the biological or mental inferiority of Arabs, Indians or other Asians. Indeed, the advanced civilizations created in these areas before the dawn of Christianity were often the envy of Europeans, although any colonialism tended to need the psychological justification of a sense of superiority.

The African reaction to colonialism is unique in its particularly keen involvement with a rectification, as it were, of the Negro's position as a member of the human race which was undermined by the dogmas of white supremacy associated with the slave trade and European colonialism. This concern, moreover, was not restricted merely to the initial reactions to colonialism of the first generation of Western educated Africans, but has in fact become more vehement and vocal as the years have gone by. Finally, this concern for the Negro's standing among men embraced all Negro peoples wherever they resided, and manifested itself not only in Africa but also in the New World areas of Negro settlement: North America, the island communities of the Caribbean (especially the British and French West Indies), and South America (especially Brazil).

Kwame Nkrumah's speech to the First International Congress of Africanists fully reflects this issue. The Congress, held at the University of Ghana in December, 1962, marked a major turning point in the nature of the study of African history and societies. Nkrumah's address summarized the meaning of this Congress in terms of the impact it would have in clearing African studies of the damage done by European ideas of Negro inferiority.

The selections from the writings of Dr. Edward Wilmot Blyden and from J. E. Casely Hayford represent the thought on this issue of the first generation of the African intelligentsia. As will be seen, these writings are of more than historical interest. Both Blyden and Casely Hayford had formulated the concept of "African Personality," which in recent times has been elaborated by a number of English-speaking African intellectuals, as well as by French-speaking Africans (who have given it a special twist) designating it by the term "Négritude" or "Negroness." (James Edward Bruce, an American Negro, who was known personally to Blyden and Casely Hayford, first used the term.[1])

The selection from Félix Éboué is unique for several reasons. Éboué was a Negro of French West Indian origin and thus not strictly African. But, as Professor George Shepperson of Edinburgh University has rightly pointed out, a major part of the ideas constituting modern African thought had its beginnings among persons of African descent in the "diaspora"—in the outer fringes of the Negro world among Negro Americans and Negro West Indians (British and French), where contact with the modern world was both more intensive and extensive.[2] Thus,

[1] George Shepperson, "Notes on Negro American Influences on the Emergence of African Nationalism," The Journal of African History, Vol. I, No. 2 (1960), pp. 309-310.

[2] Shepperson, op. cit., pp. 304 ff. For instance, James Edward Bruce, a Negro American newspaper owner and journalist in New York, not only originated the notion of "African Personality" but also offered one of the first formulations of the French African variant of this notion known as "Négritude." Responding to a speech by the Nigerian Majola Agbedi in 1902 in which Agbedi celebrated the founding of the first Independent African Christian Church, Bruce remarked on his own sense of his blackness as follows: "I am a negro and all negro. I am black all over, and proud of my beautiful black skin. . . ." (Quoted in Shepperson, op. cit., p. 310.) Some thirty years later the French West Indian poet, Aimé Césaire, coined the term "Négritude" and described its essence in the same terms—indeed the same words—used by Bruce. Césaire, a New World Negro himself, introduced this concept into the mainstream of French African

much of modern thought among New World Negroes was equally the modern thought of Negro Africans. There prevailed throughout the nineteenth and twentieth centuries a rich variety of contacts (religious, educational, economic, and political) between Africans and New World Negro intellectuals which enabled the ideas of the latter to be communicated to and take root among the former.

Félix Éboué secured a keen knowledge of and close affinity with African societies through the numerous positions which he held as a colonial administrator in French Equatorial Africa. The selection from his writings included in this volume is an official report to the French Government on the changes required to make French administration a more African-centered process, in part through an adoption and adaptation of the principles of indirect rule developed by British colonial authorities. Though written in the form of a colonial administrator's report, Éboué's *Circular* represents something more than this. It reflects his own vantage point as a person of African descent who is concerned with the cultural and personal self-identity of Africans and with preserving what is unique and universally valuable in this identity against French cultural encroachment. In other words, though the form of Éboué's report is that of a colonial administrator, the content is akin to that of the literary intellectuals among French-speaking Negroes of the period, like Aimé Césaire of Martinique and Léopold Senghor of Senegal, who were seeking to retrieve self-identity of Negro Africans through the concept of "Négritude."

Another variant of the French-speaking African response to colonialism is reflected in the selection from Félix Houphouet-Boigny. Its form is not that of the aggressive, militantly self-conscious black intellectual, casting aside the European colonial experience with one stroke as a useless, exploitative relationship, thoroughly destructive of everything African. It is rather more moderate in form, viewing the French colonial experience as basically regenerative and constructive, and in large measure accepting, as did so many of the rising French-speaking African élite, the goal of equal assimilation into a single larger France. In this he was following in the tradition of Blaise Diagne, African deputy from Senegal in the French National Assembly, who in 1922 wrote to Marcus Garvey, leader of a "Back to Africa" movement and self-proclaimed Provisional President of an African Republic, repudiating Garvey's claim to represent the Africans:

> We French natives wish to remain French, since France has given us every liberty and since she has unreservedly accepted us upon the same basis as

---

intellectual thought. But even before Césaire gave Négritude its literary expression, Negro American writers at the end of World War I had already done so, and it is likely that Césaire was aware of their work. The writings of Claude McKay, Countee Cullen, Langston Hughes, Jean Toomer, Sterling Brown, and others, during the 1920s and 1930s contain sophisticated formulations of what Césaire termed "Négritude." See, e.g., Claude McKay's novel, *Banjo* (New York, 1929).

her own European children. None of us aspires to see French Africa delivered exclusively to the Africans as is demanded, though without any authority, by the American negroes, at the head of whom you have placed yourself.

No propaganda, no influence of the blacks or of the whites will take from us the pure sentiment that France alone is capable of working generously for the advancement of the black race.[3]

An essentially conservative practical thinker and political leader eschewing intellectual formulations and philosophical categories, Houphouet-Boigny was concerned that the full network of modern life be taken into account in shaping the African response to colonialism. For him, French colonialism must be judged in this context, for the Africans, being numerical majorities in their respective countries, could take for granted their ability to "Africanize" modernity once they secured it in all its facets.

The selections contained in this Part present the reaction to colonialism of African intellectuals and political leaders. Much of what they had to say is summed up in the simple and moving words of Charles Domingo, an African Seventh Day Baptist, who wrote in Nyasaland in 1911 that

> There is too much failure among all Europeans in Nyasaland. The three combined bodies, Missionaries, Government and Companies, or gainers of money—do form the same rule to look upon the native with mockery eyes. It sometimes startles us to see that the three combined bodies are from Europe, and along with them there is a title *"CHRISTENDOM."* And to compare or make a comparison between the *MASTER* of the title and his servants it pushes any African away from believing the Master of the title. If we had power enough to communicate ourselves to Europe we would advise them not to call themselves "Christendom" but "Europeandom." Therefore the life of the three combined bodies is altogether too cheaty, too thefty, too mockery. Instead of "Give" they say "Take away from." From 6 A.M. to 5 or 6 P.M. there is too much breakage of God's pure law as seen in James Epistle, v.4.[4]

[3] Letter, July 3, 1922, from Blaise Diagne to Marcus Garvey in Raymond Leslie Buell, *The Native Problem in Africa* (New York: The Macmillan Company, 1928), Vol. II, p. 81.

[4] Pamphlet, September 21, 1911 (in Seventh Day Baptist Historical Society), "To the Pastors and Evangelists," in George Shepperson and Thomas Price, *Independent African* (Edinburgh: The University Press, 1958), pp. 163-4. The reference to "James Epistle" should properly be to Chapter 4.

1 / AFRICAN HISTORY THROUGH AFRICAN EYES / KWAME NKRUMAH

Distinguished Scholars, it is an honour and privilege for me to welcome you to Ghana and to this First Africanist Conference. Your meeting here,

From Address by President Kwame Nkrumah to the First International Congress of Africanists held at the University of Ghana, Legon, on December 12th, 1962, and published as *Africa's Glorious Past* (Accra: Government Printing Department, 1962).

within the ramparts of an African university, is a reflection of Africa's recovery and re-awakening. It is also a recognition of the new spirit which now animates the people of this great continent. It is even edifying that this Congress is taking place on African soil. I know that you who have gathered here represent various fields and branches of learning; in fact I see familiar faces of professors of universities and academies. What has impelled you, Distinguished Scholars, to gather here at such a time as this? You are here and are united by the fact that you want to find out the truth about Africa and, when you have found out, to proclaim it to the world.

Scholarly and academic interest in Africa is not a new venture. The desire to know more about Africa has been expressed from the very earliest times, because Africa has been the question-mark of history. To a Roman pro-consul: *Semper aliquid novi ex Africa.*

From the imaginings of the ancient geographers, an inaccurate and distorted picture of Africa often emerged. South of the Atlas ranges, a sandy desert was believed to extend indefinitely, with here and there a providential oasis, a rivulet, which, nibbling and corroding its way through the sandy wastes, dripped into the sea. Even so, the ancients had some genuine knowledge of the African Continent, for they had a scientific curiosity about it. Thus Eratosthenes and Aristotle knew that the cranes migrated as far as the lakes where the Nile had its source. And both of them thought that it was there that the pygmies dwelt. Among the travellers of the ancient world who tried to explore Africa, we may recall men like Strabo and Hanno of Carthage.

After these early travels, foreign knowledge of Africa became static until a new impetus was given to it by the Arabs and the Chinese.

The Arabs and the Chinese discovered and chronicled a succession of powerful African kingdoms. One of these kingdoms was that of Ghana, the pomp of whose court was the admiration of that age—and also of ours. It bred and developed within its borders the instruments of civilisation and art; its palaces were of solid architectural construction, complete with glass windows, murals and sculpture, and the thrones within the palaces were bedecked with gold. There were other kingdoms, such as those of Shonghay, Sala, Berissa, the renowned empires of Bornu, Wangara, Melli. The historians tell us that these empires and kingdoms were maintained with remarkable efficiency and administrative competence. Their splendour was proverbial in mediaeval times.

The Chinese, too, during the T'ang dynasty (AD 618-907), published their earliest major records of Africa. In the 18th century, scholarship connected Egypt with China; but Chinese acquaintance with Africa was not confined to Egypt only. They had detailed knowledge of Somaliland, Madagascar and Zanzibar and made extensive visits to other parts of Africa.

The European exploration of Africa reached its height in the 19th century. What is unfortunate, however, is the fact that much of the discovery was given a subjective instead of an objective interpretation. In the regeneration of learning which is taking place in our universities and in other institutions of higher learning, we are treated as subjects and not objects. They forget that we are a historic people responsible for our unique forms of language, culture and society. It is therefore proper and fitting that a Congress of Africanists should take place in Africa and that the concept of Africanism should devolve from and be animated by that Congress.

Between ancient times and the 16th century, some European scholars forgot what their predecessors in African Studies had known. This amnesia, this regrettable loss of interest in the power of the African mind, deepened with growth of interest in the economic exploitation of Africa. It is no wonder that the Portuguese were erroneously credited with having erected the stone fortress of Mashonaland which, even when Barbossa, cousin of Magellan, first visited them, were ruins of long standing.

I have said that the pursuit of African Studies is not a new experience. But the motives which have led various scholars to undertake these studies have been diverse.

We can distinguish first a true scientific curiosity. Most of the Persian, Greek and Roman travellers exhibited this motive. Even when, as in the case of the Romans, they had a primary military purpose, they still tried and often succeeded in preserving some sense of objectivity.

Arab explorers were also often unbiassed in their accounts of Africa, and indeed we are grateful to them for what they wrote concerning our past.

By the time the early European writings on Africa got under way, a new motive had begun to inform African Studies. Those early European works exchanged the scientific motive for one that was purely economic. There was the unbalanced trade in ivory and gold, and there was the illegitimate trafficking in men for which these writings needed to find some sort of excuse.

The point I wish to make at this stage is that much of European and American writing on Africa was at that time apologetic. It was devoted to an attempt to justify slavery and the continued exploitation of African labour and resources. African Studies in Europe and America were thus at their lowest ebb scientifically.

With the abolition of the slave trade, African Studies could no longer be inspired by the economic motive. The experts in African Studies therefore changed the content and direction of their writings; they began to give accounts of African society which were used to justify colonialism as a duty of civilisation. Even the most flattering of these writings fell short of objectivity and truth. This explains, I believe, the popularity and success of anthropology as the main segment of African Studies.

The stage was then set for the economic and political subjugation of Africa. Africa, therefore, was unable to look forward or backward. The central myth in the mythology surrounding Africa is that of the denial that we are a historical people. It is said that whereas other continents have shaped history and determined its course, Africa has stood still, held down by inertia. Africa, it is said, entered history only as a result of European contact. Its history, therefore, is widely felt to be an extension of European history. Hegel's authority has lent to this a historical hypothesis concerning Africa. And apologists of colonialism and imperialism lost little time in seizing upon it and writing wildly about it to their hearts' content.

To those who say that there is no documentary source for that period of African history which pre-dates the European contact, modern research has a crushing answer. We know that we were not without a tradition of historiography, and, that this is so, is now the verdict of true Africanists. African historians, by the end of the 15th century, had a tradition of recorded history, and certainly by the time when Mohamud al-Kati wrote Ta'rikh al'Fattash. This tradition was incidentally much, much wider than that of the Timbuktu school of historians, and our own Institute of African Studies here at this University, is bringing to light several chronicles relating to the history of Northern Ghana. . . .

But our historical records do not consist alone in the facts which we committed [to] the Arabic script. Every society has methods of preserving facts about its past. And where a society has no literate traditions, it devises rigorous methods of oral recording. Scholars who have studied this phenomenon know this well. Historical recording in Africa therefore rightly comprises the documents in Arabic and African languages on the one hand, and, on the other, the well-preserved and authentic records of oral tradition. Our inheritance of oral literature, of epic and lyric poetry of stories and legends, praise songs and the chronicles of states, Kings and dynasties preserved by palace officials, is of intrinsic interest and merit, as it is of historical importance.

The history of a nation is, unfortunately, too easily written as the history of its dominant class. If the history of a nation, of a people, cannot be found in the history of a class, how much less can the history of a continent be found in what is not even a part of it—Europe. And yet, this is precisely what many a European historian has done in the past. The history of Africa has with them been European centred. Africa was only the space in which Europe swelled up. The African past was ignored and dismissed in these tendentious works as not contributing to, or affecting the European expansion and presence in Africa.

If Africa's history is interpreted in terms of the interests of European merchandise and capital, missionaries and administrators, it is no wonder that African nationalism is regarded as a perversion and colonialism as a virtue. . . .

In East Africa, in the Sudan, in Egypt, in Nigeria, here in Ghana and elsewhere, the earth is being dug up apace—this time not for gold or diamonds only, or for bauxite and other mineral riches, but also for its rich information about our past, its testimony to our achievements and its refutation of the sombre prophets of African History. Valuable pieces have already been unearthed, including evidence of the origin of man in Africa.

We have made our contribution to the fund of human knowledge by extending the frontiers of art, culture and spiritual values.

Democracy, for instance, has always been for us not a matter of technique, but more important than technique—a matter of socialist goals and aims. It was, however, not only our socialist aims that were democratically inspired, but also the methods of pursuit were socialist.

If we have lost touch with what our forefathers discovered and knew, this has been due to the system of education to which we were introduced. This system of education prepared us for a subservient role to Europe and things European. It was directed at estranging us from our own cultures in order the more effectively to serve a new and alien interest.

In rediscovering and revitalising our cultural and spiritual heritage and values, African Studies must help to redirect this new endeavour. The education system which we devise to-day must equip us with the resources of a personality and a force strong enough to meet the intensities of the African presence and situation. . . .

2 / AFRICA'S SERVICE TO THE WORLD / EDWARD WILMOT BLYDEN

It is painful in America to see the efforts which are made by Negroes to secure outward conformity to the appearance of the dominant race.

This is by no means surprising; but what is surprising is that, under the circumstances, any Negro has retained a particle of self-respect. Now in Africa, where the colour of the majority is black, the fashion in personal matters is naturally suggested by the personal characteristics of the race, and we are free from the necessity of submitting to the use of "incongruous feathers awkwardly stuck on." Still, we are held in bondage by our indiscriminate and injudicious use of a foreign literature; and we strive to advance by the methods of a foreign race. In this effort we struggle with the odds against us. We fight at the disadvantage which David would have experienced in Saul's armour. The African must ad-

From Addresses by Dr. Edward W. Blyden to the American Colonization Society in 1880 and to the University of Liberia in 1881. Edward W. Blyden, *Christianity, Islam and the Negro Race* (London: W. B. Wittingham and Co., 1887), pp. 89-90, 139-143.

vance by methods of his own. He must possess a power distinct from that of the European. It has been proved that he knows how to take advantage of European culture, and that he can be benefited by it. This proof was perhaps necessary, but it is not sufficient. We must show that we are able to go alone, to carve out our own way. We must not be satisfied that, in this nation, European influence shapes our polity, makes our laws, rules in our tribunals, and impregnates our social atmosphere. We must not suppose that the Anglo-Saxon methods are final, that there is nothing for us to find out for our own guidance, and that we have nothing to teach the world. There is inspiration for us also. We must study our brethren in the interior, who know better than we do the laws of growth for the race. We see among them the rudiments of that which, with fair play and opportunity, will develop into important and effective agencies for our work. We look too much to foreigners, and are dazzled almost to blindness by their exploits—so as to fancy that they have exhausted the possibilities of humanity.

Men are now running to and fro, and knowledge of Africa is increasing. The downfall of Negro slavery in this country was sudden. The most sanguine philanthropists, thirty years ago, did not dream of so sudden a collapse of that hoary institution. And more has been learned of Africa in the seventeen years since slavery has been abolished, than was ever known during all the previous period of modern civilisation, or perhaps, of the world's history. And now, every possible interest that can give impulse to human activity is aroused in connection with that land; and the current which is moving the civilised world thitherward, gains every day in force, in magnitude and in importance. The man of science is interested on account of the wonderful things that must be concealed in that vast continent. The statesman and politician is interested in the possibilities of new states yet to be founded in the march of civilisation. The merchant is interested in the new and promising outlets for trade. The philanthropist is interested in the opening of a career of progress, of usefulness, and of happiness before the millions of that country.

Another indication of the suddenness of Africa's regeneration is to be found in the restlessness of her descendants in this country. There are thousands of Negroes, in comfortable circumstances here, who are yet yearning after the land of their fathers; who are anxious, not so much to be relieved from present pressure, as to obtain an expansive field for their energies; who feel the need not only of horizontal openings— free movement on the plane which they occupy—but a chance to rise above it—a vertical outlet.

Within the last thirty years, the sentiment of race and of nationality has attained wonderful development. Not only have the teachings of thinkers and philosophers set forth the importance of the theory, but the deeds of statesmen and patriots have, more or less successfully, demonstrated the practicability of it. The efforts of men like Garibaldi and Cavour in Italy, of Kossuth in Hungary, of Bismarck in Germany, of the Ashantees and Zulus in Africa, have proved the indestructible vitality and tenacity of race.

Notwithstanding the widespread progress of Mohammedanism in Africa, and though it has largely influenced the organic life of numerous tribes in the vast regions of the Soudan, yet the Arabs, who first introduced the religion, have never been allowed to obtain political ascendancy. None of the Nigritian tribes have ever abdicated their race individuality or parted with their idiosyncracies in embracing the faith of Islam. But, whenever and wherever it has been necessary, great Negro warriors have risen from the ranks of Islam, and, inspired by the teachings of the new faith, which merges all distinctions in one great brotherhood, have checked the arrogance of their foreign teachers, and have driven them, if at any time they affected superiority based upon race, from their artificial ascendancy. In the early days of Islam, when the Moors from the north attempted to establish political supremacy in the Nigritian countries, there rose up a Negro statesman and warrior, Soni Heli Ischia, and expelled the Moorish conquerors. He destroyed the ecclesiastical strongholds, which were fast growing into secular kingdoms, and erected upon their ruins one indigenous empire, having conquered all from Timbuctoo westward to the sea, and eastward to the frontier of Abyssinia, making about three thousand miles in length. Since then, Islam in Africa has been very much modified in its practices by the social peculiarities of the people. And, within the last twenty years, a distinguished native scholar and warrior, Omaru Al-Hajj, suppressed the undue influence of the Arabs at Timbuctoo—attacked that city in 1864, expelled the Arabs, and, with the same troops, confined the French to the western side of the Niger. His son Ahmadu now reigns at Sego, and, both by diplomacy and force, is checking or controlling the renewed operations of the French in the valley of the Niger.

This seems to be the period of race organisation and race consolidation. The races in Europe are striving to group themselves together according to their natural affinities. The concentration and development of the Slavonic power in deference to this impulse is a menace to other portions of Europe. The Germans are confederated. The Italians are united. Greece is being reconstructed. And so this race impulse has seized the African here. The feeling is in the atmosphere—the plane in which races move. And there is no people in whom the desire for race integrity and race preservation is stronger than in the Negro.

And I may be permitted to add here, that on this question of race, no argument is necessary or effective. Argument may be necessary in discussing the methods or course of procedure for the preservation of race integrity, and for the development of race efficiency, but no argument is needed as to the necessity of such preservation and development. If a man does not feel it—if it does not rise up with spontaneous and inspiring power in his heart—then he has neither part nor lot in it. The man who needs conviction on this subject, had much better be left unconvinced.

It is no doubt hard for you in this country to understand the strong race feeling in the Negro, or to appreciate the existence of such a feeling. As you glance over this land at the Negro population, their condition is such as to inspire, if not always the contempt, the despair, of the superficial observer, as to their future; and as you hear of their ancestoral home, of its burning climate and its fatal diseases, of its sandy deserts and its malarious swamps, of its superstitious inhabitants and degraded populations, you fancy that you see not one glimpse of hope in the dim hereafter of such a race. But let me assure that, ignoble as this people may appear here, they have brought a blessing to your shores; and you may rely upon it, that God has something in store for a people who have so served the world. He has something further to accomplish by means of a country of which He has so frequently availed himself in the past; and we may believe that out of it will yet come some of the greatest marvels which are to mark the closing periods of time.

Africa may yet prove to be the spiritual conservatory of the world. Just as in past times, Egypt proved the stronghold of Christianity after Jerusalem fell, and just as the noblest and greatest of the Fathers of the Christian Church came out of Egypt, so it may be, when the civilised nations, in consequence of their wonderful material development, shall have had their spiritual perceptions darkened and their spiritual susceptibilities blunted through the agency of a captivating and absorbing materialism, it may be, that they may have to resort to Africa to recover some of the simple elements of faith; for the promise of that land is that she shall stretch forth her hands unto God.

3 / RACE EMANCIPATION AND AFRICAN NATIONALITY
J. E. CASELY HAYFORD

In the name of African nationality the thinker would, through the medium of *Ethiopia Unbound*, greet members of the race everywhere throughout the world. Whether in the east, south, or west of the African Continent, or yet among the teeming millions of Ethiopia's[1] sons in America, the cry of the African, in its last analysis, is for scope and free-

From J. E. Casely Hayford, *Ethiopia Unbound: Studies in Race Emancipation* (London: C. M. Phillips, 1911), pp. 167-171, 173-175.
[1] Use of the term "Ethiopia" to denote African or Negro peoples was adopted from the Old Testament by the first generation of modern African thinkers. [Eds.]

dom in the struggle for existence, and it would seem as if the care of the leaders of the race has been to discover those avenues of right and natural endeavour which would, in the end, ensure for the race due recognition of its individuality.

The race problem is probably most intense in the United States of America, but there are indications that on the African Continent itself it is fast assuming concrete form. Sir Arthur Lawley, the present Governor of Madras, before leaving the Governorship of the Transvaal, is reported in a public address to have said that the "black peril" is a reality, and to have advised the whites to consolidate their forces in presence of the potential foe. The leaders of the race have hitherto exercised sound discretion and shown considerable wisdom in advising the African to follow the line of least resistance in meeting any combination of forces against him. The African's way to proper recognition lies not at present so much in the exhibition of material force and power, as in the gentler art of persuasion by the logic of facts and of achievements before which all reasonable men must bow.

A two-fold danger threatens the African everywhere. It is the outcome of certain economic conditions whose method is the exploitation of the Ethiopian for all he is worth. He is said to be pressed into the service of man, in reality, the service of the Caucasian. That being so, he never reaps the full meed of his work as a *man*. He materially contributes to the building of pavements on which he may not walk—take it as a metaphor, or as a fact, which way you please. He helps to work up revenues and to fill up exchequers over which, in most cases, he has no effective control, if any at all. In brief, he is labelled as belonging to a class apart among the races, and any attempt to rise above his station is terribly resented by the aristocracy of the races. Indeed, he is reminded at every turn that he is only intended to be a hewer of wood and a drawer of water. And so it happens that those among the favoured sons of men who occasionally consider the lot of the Ethiopian are met with jeers and taunts. Is it any wonder, then, that even in the Twentieth Century, the African finds it terribly difficult to make headway even in his own country? The African may turn socialist, may preach and cry for reform until the day of judgment; but the experience of mankind shows this, that reform never comes to a class of a people unless and until those concerned have worked out their own salvation. And the lesson we have yet to learn is that we cannot depart from Nature's way and hope for real success.

And yet, it would seem as if in some notable instances the black man is bent upon following the line of greatest resistance in coping with the difficulties before him. Knowledge is the common property of mankind, and the philosophy which seeks for the Ethiopian the highest culture and efficiency in industrial and technical training is a sound one. It is well to arrest in favour of the race public opinion as to its capability in this direction. But that is not all, since there are certain distinctive qualities of race, of country, and of peoples which cannot be ignored without detriment to the particular race, country, or people. Knowledge, deprived of the assimilating element which makes it natural to the one taught, renders that person but a bare imitator. The Japanese, adopting and assimilating Western culture, of necessity commands the respect of Western nations, because there is something distinctly Eastern about him. He commands, to begin with, the uses of his native tongue, and has a literature of his own, enriched by translations from standard authors of other lands. He respects the institutions and customs of his ancestors, and there is an intelligent past which inspires him. He does not discard his national costume, and if, now and again, he dons Western attire, he does so as a matter of convenience, much as the Scotch, across the border, puts away, when the occasion demands it, his Highland costume. It is not the fault of the black man in America, for example, that he suffers to-day from the effects of a wrong that was inflicted upon him years ago by the forefathers of the very ones who now despise him. But he can see to it that as the years go by it becomes a matter of necessity for the American whites to respect and admire his manhood; and the surest way to the one or the other lies not so much in imitation as in originality and natural initiative. Not only must the Ethiopian acquire proficiency in the arts and sciences, in technical and industrial training, but he must pursue a course of scientific enquiry which would reveal to him the good things of the treasure house of his own nationality.

There are probably but a few men of African descent in America who, if they took the trouble by dipping into family tradition, would not be able to trace their connection and relationship with one or other of the great tribes of West Africa; and now that careful enquiry has shown that the institutions of the Aborigines of Africa are capable of scientific handling, what would be easier than for the great centres of culture and learning in the hands of Africans in the United States to found professorships in this relation? In the order of Providence, some of our brethren aforetime were suffered to be enslaved in America for a wise purpose. That even in the history of the race has made it possible for the speedier dissemination and adoption of the better part of Western culture; and to-day Afric's sons in the East and in the West can do peculiar service unto one another in the common cause of uplifting Ethiopia and placing her upon her feet among the nations.

Looking at the matter closely, it is not so much *Afro-Americans* that we want as *Africans* or *Ethiopians,* sojourning in a strange land, who, out of a full heart and a full knowledge can say: If I forget thee, Ethiopia, let my right hand forget its cunning! Let us look at the other side of the picture. How extraordinary would be the spectacle of this huge Ethiopian race—some millions of men—having imbibed all that is best in Western culture in the land of their oppressors, yet remaining true to racial instincts and inspiration, customs and institutions, much as did the Israelites of old in captivity! When this more pleasant picture will have become possible of realisation, then, and only then, will it be possible for our people in bondage "metaphorically to walk out of Egypt in the near future with a great and a real spoil."

Someone may say, but surely, you don't mean to suggest that questions of dress and habits of life matter in the least. I reply emphatically, they do. They go to the root of the Ethiopians' self-respect. Without servile imitation of our teachers in their get-up and manner of life, it stands to reason that the average white man would regard the average black man far more seriously than he does at present. The adoption of a distinctive dress for the cultured African, therefore, would be a distinct step forward, and a gain to the cause of Ethiopian progress and advancement. . . .

Here, then is work for cultured West Africans to start a reform which will be world-wide in its effects among Ethiopians, remembering as a basis that we, as a people, have our own statutes, the customs and institutions of our forefathers, which we cannot neglect and live. We on the Gold Coast are making a huge effort in this direction, and though European habits will die hard with some of our people, the effort is worth making; and, if we don't succeed quite with this generation, we shall succeed with the next.

4 / REQUIREMENTS AND PRINCIPLES OF A NATIVE POLICY
FÉLIX ÉBOUÉ

French Equatorial Africa has reached a decisive moment in her history. It is useless to dwell on the errors of the past; we have better things to do than to criticise and regret. An already long experience and the lessons of the war permit us to sum up our achievements and our failures and to see clearly the colonization program which is prescribed for us. We know what we must do, and we know how to do it. . . .

Any attempt to create or re-create a society in our own image, or even in conformity with our mental habits, is bound to fail. The natives have habits, laws, a homeland of their own, which are unlike ours. We shall not ensure their happiness by applying to them the principles of the French Revolution, which is our Revolution, or the Napoleonic Code, which is our Code, or by substituting our government officials for their

From Félix Éboué, *General Circular on Native Policy*, reprinted in *Free France*, Special Issue No. 2 (New York: French Press and Information Service, September 1944), pp. 17-26.

chiefs, because our officials will think instead of the natives, but they will neither think for them, nor express their viewpoint.

On the contrary, we shall ensure the mental equilibrium of the natives if we treat them so to speak, from the inside, not as isolated and interchangeable individuals, but as human beings with traditions, as members of a family, a village or a tribe capable of progress within their own environment but very probably lost if they are removed from it. We shall concentrate on developing their consciousness of their own dignity and responsibility and on ensuring their prosperity, thus providing at the same time for their moral and their material progress; but we shall do this within the framework of the natives' natural institutions. If these institutions have deteriorated as a result of contact with us, we shall reorganize them, under new forms necessarily, yet sufficiently close to the natives to preserve their attachment to their country, and to encourage them to demonstrate their ability to manage their own affairs. Then further steps can be taken. Briefly, we shall restore to the native what no man can be deprived of without harm; we shall make him no illusory gifts, but we shall restore to him the deepest meaning of life and the desire to perpetuate it.

Lyautey has shown us the way. Let us listen to his quotations from Lanessan, his first teacher in colonial affairs: "In every country there is an organized leadership, an élite. The great mistake for a European nation which enters such a country as a conqueror is to destroy this leadership. Deprived of this organization, the country becomes a prey to anarchy. You have to govern with the mandarin, and not against the mandarin. The Europeans do not have numerical superiority and cannot substitute themselves for the natives. But they must guide them." And Lyautey himself adds: "Consequently, it is imperative not to interfere with any tradition, not to change any custom. *In every society, there is a leading class, born for leadership and without which nothing can be accomplished.* It must be drawn into the orbit of our interests."

Guided by such a principle, we shall have, first of all, to consolidate or reinstate and, in all cases, to promote the political institutions of the natives. Let me make this clear: political customs are not to be considered as something fixed and immutable. Our aim is not to perpetuate museum curios. It is obvious that customs change and will change, and that it is not our purpose to make them sterile and stagnant. What we must do is penetrate the depth of their meaning and consider them as no less essential than the tradition and the feeling from which they originated. This tradition is that of the country or the tribe; this feeling is that of the homeland. To deprive the natives of these two driving forces of human life would be to take from them without any compensation. It would be as absurd as to take away from a French peasant his field, his vineyard, his cows and his vegetable garden and to make of him just another chain-worker whose job is to handle the products of an industrialized countryside.

Moreover, if we fail to consolidate the political institutions of the natives in their very foundation, this foundation itself will give way to unbridled individualism. And how shall we awaken this agglomeration of individuals to action? When I see impatient administrators install, dismiss, condemn native chiefs and replace them with others and thereby undermine traditional institutions, I cannot help feeling that they do not realize what will happen when these institutions will have lost, through their errors, all their effectiveness and their living spirit. I can tell them: the only means that will be left to remedy the decline of the natural authority will be to administer through native functionaries. Since the administrator in charge of a subdivision cannot possibly look after the well-being of all the inhabitants of the territory under his control, he will have to resort to native officials to act as intermediaries in place of the chiefs whom he will have lost. I leave it to the experience of those concerned to decide which is the better solution. If an ambitious administrator seeks to dispense with both chief and functionary, or at least to reduce the former as well as the latter to the role of mere puppets in his hands, of docile and efficient instruments of his will, I am sure that he is making a grave error, or in any event, that his successor will not be able to follow his practice. Continuation of the effort, when dependent upon the decisive superiority of one individual administrator, will be jeopardized the moment he departs. He will have built cathedrals on sand.

I have spoken of the chiefs. As a matter of fact, though the native institutions are frequently monarchies, this is not always the case. The nomadic tribes of the North, for example, actually live under a regime of organized anarchy. In the monarchic state itself the chief is not the sole political institution. His power is modified, limited by more than one principle, by more than one tradition. None of these factors should be overlooked or rejected. No existing council should be abolished, no tutor dismissed, no religious law neglected, on the pretense that it is ridiculous, troublesome or immoral. The task is neither to deny nor to condemn what exists and what imports, but to make it evolve.

However, the institution of the chief is the most important, and we shall devote our greatest attention to him. Here a preliminary question arises: Who is to be chief? I shall not answer, as was the custom in Athens: "The best." There is no best chief, there is just a chief, and we have no choice. I have already dealt with the frequent changes of chiefs; they are deplorable as well as preposterous. There is a chief designated by custom; he must be *recognized*. I use this term in its diplomatic sense. If we replace him arbitrarily, we divide the authority into two parts: the official authority and the real one; by this we deceive no one but ourselves; and if we have the illusion of obtaining more from *our chief*, we are unaware, most of the time, that he himself obeys the *real chief,* and that we have been cheated in the deal.

The chief is not interchangeable; when we depose him, public opinion does not confirm it; the chief pre-exists. This pre-existence frequently remains unknown to us, and often the most difficult thing is to discover the real chief. This is the task to which I want the Governors and the Administrators, from now on, to devote their efforts. I intend to see to it that the practice of placing in power upstarts, menials or native "tirailleurs" whose services must be rewarded, is discontinued once and for all (there are a thousand other ways to reward them). Moreover, it is my desire that the legitimate chiefs be sought out, wherever our ignorance has allowed them to go into hiding, and that they be reinstated in all their external dignity. I know what is being said: all that has disappeared; it is too late; we will only find miserable and despicable wretches from whom nothing whatever can be expected. It is my contention that this is not true; the occult power persists because it is the traditional power. It must be discovered, placed in the limelight, honored and educated. There can be no doubt as to the results.

In order to preserve the full practical value of this precept, the Governors in charge of the administration of territories shall henceforth see to it that no recognition—I insist on the word—be granted without a preliminary and thorough study made by the head of the subdivision and the head of the department; this study must prove conclusively that the candidate for recognition is the real chief and that he really enjoys, to the fullest extent, the authority which we are going to confirm in him. Thus we shall give back to the country its own elite, and we shall be able to entrust them, in all sincerity, with the share of responsibility which belongs to them in the administration of local affairs.

I presume that this will meet with many objections. Shall we resort to indirect administration in a colony where the natives have given so little proof of their ability? The answer is: no. With the exception of some regions of the Chad, we shall not yet apply indirect administration, but our policy, constantly and everywhere, will tend to place the delegated power in the hands of the native chiefs. In other words, we shall no longer try by ourselves to stimulate the bulk of the natives; we shall, instead, seek out the legitimate chiefs and devote all our efforts to them, and it is through them that we shall reach the masses and achieve their education.

The perfect head of a subdivision will be the one who, after having found those chiefs who command the greatest obedience, that is to say those who are the most deeply rooted in the country, will succeed in educating them by patient endeavor; he will then have in them reliable assistants who will relieve him of most of the actual work, and his role will merely be to suggest, to advise, and to control.

I know that some people will tell me that this is an illusion. Nevertheless, this illusion has been responsible for the building up of Morocco and British Nigeria. They may add that the comparison is not valid. I would like to know why. The cultural level and the number of inhabitants have no bearing on the matter. Wherever there are men who respect an authority, it is this authority which, addressing them in their own language, is the best fitted to lead them, provided it is itself enlightened.

And this is our great duty. Our aim is not to create, by contact with us, a mob of proletarians, more or less ill clothed, more or less able to speak the French language; it should be the creation of an elite, beginning with the elite of the chiefs and notables who, entrusted by us with the personal responsibility of power, will progress in the face of difficulties, will apply themselves to the task and thereby gain a deserved pre-eminence in their country to the benefit of their country. Is this not better than to have a multitude of embittered individuals, liable to respond to slogans of doubtful origin and unfit for them?

But our aim cannot be attained unless we insist from the outset, and once and for all, upon the notion of respect. The chiefs must have the respect of those they govern; they must also have ours. We shall take the practice of viewing them as the traditional masters of the country, as members of a natural aristocracy, whose leadership must not be jeopardized.

The colony possesses two elements of stability: French sovereignty and the native authority rooted in the soil. The administrators *represent* the sovereignty of France, the chiefs *hold* the local authority. The former commands respect and obedience by virtue of their function, the latter because of their birth rights. This distinction is fundamental, and my advice to all administrators is to meditate profoundly upon it; it explains the respect due to the chiefs, it also determines its nature. . . .

Even though he may be guided by the very best intentions, the administrator is often liable to do more wrong to the population than a disreputable chief. For the latter knows, while the former does not. Let us leave the case of administering the people directly to the one who has the knowledge; and if he continues to misuse his authority, let us show infinite patience in setting him straight. . . .

Finally, we also find certain individuals who are isolated in the traditional native society and unable, because of their personal degree of evolution, or by reason of their mixed blood, to find in it their natural place.

In their present state, I can see only two towns of French Equatorial Africa which could properly fall within the first definition I have offered; they are Libreville and Bakongo. The other agglomerations: Bangui, Ponte-Noire, Poto-Poto, even Port-Gentil, and the less important centers, do not possess that characteristic which is required of an urban community, and shall be treated in a different manner.

The towns have followed an evolution of their own and have acquired a personality which excludes them from the native political custom. Individuals of fairly advanced evolution owing to contact with us have formed in these towns the habit of an urban life. It is no exaggeration to speak in this connection of a genuine native middle-class. And let us beware of a rather common mistake: it is often difficult to refrain from smiling at these "civilized" natives or from becoming impatient at their pretensions. We must, on the contrary, consider the effort they have made in order to raise themselves to our level, and show them that this effort is but a beginning. A certain naive, and sometimes arrogant, satisfaction of the more civilized natives will gradually disappear when they are made to face serious problems and are compelled to solve them. Until now, they have adopted hardly more than the external aspects of European civilization: beautiful clothes, refined language, easy manners. Henceforth, they must be made to tackle the real tasks and made to realize that results cannot be achieved without a great deal of exertion. They will win the honors of which they are so fond by their capacity for concentration, for reflection and for work. It is with this in mind that we are going to establish the native "communes." The native "commune" will give a public personality to the already existing homogeneous towns which are in fact exempt from the customary political laws. It will govern the life of all the inhabitants of the municipality, but only the class of "notables évolués" will participate in the municipal administration. It is from this class that the members of the municipal staff will be selected; the administration, placed under the control of a European official, will not deal in the beginning with financial matters, but it will have full authority in all questions pertaining to town life, thoroughfares, sports, professional and adult education. Its activity will be directed particularly toward the physical, intellectual and moral education of the inhabitants of the municipality. It will act in cooperation with the "Sociétés de Prévoyance" which, under its guidance, will assure its members lasting advantages, particularly through building loans. By developing the sense of property, the urban character of the town will be more firmly established and the families of the town will have that factor of personal progress which is still lacking. Finally, a simple police court, composed of members of the municipal staff, will give the latter an added feeling of responsibility toward those under its administration.

The French citizens of local origin, of colored or mixed blood, will, by right, belong to the class of "notables évolués" but it will not be limited to them; all those who will have reached a certain position in the town will also belong to it. A political statute for the "évolués" will be promulgated to this effect. The "évolués" defined under this statute will thus become genuine citizens of the colony and in this capacity, under our control, they will have to prove their ability in the administration of their own community. The former practice of granting illusory titles and rights without demanding in exchange any personal effort whatever, will be abandoned and replaced by a program of collective and well adapted work which will determine the titles and rights to be conferred on those who deserve them. . . .

5 / THE AFRICAN CONTINENT IN MOTION / FÉLIX HOUPHOUET-BOIGNY

Where is Africa going?

Before trying to answer this question, curious for some, distressing for others, we would like, for the sake of clarity in what is to follow, to make certain declarations. We would be unfair (one does not have the right to be unfair when one claims to combat injustice) if we wanted to deny the works accomplished in Africa by France.

That against which we rise and against which we shall always rise, are the privileges abolished in France and reestablished in Africa. Those who had victoriously fought the monarchy did not deny the immense work of the kings: national unity, the sciences, the letters, the arts (famous and matchless monuments). What they could not bear was the incredible luxury of some and the horrible misery of others, all rights acknowledged to the former and denied the latter, full and entire liberty to the one, chains for the others, taxes, duties inversely proportional to the social status of subjects of the same king.

We denounce the abuses, we do not deny the benefits. We love those who love us. Love cannot be and should not be in one direction only. Let them cease, then, to give us ideas and sentiments that we do not have. They did not place only arithmetic books in our hands; we have read with fervor and with passion other books, other leaflets: the History of France, the "Declaration of Rights." Those who, for a selfish goal, opposed the peaceful evolution of Africans would like to push us in the direction of revolutionary movements, as a pretext for brutal repression and political and social reaction.

Hopes of Liberty Disappointed

During the last century, the great manhunt which fed the foreign slave trade ended thanks to the abolition of slavery. However, until the beginning of this century, at least in certain regions, the domestic [slave]

From Félix Houphouet-Boigny, "Le continent Africain en marche," *Démocratie Nouvelle*, No. 2 (Février, 1947), pp. 74-79. Reprinted by permission of *Démocratie Nouvelle*.

trade continued. A slave often changed masters, with the accompanying vicissitudes of numerous internal wars, waged by our emperors, kings, and sub-kings. The suffering of the people was great.

One understands, then, the immense hope which arose among the African masses in many regions at the coming of the French. Explorer or conqueror, it was always in the name of liberty that the French made contact with the Africans. The grandsons of those who fought at the risk of their lives for the abolition of the corvée, of the tithe, of the harvest tax, came to liberate the unhappy Africans. How not to understand, then, the enthusiasm, the heroism with which the African people contributed to their own liberation. Under this sun of fire, on this burning desert sand, in these swampy forests, these elusive wilds, under these flooding rains, the pacification of Africa by European soldiers alone would have been extremely difficult, ruinous, if not impossible in an age when one could not count on the aid of modern military techniques, notably radio and aviation. Together, fearless liberators, valorous, confident, devoted and thankful, planted the victorious tricolored flag in every hamlet from Senegal to the Congo.

For this immense population, France was the country of liberty. It was for this liberty that, without betraying Africa, our riflemen fought their own chiefs: El Hadj Omar, Samory, Behanzin, to cite only the most famous.

Peace having been secured, it was necessary for the colonial government to organize our countries. There emerged the following numerous contradictions:

Contradiction between the abolition of slavery and the institution of forced labor, that other form of serfdom, if not as debasing, at least more painful, more deadly;

Contradiction between the maintenance of chiefs and the failure to reprimand them for their misdeeds for the sole end of associating them with the shameful exploitation of that mass which one claims to liberate, educate;

Contradiction between the generous idea of teaching an ignorant people and the systematic sabotage of teaching;

Contradiction between respect of culture and the infamous code [the *indigénat*] which gave to its administrators the right to accuse, try, and judge;

Contradiction between the recognition of rights and the expropriation of the collectives;

Contradiction between the plan for the full usage of, and the systematic pillaging of, colonial resources;

Contradiction between the recognition and utilization of our military worth and the miserable situation in which our riflemen and our pension-holders find themselves;

Contradiction between the condemnation of privileges and the installation of privileges;

Contradiction between the declaration of free association between colonizers and colonized and the effective discrimination against the latter in the administration of their country's interests;

Contradiction, in a word, between the generous principles declared in Paris and their faulty application in Africa.

Elevation of the Masses

We shall not cease repeating it: union as a foundation is the key to success. In black Africa where the mercantile exploitation of the colonialists brings together all Africans from whatever class in a common struggle, to want to establish capitalistic relationships between classes and the resulting political struggles would be a profound error. To transpose to Africa the ideological struggles of the metropolis would be to completely distort the basic nature of the problem confronted by Africans.

Certainly, between exploiters and exploited, reactionaries and democrats, we would not hesitate; we would be, body and soul, with the progressive forces and against the retrograde forces.

But one must not believe, because of this, that we are obliged to organize in black Africa a simple repetition of metropolitan political organizations. We have our own originality which we plan to defend, preserve, and develop.

This much said, there can be no question of Africans isolating themselves in a fight in which the diverse peoples of the French Union, and the French people in particular, are concerned. There is no doubt that we shall rely on, and associate ourselves with greater confidence to those political forces of the metropolis which will offer us the best opportunities by their attachment to the democratic ideal, and by the firmness and efficacy of their means of action.

Emptied of the best of its resources and of the blood of the best of its children, weakened by the internal divisions created by the colonialist reaction, Africa is seeking her salvation through unity, unity of action. The diverse tribes, races, and peoples do not understand each other, but there is a language which all the oppressed people of the world can understand, it is that of democracy, the call to fraternity.

Africa has known the great suffering of peoples; she had expected much; she has been disappointed, but she has again taken hold of herself. She is finally becoming aware of herself. She will, painfully but confidently, advance toward her destiny, a luminous destiny: the sun comes from Africa.

Africa has not yet said her final word. Open to all peoples, she shall reconcile all peoples. From its hot greenhouse will grow a sturdy democracy, a new democracy, which, by suppressing struggles, sordid internal wars, shall make the fraternity between peoples reign forever. One can slow down an evolution, one cannot stop it . . . .

Africa is in motion.

II / IDEAS AND CONTEXT OF AFRICAN NATIONALISM

INTRODUCTION

The selections included in Part II reflect more explicitly than do those in Part I a concern for the political element in the African reaction to colonialism. As such they go beyond the mere formulation and definition of the African's relationship as a man to the European and his institutions. They do not neglect such formulation, but rather make it a part of the general political context within which the African might release himself from all forms of colonial subordination. The selections in Part II are thus "nationalistic," representing the self-assertion of the interests of a given African community (whose politico-geographical limits are those of the colonial territory) against those of the foreign colonial oligarchy.[1] The ultimate political goal of this self-assertion is the establishment of a modern African community, perhaps along the lines of the nation-state as represented in the Western world.

It is fitting to begin the selections in Part II with the writings of J. E. Casely Hayford. Unlike any other African leader represented in this volume, he cuts across both periods of the African reaction to colonialism. Next to Dr. Edward Blyden, Casely Hayford was the most eloquent spokesman of the initial period of the African reaction which concentrated upon the question of racial self-definition; and, at the early stage of the secondary period of the African reaction which emphasized political nationalism, Casely Hayford was unquestionably without a peer, in either British or French Africa, as formulator of the ingredients of incipient African nationalism. In both thought and action Casely Hayford was the quintessence of an African nationalist. A man cultured and learned in modern ways, and equally conversant with his own traditional African society, his thought and action constituted a synthesis of the two

[1] See Thomas Hodgkin, *Nationalism in Colonial Africa* (New York: New York University Press, 1960); Rupert Emerson, *From Empire to Nation* (Cambridge, Mass.: Harvard University Press, 1960; Boston: Beacon Press, Inc., 1962); Martin Kilson, "The Analysis of African Nationalism," *World Politics* (April 1958), pp. 484-97.

main facets (the self-definitional and the nationalistic) of the African response to colonialism.

This is readily apparent from a perusal of any of his writings (such as *Ethiopia Unbound: Studies in Race Emancipation* [1911], *Gold Coast Native Institutions* [1903], and *The Disabilities of Black Folk and their Treatment* [1929]), and from his manifold political activities. In 1897 he was one of the founders and, subsequently, a leader of the Aborigines Rights Protection Society in the Gold Coast—one of the first institutions among both the intelligentsia and the middle class of West Africa which sought practical solutions for the problem of Negro self-identity along lines of self-help and self-protection.[2] The ARPS organized a Botanical Garden for experimentation and training in modern agriculture; it endeavored to protect traditional land rights and customs against encroachment by colonial authorities; and it represented the interests of both the chiefs and the new elite in disputes with the colonial government. Casely Hayford was also founder and leader of the National Congress of British West Africa in 1920. The NCBWA was an incipient pan-African nationalist body embracing members of the intelligentsia in all of British West Africa (Gold Coast, Nigeria, Sierra Leone, and Gambia), and, until his death in 1930, Casely Hayford was its leading light and most prominent thinker, as evidenced by the selection in this volume from his Presidential Address to the Third Conference of the NCBWA.

Dr. J. B. Danquah, author of the second selection in Part II, was another of the many prominent contributors to modern African thought produced during this century by Ghana—the name chosen by the Gold Coast government upon the attainment of independence in 1957. Danquah assumed leadership of the second generation of Ghanaian nationalists following the death or retirement from active political life of such leaders as Casely Hayford, E. J. P. Brown, a leader of the ARPS, and T. M. Hutton-Mills, a leader of the NCBWA. Like Casely Hayford, Danquah was both highly cultured in Western terms and superbly informed about, and personally close to, traditional Ghanaian society. The latter characteristic had the effect of tempering his nationalist response to colonialism—as it also did for Casely Hayford. A member of a traditional ruling family in Ghana, Danquah was never quite able to modify his sense of traditional high status in order to become a nationalist leader who mingled easily and familiarly with the common folk.

The Gold Coast Youth Conference, which Danquah helped to found and lead from 1937-1947, carried on in the vein of the earlier NCBWA, organizing nationalist activity among the intelligentsia and the emergent middle class. Its social and political thought was the expression of the

[2] For an excellent account of the ARPS, see David Kimble, *A Political History of Ghana: The Rise of Gold Coast Nationalism, 1850-1928* (London: Oxford University Press, 1963).

needs of these groups, and, as is apparent in the essay in this volume, the Youth Conference's leaders were quite incapable, for ideological and personality reasons, of moving beyond this to a mode of thought coincident with the needs of broader elements in the community. As future events revealed, political success in postwar Ghanaian nationalist politics went to the section of the new political elite that was able and willing to formulate nationalist thought and practice in terms of the broader mass elements. In this connection, there is a rather pathetic irony about Danquah's account of the policies of the Gold Coast Youth Conference up until World War II. The methods and tactics which Danquah's critics claimed he lacked—which Danquah admitted—were precisely those successfully used by Kwame Nkrumah and the Convention People's Party in the postwar period.[3]

Like Danquah, Dr. Nnamdi Azikiwe entered organized African nationalism in the late 1930s when the first generation of Nigerian nationalists like E. O. Moore, Egerton Syngle, Sir Kitoyi Ajasa, and Herbert Macaulay had retired from active political life. Azikiwe was unique, however, in that he was the first West African nationalist of prominence who had been educated in the United States, where he attended two Negro Colleges—Lincoln University, Pennsylvania, and Howard University—and then the University of Pennsylvania. He was also unique insofar as he was the first West African nationalist to pursue successfully both a political and a business career. No small part of Azikiwe's definition of the content of Nigerian nationalism was influenced by his dual function as a politician and a capitalist, and his political career demonstrated the significant relationship between political power and success in business in a developing African society. As evidenced in the blueprint for postwar Nigeria reprinted here, his sense of proportion, of the politically possible within a colonial society, was linked to his wide business experience.

Azikiwe was equally unique among Nigerian nationalist personalities as the first to demonstrate the possibility of establishing a nation-wide political organization. Unlike Danquah in Ghana, Azikiwe's social origin was that of a commoner and this facilitated his campaign to project and organize Nigerian nationalism among the masses. Though his formal projection of the requirements for an effective nationalist movement in Nigeria was free of tribalist assumptions, when he finally succeeded, in 1944-45, in organizing the first territory-wide nationalist party in the form of the National Council of Nigeria and the Cameroons, Azikiwe discovered that the practical realities of Nigerian political life, divided as it was among a hundred or more tribal groups, necessitated the initial organization of the NCNC among his own tribal kinsmen, the Ibo. Traditional and modern forms of associations were employed as the core of

[3] See Kwame Nkrumah, *Ghana: The Autobiography of Kwame Nkrumah* (New York: Thomas Nelson & Sons, 1957).

the structure of political influence and power in the NCNC, and this situation has persisted to the present.[4]

A major consequence of the Ibo-centered basis of power in the NCNC was that it stimulated political response by other major tribal groups in Nigeria against the tribal-centered organization. This was especially true for the Yoruba in Western Nigeria whose main political leader since the end of World War II has been Obafemi Awolowo. Whereas the tribal element in the nationalist politics of Eastern Nigeria under Azikiwe's leadership was varied with practical necessity and never rationalized as an ultimate good, the role of Yoruba tribalism in the nationalist politics of Western Nigeria under Awolowo's leadership was from the start conceived and projected as inherently desirable. As may be seen in the selection from Awolowo's writings included in this volume, the Yoruba actually conceived of themselves—and thus, by implication, other tribes as well—as a definable national group historically worthy of controlling its own nation-state political system. Furthermore, it is apparent from Awolowo's writings and those of other Yoruba political personalities that, as a people, the Yoruba considered themselves somewhat superior to other Nigerian tribes, and especially to the Ibo in Eastern Nigeria.[5] This sense of Yoruba superiority was introduced into the thought and behavior of the first major postwar nationalist organization among the Yoruba, the Action Group, and, since its foundation in 1948-1949, the Action Group's use of ideas of Yoruba superiority has contributed greatly to Nigeria's regional-based nationalist politics. Indeed, at the point where the joint forces of Nigerian nationalism succeeded in getting the British to agree to the ultimate transfer of political power to Africans, this transfer was effected only through the establishment of a Federal political system composed of three regional states in which the three major tribal complexes in Nigeria (viz., Hausa-Fulani in the North, Yoruba in the West, and Ibo in the East) held sway.

An indication of the forces underlying the formation of the Federation of Nigeria in 1960 was revealed in the debates in the House of Representatives in 1957-1958 concerning the grant of regional self-government to the Western and Eastern Regions. The statement of S. L. Akintola reprinted here emphasizes the need for Nigerian unity to facilitate African demands for full independence, while that of Mallam (now Sir) Abubakar Tafawa Balewa concerns the interests of Northern Nigeria and its Hausa-Fulani population, Muslim in religion, whose modern development lagged significantly behind the Eastern and Western Regions which together made up the South. Today these ethnic differences and the differential in development between Northern and South-

[4] See Richard L. Sklar, *Nigerian Political Parties: Power in an Emergent African Nation* (Princeton, N.J.: Princeton University Press, 1963).

[5] See James S. Coleman, *Nigeria: Background to Nationalism* (Berkeley: University of California Press, 1958).

ern Nigeria still influence a major part of Nigerian political thought and practice.

The next three selections in Part II represent the ideas and context of nationalism in French-speaking West and Equatorial Africa. Gabriel d'Arboussier, author of the selection from the Report on the *Rassemblement Démocratique Africain* (RDA) Conference at Bamako, French Sudan (now Mali Republic) in 1946, stands out in striking contrast to Houphouet-Boigny and Félix Éboué who are represented in Part I of this volume. Of mixed French-African extraction, d'Arboussier was one of the sizeable number of French Africans whose education and intellectual development in France was greatly influenced by the Marxist and Communist Left. Whereas Houphouet-Boigny and Éboué took most of their intellectual definition from the legitimate or dominant ideologies of metropolitan France, d'Arboussier rejected these ideologies, embraced Marxism as a philosophy, and was closely associated with the French Communist party as a practical politician.

However, d'Arboussier and other French Africans of his outlook were never dogmatic in their attachment to Marxism. D'Arboussier makes this perfectly clear in his 1946 report to the RDA Congress, which was, in fact, the first statement of the French pragmatic approach to Marxism. (It is often erroneously assumed that Sékou Touré of Guinea was the first to express such an approach.) Despite its non-dogmatic qualities, the core of the thought of the radical French Africans remained basically Marxist and, within this framework of political ideas and methods, they organized their nationalist attack against French colonialism, although, in keeping with the French outlook, no major group or party spoke up for independence until late in the 1950s. The influence of Marxism upon the territorial nationalist party branches of the RDA was greatest in Guinea, Mali, and Senegal. But it was not insignificant even in the Ivory Coast, for Houphouet-Boigny, the first President of the RDA, recognized the value of the organizational skills of the convinced Marxists and agreed to the association between the RDA deputies and the French Communist party in the French National Assembly during 1946-1950. This was, however, a matter of expedience and not of conviction for Houphouet-Boigny. At the end of 1950, he influenced the RDA to sever its ties with the French Communists, and his own territorial branch of the RDA, the *Parti Démocratique de la Côte d'Ivoire*, likewise eased the Marxists into the background.

Majhemout Diop stands out among the French African Marxists as one of the few who became orthodox in Marxist thought and practice. His party, the *Parti Africain de l'Indépendence*, is considered essentially communist and was outlawed as such by Senghor's government in Senegal in 1960. The selection from Diop's writings is given as representative of the orthodox Marxian version of colonialism, as seen through African eyes.

The last four selections in Part II relate to the ideas and context of nationalism in East, Central and South Africa. The first selection by Tom Mboya provides the basic elements in the colonial situation in East and Central Africa that distinguished it so sharply from that in West and Equatorial Africa. White settlement in the highland areas of East and Central Africa was the crucial element distinguishing the colonialism in these territories. Thus African nationalism confronted not only a colonial oligarchy of bureaucrats and expatriate businessmen and firms, but also a unified community of Europeans who came to East and Central Africa to stake out a permanent home.

As the colonial territories in these areas began their political evolution, the settled European communities secured a dominant position in the new self-governing institutions. Throughout East and Central Africa British policy had committed itself to such a course from the very beginning of European settlement at the turn of the twentieth century; and in Southern Rhodesia in 1923 the British colonial authorities actually granted full internal self-government to the European settled community (numbering in 1964 around 225,000 among 3,000,000 Africans). Similar status was sought by the settled community in Kenya (at its peak numbering around 30,000 among 6,500,000 Africans) but, recognizing the error of their ways in the Southern Rhodesian decision and the differences in the racial and political balance, the British colonial authorities refused to grant it. Short of this, the colonial authorities gave preferred treatment to the European community in all spheres of the colony's life, especially in the realms of government and economics. The African nationalist response to this situation was decidedly more aggressive and violent here than in West Africa where more peaceful political outlets were available, culminating in Kenya in 1951-58 with a full fledged revolt against colonial rule, known as the Mau Mau Rebellion.

Mboya's essay is a critique of the particular type of colonial regime established in East and Central Africa, and it warned the Europeans that unless their ways were mended and full political rights extended to Africans, their whole future in Kenya, and elsewhere in East and Central Africa, would be jeopardized. At the same time, he offered them the alternative of open cooperation with the new African political elite in the development of an independent Kenya. Fortunately for both sides, the majority of the Europeans in Kenya accepted the position argued by Mboya and other Kenya leaders like Jomo Kenyatta, first Prime Minister and then President of Kenya, and when independence was attained in December 1963 most of them remained in the country.

A different response, however, occurred among the much larger and more powerful European community in Southern Rhodesia. As already noted, this community gained full internal control of the government in 1923, while the British colonial authorities retained only remote and ineffective jurisdiction over governmental actions which discriminated against the Africans. Late in 1953 the power of this community, the largest of its kind in all of East and Central Africa, was significantly enhanced through Southern Rhodesia's federation with the two British protectorates to the north, Nyasaland and Northern Rhodesia. Fortunately for African interests in the latter two territories, however, the British remained the primary authority with regard to the ultimate political future of these areas. Thus, when the nationalist movements in Nyasaland and Northern Rhodesia demonstrated total African opposition to the Federation, British authority was willing to permit them to withdraw, which they did in 1963.

In Southern Rhodesia the remnants of British colonial authority deny that they retain the power to alter the authoritarian white supremacist system controlled by the locally established Europeans. The selection from the writings of Ndabaningi Sithole represents the moderate strain of African nationalist politics in Southern Rhodesia. It holds out hope for a possible accommodation of European and African interests on behalf of the future development of a multi-racial society. Yet Sithole is firm in his identification and castigation of white responsibility for the backward, oppressed plight of his countrymen.

The emphasis upon white-black interaction as a grossly dehumanizing fact for Africans is equally apparent in the powerful and eloquent brief that Nelson Mandela delivered in his own defense before a South African court that tried and convicted him on a charge of treason. By far the most oppressive anti-Negro political system on the continent, the Republic of South Africa differs from the other African states considered in this volume. It has been an independent, sovereign political unit since Britain granted Dominion status to it in 1910. Though a significant portion of the South African white population is of British extraction and somewhat more liberal in political outlook, since 1948 the government has been controlled by the Afrikaans-speaking Boers who were the original white settlers in South Africa in the seventeenth century. Together these white groups represent about one-fifth of the 16,000,000 people in South Africa.

As adherents of the Dutch Reformed Church whose interpretation of Christianity has it that Negro peoples were cursed by God and destined to be hewers of wood and drawers of water, the Boers have imposed a system of race relationships that is known by the Afrikaans word "apartheid," or complete racial separation. This system is currently under increasing attack from the African population whose present leaders have slowly moved away from the constitutionally oriented nationalist politics of the earlier leaders of the African National Congress, such as Chief Albert Luthuli, toward a militant black nationalism which, if need be, will embrace armed revolution to overturn the well armed fascist-type police state in South Africa. As the selection from Mandela suggests, the new leadership of the African National Congress has not quite yet reached this stage (though its competitor, the Pan-Africanist Congress has).

The last selection in this Part consists of excerpts from the first major political manifesto to be issued in the Belgian Congo. It followed upon the heels of the publication in 1954 by Professor A. A. J. van Bilsen of a "Thirty Year Plan for the Political Emancipation of Belgian Africa." This proposal, despite its studied moderation, was of earth-shaking consequence since Belgium had as yet come to no awareness that independence for the Congo was conceivable, even at the end of a thirty year period, nor was it prepared for the kind of criticism of its African policies undertaken by Professor van Bilsen. It was even more startled when, in 1956, a group of Congolese *évolués* in Leopoldville, associated with the little-known journal, *Conscience Africaine,* published a manifesto which looked to a thirty year advance toward the total emancipation of a people whom they saw as destined to become "a great nation in the center of the African continent." The progression was swift: independence came to the Congo not in thirty years but in four.

6 / LEADERSHIP AND AFRICAN COOPERATION
J. E. CASELY HAYFORD

It will be recalled that at our first Session it was laid down that the objects of the Congress should be to press for "a Legislative Council composed of representatives, of whom one half shall be nominated by the Crown and the other half elected by the people, to deal with Legislation generally. Next a House of Assembly composed of the Members of the Legislative Council together with six other Financial representatives elected by the people, who shall have the power of imposing all taxes and of discussing freely and without reserve the items on the Annual Estimates of Revenue and Expenditure prepared by the Governor in the Executive Council and approving of them." This, it will be seen, aimed at effective representation which was emphasised in the resolutions passed upon that head at our second Session. It will be our duty to study the provisions of the Constitutions extant, see in what way they fall short of Congress proposals, and to make representations accordingly.

The advance of Science has brought about a contraction of our globe, which compels contact and inter-dependence among peoples, creeds, and races. So strong is the impact that you cannot escape it, if you may. As a Congress, therefore, we cannot be indifferent to world problems which affect us more nearly than we have yet realised. The African, for one thing, is called upon for his contribution to the maintenance of the

From Presidential Address by Casely Hayford to the Third Session of the National Congress of British West Africa, held in Bathurst, Gambia, December 1925. Reprinted from Magnus J. Sampson, *West African Leadership: Public Speeches Delivered by the Hon. J. E. Casely Hayford* (London: Arthur H. Stockwell, n.d.), pp. 78-85.

conditions of modern life, and often the call comes upon him so insistently and in a way which may easily make him the slave of circumstances.

Within the Empire itself there was at the beginning of the Congress movement the activities of the Empire Resources Development Committee, which distinctly aimed at African exploitation and which we had cause to condemn at the time. There is reason to believe that even now British West Africa is not free from danger of that sort; and it will be for us to examine the facts and resort to that eternal vigilance which is the price of liberty.

Nor is that enough, as a Congress, we must be in advance of the current racial thought of the day. We must, to a certain extent, be able to guide and control it. There is intense activity in racial progress both in the United States and in the Islands of the Sea.[1] But, admittedly, in the last analysis, the right inspiration must come from the mother continent; and in no part of Africa can such inspiration be so well supplied as in the West. Our work, therefore, must be constructive; and we must take long views and look far ahead of our times in racial reconstruction. As there is an international feeling among all white men, among all brown men, among all yellow men, so must there be an international feeling among all black folk. And it is no good pretending otherwise. To-day, where two or three of our race are gathered together, the thought uppermost in their minds is how to attain African emancipation and redemption. At the same time it is true that we are all intensely attached to our several nationalities. Trained under the constitution of the British Flag, we in British West Africa, for example, are intensely patriotic, and we have given blood and treasure for that Flag and may yet do it again. But let no one make the mistake to think that the general disabilities of our race in the four corners of the Earth do not concern us. If we, as a people, sow in order that others may reap, we are sure it is not so much from an innate inability to command success as from want of equipment; and if that is the result of improper education, we hope to remedy it. There is no reason why we, as Africans, should not also harness the discoveries of Science to our everyday need and make them productive of Wealth and prosperity within our own borders. We have been burden-bearers far too long for others. We must set to work to realise some of the assets for ourselves. And how to bring that about must form a topic of our deliberations.

At the same time it must be recognised that co-operation is the greatest word of the century. With co-operation we can command peace, goodwill and concord. Without: chaos, confusion and ruin. But there can really be no effective co-operation between inferiors and superiors. Try as they may, there must come a time when the element of superiority

[1] That is, among Negro Americans and Negro communities in the British and French West Indies. [EDS.]

will seek to dictate, and the inferior ones will resent such dictation. It logically follows, therefore, that unless there is an honest effort to raise the inferior up to the prestige of the superior and the latter can suffer it, all our talk of co-operation is so much empty gas. For instance, so long as you regard the African as a person who must be held in perpetual tutelage for your convenience, there cannot, in the nature of things, be that spirit of confidence essential to true co-operation.

While co-operation between race and race is preached, and it is desirable that it should be preached, surely there can be nothing wrong in suggesting that there should be closer and yet closer co-operation between members of our own race. While there has been a tremendous wave of race consciousness, our coming together for practical purposes is yet uncertain, and our organisations are very loose. In the dominant race while there is rivalry and competition in business and other concerns, yet do you see a general co-operation between banking and shipping and mercantile elements which tends to ensure the prosperity of a progressive society. If the black man hopes to survive, he must assimilate and adopt this sort of intensive co-operation. However great the philanthropist, it is startlingly true, that unless he be a Christ, there comes a time when he must choose between his country and another's, between his own people and other people. And you cannot blame him. It is but natural. Therefore there must come a point when we must make up our minds to shoulder our own industrial, educational, political, and religious burdens, expending thought upon them, and resolute in taking action. . . .

To summarise much of what has been said in this address, we want to get to the essence of things. We, as Africans, want to reach the kernel and will not be satisfied with the husks. If the civilisation which we have imbibed leaves us without backbone and makes us incapable of helping ourselves economically, politically, educationally, and religiously, we must be prepared to shed off that civilisation. In a community where educational aspirations are high and there is an ostensible intention to train for leadership, if leadership by leading minds is in fact tabooed, we must have to examine the situation in the light of the facts and to apply the necessary remedy. We shall have to examine the constitutions of British West Africa and discover in how far they make for national progress, and, where they fall, it will be our duty to say so explicitly and without reserve. If we find that the instrument which we have forged in defence of our national rights, our national integrity, is not sufficiently effective, we shall have to devise means to strengthen it. What is obsolete must be scrapped, and unwieldy agencies and obstacles in our path must be weeded out. Personalities must not stand in the way of principles, and the national soul must be more important to us than the trappings of mere conventionality to the end that we, Africans, who have borne the heat and burden of the day in the world's work and in the world's progress, may benefit fully by the resultant harvest. . . .

7 / SELF-HELP AND EXPANSION / J. B. DANQUAH

Faith in the Gold Coast

If history is any guide, the world's most oppressed race are the Jews. Black men come off second best, or perhaps I should say, the second worst. By the same standard the Jews are the luckiest of all the human races. The Almighty made them his own chosen people.

As I understand the term, a chosen people are those who have no need for a national or battle cry like "Plan, or perish!" When Adam delved and Eve span, who then was the planner? Whether a chosen race plan or not, they either prosper or perish. If, for instance, they have a Red Sea to cross, they are not bound to plan, as we are bound to plan in the Gold Coast. They do not have to make ships, or canoes, or bridges to enable them to cross the Red Sea. A ready-made and super-scientific crossing is provided for them. The sea is held up like a Policeman holds up the traffic in Station Road, and "Hey, Presto!" the lucky Jews cross over and disappear on the other side. They are so lucky, so much a chosen race, they did not have to help themselves before God helped them to reach Palestine, the land flowing with milk and honey. A blessed, most oppressed, and lucky people, the Jews, a chosen people.

What of us in the Gold Coast: Our case is quite the reverse, if one is to believe the newspapers. And I, of course, believe them—our newspapers. We are not a chosen race. Day in and day out our newspapers remind us: "God helps those who help themselves," and they sell the newspapers to us for a penny, and they believe they have done their duty. How are we then to help ourselves? . . .

Sometimes I am driven to desperation by those who ask for action without knowing just what sort of action they want, or whether the sort of action they want is worth while at all. Some time ago, someone, who was pressing that I should do something, was asked: "What do you think is the best thing I can do?" "Oh!" he said, "you must be prepared to go to prison for your country. You must be prepared to do something that will send you to prison." Is that so? That man wants me to rush to the next Policeman I meet, knock him down, and then go to prison for it. Then he will call me his hero, a Gold Coast hero! Or, probably, he wants me to collect two or three hundred people, rush to the Castle, climb up to the Governor's private office and tell His Excellency to clear out of the Gold Coast, and, says this man, I should be damned glad to

From Dr. J. B. Danquah, *Self-Help and Expansion: A Review of the Work and Aims of the Youth Conference, with a statement of its policy for 1943, and the Action Consequent upon that Policy* (Accra: Gold Coast Youth Conference, 1943), pp. 1-7, 20-25.

go to prison for doing such a "noble" and "patriotic" act. And when I am in prison my questioner will probably expect me to go on hunger strike for three weeks, twenty one days, and come out to wear a loin cloth around my waist. I asked him what was to happen to the Youth Conference whilst in prison. "Oh," he replied, "I have not thought of that. That is your job. In India they sent one editor to prison, and another took his place."

Ladies and gentlemen, it is no joke. Almost every man in fifty you meet may tell you that unless you are prepared to go to prison like Wallace Johnston or Gandhi, then you are a fraud, you have no right to speak to the public. O.K. We all know it takes a saint or "Mahatma" like Gandhi to go to prison and come back to wear a loin cloth, but I hope that you, ladies and gentlemen, whom I address now, do not consider that I do anything fraudulent in addressing you although I am not a political ex-convict. There is far too much in the Gold Coast to be done than to go to prison for it.

The Dual Policy

What then is the remedy offered by the Youth Conference? What is the line of action the Youth of the country are placing before the Elders and People and Government of the country in order to obtain for the people Power, world citizenship and a government, or a will of their own, autonomy, self-rule? . . .

In the past we had only declared what was the constitution of the Conference, to educate the people on the need for a common platform and to go out with them in search of that platform. Today . . . we have clear in our minds, as we believe in the minds of the people and the Chiefs, what sort of platform would obtain the general assent of the vast majority of the thinking people in this country.

In declaring that policy, let it not be thought by any one that it is the duty solely of the Youth Conference to see that it is carried out. The Youth Conference is not the only public organ of expression in this country. We have the Press, we have the Provincial Councils, we have the State Improvement Societies, and we have literary and social clubs, some of which are semi-political institutions. We have also, still with us, the Aborigines Society. All these organs of public expression, as well, of course, as the schools and colleges, especially the Colleges and Old Boys Associations, will have to devise their own ways of action for bringing that policy into being, for the word to be made flesh. In fact, without the willing cooperation of the general public and the Press, the Youth Conference alone can achieve but little. . . .

In brief, then, the policy we declare to you this day is dual, self-help and expansion. We must have power, and we must adequately fill in that power to give us world citizenship.

As regards self-help, we support the resolution passed on November 4, 1942 at the public meeting addressed by Mr. K. A. Gbedemah and presided over by the Honourable K. A. Korsah, that a national fund should be established for the people of the Gold Coast. The resolution was as follows:

> To enable the Gold Coast as a whole to make adequate provision for the country's needs, such as scholarships, in addition to any provided by Government, a national fund or people's fund, should be established by the appropriate authorities under a Board of Trustees appointed by the said authorities.

The terms of the resolution are susceptible of a single interpretation, that the national fund is to be subsidiary to anything the Government itself might do. Were this country a self-governing country, a national fund would not be necessary, because the people could easily ask their government to raise the necessary funds through its Treasury to meet the adequate needs and demands of the people. Not being a self-governing country, and not being really sure that the Government will at all times provide fully for the immediate and urgent needs of the country, the national fund is to be brought in to accelerate the process of expansion, our accession to power, and to fill in the gaps during the periods of discontinuity when the Governor of the day may be unwilling to meet the people half-way, or at all.

Further, the national fund is not to be collected by any but the appropriate authorities. That is to say, it is to be a compulsory fund. All talk of voluntary national fund is so much waste of people's time and energy. You may get the people to subscribe voluntarily in the flush of the moment, but you will not get the people to subscribe willingly all the time. . . .

As to the purpose to which the fund will be put, it is quite clear from the terms of the resolution that national education and scholarships for study abroad will stand at the top of the list. But apart from academic scholars we shall have to send teachers, industrialists, farmers and other workers to go abroad and learn, and handle the tools and come back to the country to be the pioneers in the total and complete industrialization of their country's resources, including, of course, the mines.

That, then, is our policy as regards self-help.

Next, as regards expansion, it follows that if the people of this country were autonomous, all one would have to do would be to place in power a Cabinet of men who are prepared to carry into effect that policy of raising the status of this country to that of world citizenship, *industrially and economically*. Since, however, this country is not autonomous, it behoves us to accelerate the pace of the expansionist policy by setting up a central council of the nation whose duty will be to see that the policy of developing the economic resources of this country by means of maximum industrialization, and not merely by hand pressed and village industries, is carried into effect. . . .

Quite obviously, the Central National Council must be composed of the Chiefs and intelligentsia, namely the rapidly rising element of highly instructed people, who because of their education and opportunities, will be in a position to cooperate with our Chiefs to translate the policy of the country into action.

8 / POLITICAL BLUEPRINT OF NIGERIA / *NNAMDI AZIKIWE*

Now is the time to make a blueprint of our political aspirations so that all who are interested in the formulation of the political reconstruction programme of this country will read, mark, learn, and inwardly digest what the awakened Nigerian thinks and feels of the Nigeria of tomorrow. This political blueprint which I am about to publish is based on previous views espoused by me in the newspapers and other mediums for the expression of public opinion, and it is in accordance with some resolutions and manifestoes issued by certain groups and individuals who had given this subject serious study and deep thinking.

I will concede the following:

(1) Democracy as a political philosophy is the goal of progressive humanity; it appreciates the worth of the individual and seeks to crystallise in any aspect of human society this way of life.

(2) Indigenous political philosophy of Nigeria, in the main, is essentially democratic; it respects the will and wishes of the masses, and seeks to promote the welfare and well-being of the many, through ministers (not autocrats) of the State.

(3) The professed goal of British connection with Nigeria is said to be self-government.

(4) There have been contradictions between principle and practice towards the realisation of self-government in Nigeria.

(5) The period of tutelage and conditions for emancipation from political servitude are yet to be stated in categorical terms.

(6) A workable formula for attacking the vagaries which are inherent in such a system of government and administration is a desideratum.

The facts postulated above being self-evident truths, therefore, I submit the following as foundation for the erection of a political structure, which progressive dreamers and schemers should bear in mind in planning a free Nigeria.

From Nnamdi Azikiwe, *Political Blueprint of Nigeria* (Lagos: African Book Co., Ltd., 1943), pp. 8-11, 16-22, 56-58, 62-64. Reprinted by permission of the author.

Two Basic Stages of Development

Two basic stages in the political evolution of Nigeria are essential to-wards the crystallization of Nigerian autonomy: the Preliminary and the Intermediate.

The Preliminary Stage should last for a duration of no more than 10 years, and should start either now or immediately after the World War II. During this stage there should be a conscious process of Nigerianization in all aspects of our political and administrative life. The economy of the country should be planned in order to adjust and adapt it to the conscious process. At this stage, 200 scholarships should be awarded to the sons and daughters of Nigeria annually, for five years, to enable them to proceed abroad for specialised training in all branches of human endeavour; this will cost the country less than £50,000 a year. If Britain means to reduce the period of tutelage during which this country must suffer political servitude, then it should realise that only by this country producing trained men and women in all aspects of human endeavour can political progress be accelerated. . . .

The Second Stage in the political evolution of Nigeria is that stage which finds the process of Nigerianization taking shape and makes it necessary for non-Nigerian appointees in the Civil Service to act in an advisory and not in an administrative, capacity, in all aspects of Nigerian political life. This stage should last for five years, and at the end of period of tutelage, namely, 15 years (First Stage ten years, and Second Stage five years), the process of Nigerianization should be complete and non-Nigerian political experts should "hands off" our affairs administratively.

What I mean is that during the First Stage, Nigeria should be ruled by non-Nigerians, and Nigerians should undergo a period of tutelage which should prepare them for self-government. The key positions in the Nigerian State should be shared between Nigerians and non-Nigerians, and the former would act in an administrative capacity in concert with the latter. By the time 1,000 Nigerian scholarship holders shall have returned the country will be ready to stand on its own feet, politically. The period of training should last for seven years; it would take three years for the "handing over" process to be completed, to enable Nigeria to try "walking" and see whether, by the process of *experimenta lucifera,* it can also run.

With the First Stage over, Nigeria should be ready to put into practice what it had learned, in the past 10 years of Nigerianization of all the political institutions of the Nigerian State, and so it would enter the Second Stage to learn to do, by doing, which is the fundamental of all pedagogical methodologies. The period of learning to do by doing should take five years, after which the Mother Country should be prepared voluntarily (not reluctantly or compulsorily) to transfer the sceptre of sovereignty to the Nigerians who should have earned a "pass," and be diplomated. This shall automatically mean recognition of Nigeria as an autonomous community, equal in status and in no way subordinate either to the Dominions or to the Mother Country, in any respect of their domestic or external affairs, though united by a common allegiance and freely associated as a member of the commonwealth of nations. . . .

During the Preliminary Stage, there should be established a Nigerian Army, Nigerian Navy and Nigerian Air Force, in addition to the usual complements of such military organizations elsewhere, e.g. paratroops, home guards (for guerilla warfare), auxiliary and volunteer services, etc. In these military services, the rank and file should comprise Nigerian nationals, and should be officered by Nigerian and non-Nigerian nationals.

During the Intermediate Stage, there should be a complete Nigerianization of Nigerian man-power in the military services. At this stage, the Nigerian Army, the Nigerian Navy, and the Nigerian Air Force should be staffed in the rank and file by Nigerian nationals, and should be officered by commissioned persons of Nigerian nationality. The services of persons of non-Nigerian nationality will be required, since the development of military science and tactics is not static; in that case, such military experts can be employed or co-opted on special arrangement.

Once the man-power of Nigeria is organized and mobilized so that our national energy is directed and canalised into useful channels of community security and national preservation, the invitation which a state of martial weakness encourages is bound to recede; this should be a signal to sound the death knell of imperialism in Nigeria. . . .

Administrative Service

I wish to make it clear that, at present, the Administrative Service is almost a separate department from the rest of Government departments in Nigeria. From time immemorial it was regarded as a sacrosanct institution from whose ranks indigenous Nigerians were barred. It is true that there have been isolated instances when Nigerian nationals were appointed Administrative Officers, but if one should say that these people were tolerated, that is not stretching the point.

There is no doubt that we have had Africans who rendered efficient and loyal service in the Administrative Service, either as heads of departments or as junior executives, but the fact still remains that until relatively recent times, it was impossible for any Nigerian ever to dream of becoming a District Officer or a Resident, posted to serve and to take charge of a Division or Province, as had been the case with non-Nigerians. In the circumstances, it is imperative that in the political blueprint of Nigeria the role of the Administrative Officer of Nigerian nationality must be given due prominence. Without Nigerian Administrative Officers, the political future of Nigeria is bound to be retrogressive because only Nigerian political officers are capable of having the psychological and biological weapons with which one can adapt oneself to the complex political issues which face our political entities from time to time.

Nigerians have often viewed with alarm the tendency of the Colonial Office to impose on them alien political officers in the Administrative Service, with the result that in certain instances alien ideologies have replaced indigenous political philosophy of government and administration, despite the worship of the political cult of the so-called "Indirect Rule." For example, the idea of "Sole Native Authority," I maintain without fear of contradiction, is incompatible with the tenets of democracy, and I say most emphatically that most indigenous Nigerian political institutions are essentially and basically democratic. . . .

As I see the blueprint of rural government and administration in the Nigeria of my dreams, the so-called "Indirect Rule" must not be used as [a] weapon of reactionary ideas in an attempt (perhaps unconscious) to stay the hands of social progress in the country. The existence of so-called "Native Authorities" some of whom may be a "Sole Native Authority," and some of whom may be a "Chief-in-Council," and some of whom may be an Administrative Officer (although he cannot be a "Native" within the meaning of the Interpretation Ordinance) strikes one as odd and definitely anachronistic. If one should allege that the "Indirect Rule" system is outliving its usefulness, if its mission is to encourage the existence of feudal autocracies and medieval political institutions, one should not be regarded as a firebrand or a destructive critic necessarily. Admittedly, there is some good in the "Indirect Rule" system, but, in practice, some of the problems raised, and the attempted solutions to them— legal, political, social, etc.—have given ground for justified apprehensions. . . .

During the First Stage, rural government and administration should be continued as at present but with modifications of a fundamental nature, in so far as the practice of political philosophy is concerned. I mean that democratic institutions should substitute any undemocratic one, wherever the political system is basically democratic.

The existence of chieftaincies and emirates should not be encouraged; rather, chiefs and emirs should be incorporated in the indigenous structure of representative institutions inherent in the locality and should be specially appointed Presidents of such rural councils (for life) in so far as present chiefs are concerned, subject to good behaviour. In the rural councils, we have the germs of representative institutions; they should be the centre of gravity of rural government and administration. In any definitely demarcated area, the council responsible for government of the locality should be known as "The Local Authority" or "The Rural Authority" which should be a competent authority for the government of that particular area. By so doing, this country would have advanced politically in rapid progression, because, instead of relying on any Administrative Officer for guidance and administration, as at present, the rural population will rely on their own executive, legislative and judicial institutions, aided by experts of Nigerian and non-Nigerian nationality whose powers and terms of office should be clearly defined and limited constitutionally. . . .

Criteria of Political Autonomy

Now that we see that political autonomy is the *summum bonum* of political existence, globally, the question arises as to what are the tests of fitness for one country to arrogate to itself to wear the *toga virilis* of statehood? Usually, there are two tests, internal and external. The internal tests take into consideration such factors as (1) The desire of a people for self-government—is it real or superficial? (2) Are the population and territory capable of nurturing such political entities as would conduce to the corporate existence of a State? (3) Assuming that political autonomy is realised, will the beneficiaries be able to meet the universally accepted obligations of international society?

These internal tests could have been easily tackled, but for the fact that, excepting where revolutionary methods and means had been employed, interested States have always placed themselves as the sole arbiters to decide when a ward is fledged for political autonomy. I endorse the view postulated by international lawyers that political power is an attribute of sovereignty of every political entity and it is up to the people of such State or quasi-State to establish their claim. In this respect, I see no reason why Nigeria should not be able to satisfy the above criteria: (1) There is sustained desire on the part of our people for self-government. Old or young, literate or illiterate, they are clamouring for political autonomy: some for a Nigeria *risorgimento,* and some for a Nigeria *irredenta.* (2) With a population exceeding 30,000,000, and an area which is four times the size of the British Isles, Nigeria ranks higher than most sovereign States, in these two particular respects. (3) There is, therefore, no reason why Nigeria should not meet its international obligations, in view of the fact that during the period of tutelage, we had not given cause for anxiety in this respect, and moreover we had lived up to the spirit and letter of various international agreements, conventions, treaties, etc., signed, for and on our behalf. . . .

We demand political autonomy for our country. At this stage, we are only prepared to concede to Great Britain to take care of our defence, currency problems, as well as our external affairs. In 10 years we should be able to perform these functions, under her guidance; after 15 years, we should be free to conduct our internal and external affairs, as we see fit. Should Great Britain have the statesmen with vision and imagination to appreciate our request and facilitate self-government for our country, then a happy future can be envisaged for Anglo-Nigerian relations. Otherwise, the temper of the people might alter the present "mild" offer and an unconditional surrender of the sovereign rights of the people of the Protectorate of Nigeria might be demanded in more positive terms and action.

Nigeria at the Cross Road

Nigeria stands at the cross road of her national existence. One way leads towards the goal of political autonomy; another leads towards political servitude. Perhaps, our people might have preferred the latter road, yesterday. But then they saw their problem in a different light and perspective. Today, that cannot be the case. We are bound to move towards political freedom or know the reason why.

If there is any doubt about the yearnings of Nigerians for self-government it should be dispelled forthright. We are fed up with being governed as a Crown Colony, which we are NOT. We are nauseated by the existence of an untrammelled bureaucracy which makes, administers and interprets our laws, without our knowledge and consent. The idea of our paid civil servants ruling and lording it over us is a challenge to our manhood, both as a nation and as a race. We are now on the brink of great events: either we move forward and achieve political freedom, or we remain complacent and continue to be political serfs. We must not be complacent.

That I am interpreting correctly the temper of young Nigerians may be checked up from three important events which occurred recently. One was the historic 1942 resolution of the West African Students Union in London demanding immediate self-government. That resolution was also supported by the West African Press Delegation to London, in August, this year. Four months later, hundreds of young Nigerians met at a conference, which was held at Ojukoro Farm, near Lagos, when one of these young men proposed a resolution (which was unanimously adopted) on identical terms with those made by the West African Students Union and West African Press Delegation above. He said:

> The present Crown Colony system of government is obsolete and has no usefulness left in it. It is opposed to democracy and must be abrogated. It is the most ardent desire of our people that we must be granted internal self-government. We are finally convinced that the country is ready and prepared for same, and is matured to have it. This is apparent enough from the change of colonial policy from that of trusteeship to that of partnership. Nothing less than this form of government can bring to reality this new doctrine of partnership.

Self-government we must have. Great Britain cannot deny us this birthright of ours. Britain cannot be fighting a war of liberation and yet keep millions of Nigerians in political bondage. . . .

Nigerian soldiers are now shedding their blood. In the deserts of the

Middle East, in the jungles of Burma, in the wilds of North Africa, in the mountains of East Africa, they are sacrificing in order to make the world safe for democracy. They fight and die so that Nigerians and the rest of the world may have life and enjoy political freedom. Their valour and gallantry have been apotheosized by great soldiers and statesmen. Will their sacrifice be in vain?

9 / NIGERIAN NATIONS AND FEDERAL UNION
OBAFEMI AWOLOWO

When imperial Powers ratified the final share-out of Colonial territories at the Berlin Conference in 1885, Nigeria existed as three separate political units. These corresponded roughly with the present three Regions, and were administered by three different authorities. In 1906, the Eastern and Western zones were merged into what was then known as the Colony and Protectorate of Southern Nigeria, while the Northern Zone became the Protectorate of Northern Nigeria. These two zones were administered under separate authorities until 1914, when they were amalgamated and became the Colony and Protectorate of Nigeria.

Since the amalgamation all the efforts of the British Government have been devoted to developing the country into a unitary State. This is patently impossible; and it is astonishing that a nation with wide political experience like Great Britain fell into such a palpable error.

. . . some attempt is being made to rectify this original mistake. But it is only a partial attempt; and in many respects falls short of effectively checking the retarding influences of the existing unitary Constitution. The division into three Regions was arbitrary, and made only for administrative convenience. The proposed Constitution maintains the present division. It goes further, to devolve autonomous legislative and administrative functions on each Region, and thus to strengthen the existing decentralization. There are a few sentences in the White Paper which indicate rather vaguely that the British Government now recognizes the federal character of Nigeria.[1] But nothing is done beyond this paper recognition.

If rapid political progress is to be made in Nigeria it is high time we were realistic in tackling its constitutional problems. Nigeria is not a nation. It is a mere geographical expression. There are no "Nigerians" in the same sense as there are "English," "Welsh," or "French." The word "Nigerian" is merely a distinctive appellation to distinguish those who live within the boundaries of Nigeria from those who do not.

There are various national or ethnical groups in the country. Ten such

From Obafemi Awolowo, *Path to Nigerian Freedom* (London: Faber and Faber, Ltd., 1947), pp. 47-53. Reprinted by permission of Faber and Faber, Ltd.
[1] See *Proposals for the Revision of the Constitution of Nigeria*, Cmd 6599 (London, 1945), from which the so-called Richards Constitution was derived. [EDS.]

main groups were recorded during the 1931 census as follows: (1) Hausa, (2) Ibo, (3) Yoruba, (4) Fulani, (5) Kanuri, (6) Ibibio, (7) Munshi or Tiv, (8) Edo, (9) Nupe, and (10) Ijaw. According to *Nigeria Handbook*, eleventh edition, "there are also a great number of other small tribes too numerous to enumerate separately, whose combined total population amounts to 4,683,044."

It is a mistake to designate them "tribes." Each of them is a nation by itself with many tribes and clans. There is as much difference between them as there is between Germans, English, Russians and Turks, for instance. The fact that they have a common overlord does not destroy this fundamental difference.

The languages differ. The readiest means of communication between them now is English. Their cultural backgrounds and social outlooks differ widely; and their indigenous political institutions have little in common. Their present stages of development vary.

Politically, the best organized groups are the Hausas, including the Fulanis, who form the ruling class in the north, and the Yorubas. They had a highly developed system of government long before the white man came. The political institutions of the others, however, were primitive and are still amorphous. The constitution of the Yorubas is analogous to what is known as constitutional monarchy. The dictatorial powers which some Yoruba chiefs are wielding to-day are the making of the British Government, who at the beginning misconceived the true nature of Yoruba monarchy. The Fulani conquerors were autocrats pure and simple. They were just consolidating their conquest over the Hausas and a small portion of Yorubaland when the British came in the "scramble," to strengthen their hands. The Ibos, on the other hand, are essentially individualistic. The unit of government is the family; and the biggest autonomous aggregation for all purposes of government is the clan, with all the heads of families combining to form the governing body. The Ibos or Ibibios cannot tolerate anyone assuming the authority of a chieftain among them. For this reason the experiment of the "Warrant Chiefs" in the Eastern Region failed.

There are also vital differences in the potential abilities of the various national groups. In embracing Western culture, the Yorubas take the lead, and have benefited immensely as a result. The Efiks, the Ijaws, the Ibidios and the Ibos come next. The four last named are particularly keen and ambitious, and are doing all they can to overtake the Yorubas. The Hausas and Fulanis on the other hand are extremely conservative, and take very reluctantly to Western civilization. Their eyes are turned to the East, from whence light and inspiration had come to them in ages past; and they seem to spurn to look westward. And if the race is to the swift, in spite of their lower cultural background, the Ibos or the Ibibios would certainly qualify for self-government, long before the Hausas.

Above all, a deep religious gulf runs between the Northern and Southern portions of the country. The peoples in the Western and Eastern Regions of the south approach religion with remarkable moderation and nonchalance: Christians, Mohammedans, and so-called Pagans mix in society without restraint. The people in the North, however, are extremely fanatical about Islamism. They have an open contempt for those who do not share their religious belief.

All these incompatibilities among the various peoples in the country militate against unification. For one thing they are bound to slow down progress in certain sections, and on the other hand they tend to engender unfriendly feelings among the diverse elements thus forced together. The more alert and ambitious groups, like the Yorubas, Ibos, and Ibibios, are impatient, and want an increase in the pace of political, educational, and economic advancement; while the Hausas are indifferent. The Yorubas, in particular, have suffered feelings of frustration for years. Under a system which aims at getting all the peoples in the country to the goal of autonomy at the same hour and minute, the Yorubas have been compelled to mark time on their higher level while the other sections hasten to catch up with them. Because of this, it is wrongly believed by some that the Yorubas are deteriorating.

It is evident from the experiences of other nations that incompatibilities such as we have enumerated are barriers which cannot be overcome by glossing over them. They are *real*, not imaginary, obstacles. Those who place these groups under the same Constitution ignore them at their peril. More so, as it appears that these incompatibilities tend to grow in size as those concerned become more educated and civilized. . . .

Experts can propound learned theories as to why people having different languages and cultural backgrounds are unable to live together under a democratic unitary Constitution. But the empirical facts of history are enough to guide us. It has been shown beyond all doubt that the best constitution for such diverse peoples is a federal Constitution. This is exemplified by the Constitution of Switzerland, which is acclaimed to be the best and the most democratic in the world, since it gives complete autonomy to every racial group within the framework. The amended Constitution of the U.S.S.R. wherein each republic becomes autonomous is also an instance in point.

With regard to the effect of religious differences on political unity, India is an outstanding example. Her experience is well worth bearing in mind in tackling the constitutional problems of Nigeria. Lord Wavell's constitutional proposals are just a wee bit short of complete self-government. But to the astonishment of India's friends and admirers, she is unable to get what she has for years been painfully working for, because of religious fanaticism.

It is now no more the Congress leaders, but the Indian Moslems of the Moslem League who stand in the way of India's political advancement.

And it must be said at once that the Moslems of Northern Nigeria are no less fanatical and intolerant than Jinnah's Indian Moslems. What is more, the Government of Nigeria has all along helped to keep the flame of this fanaticism and intolerance burning brightly by pursuing a separationist policy in the North. . . .

The important point to note is that a federal Constitution is the only thing suitable for Nigeria. And for the sake of smooth and speedy progress, steps must be taken now to develop the various ethnical groups in the country along this line.

We must not wait until the situation becomes unduly complicated by long mutual friction and irritation. Already there are enough signs to put us wise. Strictly speaking, the political structure of any particular national group is primarily their own domestic concern. The others may criticize it in the same way as French and Russians may criticize the British Constitution. But they have no right to try to interfere effectively in the shaping of such a Constitution. But this is exactly what is happening in Nigeria now. The Ibos, for example, unused to having chieftains, cannot understand why the Obas in Yorubaland or the Emirs in the North should be entitled to the positions they occupy. On the other hand, the autocracy of the Emirs cuts the Yoruba people to the quick. And what is worse, the Ibos and the Yorubas think it is their business actively to work to bring about a drastic change in these Constitutions. This is certainly not the correct attitude. But as long as every person in Nigeria is made to feel that he is a Nigerian first and a Yoruba or Ibo, or Hausa next, each will be justified to poke his nose into the domestic issues of the others. The only thing of common interest to all Nigerians as such, and in which the voice of one must be as acceptable as that of any other, is the constitution of the central and federal Government of Nigeria. The constitution of each national group is the sole concern of the members of that group.

If the idea of a federal constitution for Nigeria is accepted, and if it is sincerely desired by the British Government to create "a system within which the diverse elements may progress at varying speeds, amicably and smoothly, towards a more closely integrated economic, social, and political unity, without sacrificing the principles and ideals inherent in their divergent ways of life . . . ," then the present administrative boundaries within the country must be redrawn. . . .

Under a true federal constitution each group, however small, is entitled to the same treatment as any other group, however large. Opportunity must be afforded to each to evolve its own peculiar political institution. Each group must be autonomous in regard to its internal affairs. Each must have its own Regional House of Assembly. Just now, however, it would be difficult to provide enough administrative staffs to handle the affairs of well over ten Houses of Assembly throughout the country. Even if such staffs were available the revenue of the country is unable to bear the expense. For the present, it is enough if it is borne in mind that this is our ultimate goal, and if we begin forthwith to take steps which would ensure the speedy attainment of this end.

We need not be alarmed at the number of autonomous States which would thus emerge. The population of Switzerland is about 4,000,000, just about one-sixth of that of Nigeria. This country consists of four racial groups. These are divided into twenty-two cantons, each of which has its own Parliament and Government. The Romansch, who form the fourth racial group, are only 44,000 in number. They, too, have regional autonomy with a Parliament and Government of their own. Canada, with a population of about half of that of Nigeria, has nine Provinces, each of which has its own Legislature. According to these and other well-known and well-tried constitutional precedents, even as many as thirty to forty Regional Houses of Assembly would not be too many in the future United States of Nigeria.

With this end in view, there must be a readjustment in the composition of some provinces. It is essential that each ethnical group be constituted into a separate Province or a number of Provinces. The present practice, whereby small ethnical groups are divided among neighbouring Provinces irrespective of ethnological differences, must be reversed. An outstanding example of this practice is the case of the Ijaw people. They are at present divided among the neighbouring Provinces of Calabar, Owerri, and Benin, with whom they have nothing in common but British overlordship.

A step in the right direction would be to constitute this and other similar scattered units into separate Provinces. This would make for better understanding and unity among the tribes and clans of the national groups concerned. This in turn would enable each group to make more rapid progress than at present; and as a result the pace of the country as a whole would be considerably quickened towards a federal unity.

10 / NIGERIA DEBATES SELF-GOVERNMENT / S. L. AKINTOLA and TAFAWA BALEWA

CHIEF AKINTOLA: Mr. Speaker, Sir, I rise to move the Motion standing in my name on the Order Paper. The Motion reads as follows:

> That this House instructs the delegates specifically added to the Federal Delegation to the forthcoming Constitutional Conference to express the views of this House to do all in their power to secure the grant of self-government to the Federation of Nigeria in 1957.

From Federation of Nigeria, *House of Representatives Debates. Official Report, Vol. II. Session 1957-58* (Lagos· Federal Government Printer, n.d.), pp. 728-741.

I start by assuring the House that, in moving this Motion, we are animated with the best intention in the world. The Motion, as it proceeds, will show that there will be no element of recrimination whatsoever and that, in moving it as best I can, I would express what I believe to be the legitimate desire not of just one party or one section but of the whole of the Federation of Nigeria.

I would say that this Motion presupposes that the time has come to put an end to imperialism as far as it applies to this country. Colonialism and imperialism are synonymous and I need not recount that imperialism is an evil; it has a lot of the elements of evil in it and, in saying that, I would not rely just on my own word: I would cite an instance in which one of the imperialists admitted that imperialism contains a lot of the elements of evil: I quote the words of a former Governor of Nigeria. On the 29th December, 1920, Sir Hugh Clifford made this statement to the old Legislative Council:

> The first and most obvious results of the clash of the higher with the less advanced civilizations are the demoralisation which it almost inevitably causes, alike in the possessors of the one and of the other, and of this the history of West Africa has furnished in the past—and, in a measure, furnishes even to this day—only too rank a crop of illustrative examples.
>
> The motives which brought about the first harsh impact between Europeans and the peoples of Nigeria were supplied by a hunger for wealth on both sides and by the traffic in human beings by means of which that hunger was assuaged for white man and for black man alike. The inevitable evils which arose therefrom call for no description or emphasis and, even when the Slave Trade had, at length, been stamped out, that miserable era was succeeded by the age of the traditional "palm oil" ruffians: broken men of almost every nationality who placed no limit upon the extravagances of their ill-doing and found in the African tribes which they exploited and corrupted hundreds who were eager to aid and to abet them.

In other words, imperialism is a hunger and it creates a lot of predatory instincts in man, whereby man becomes a wolf to man. The objective in this case, therefore, is to put an end to this evil of imperialism or colonialism.

Now, it is not only greed that is the evil effect of imperialism. Practically all wars that have been fought in human history arose, either directly or indirectly, as a result of imperialistic tendencies in some people. If, therefore, the abolition of imperialism is brought nearer, it may bring us nearer to peace, perfect and absolute peace, among human beings. In moving this Motion, therefore, and if this Motion is accepted, to put an end to imperialism in this country, it might be a contribution which Nigeria can make towards the establishment of universal peace.

The first evil of imperialism is that it destroys man's confidence in himself. Among imperialists there are people who have lived so long as the underdog that they have lost every confidence in themselves; they believe that, if all the countries of the world are free, it will render them poor in their own country; so it destroys their own confidence in themselves and among the backward people imperialism also destroys our own faith in ourselves.

There are people who have lived so long in bondage that they have lost every trace of liberty. Those who are interested in the history of the slave trade will remember that when those gallant lovers of peace all over the world were fighting to put an end to slavery, among their greatest opponents were slaves themselves. Slaves who had lost every confidence in themselves, who believed that they could never live again as free-born. By passing this Motion, therefore, we shall succeed in re-establishing in ourselves faith in our people and in our future.

Well, I have been able to satisfy the hon. House to some extent that imperialism is an evil, but is it an unmitigated evil? That is the question. Imperialism is an evil, but I respectfully submit that it is not an unmitigated evil. It is said that there is an element of goodness even in things evil. Bad as it is, imperialism, as far as it applies to Nigeria, has not been without some element of goodness.

Now what is the element of goodness in this part of imperialism? I must start by saying this in fairness to Britain, that Britain was not the author of imperialism. There have been several imperialist powers long before Britain. With due deference to the historians in the House, I would say that Britain has one distinctive distinction among imperialist powers. Britain succeeded in a large measure to humanise imperialism, and if ever there was anything known as benevolent imperialism, Britain was the author of it. As a result of this new faith in imperialism, Britain has been able to bring about a lot of useful changes in this country.

One outstanding contribution which will immortalise the name of Britain in this country is the creation of the country now known as Nigeria. Nigeria is a conglomeration of peoples, but Britain has, as a result of her imperial power, been able to weld together a number of people who perhaps otherwise would have remained to this day as warring tribal groups. I would therefore respectfully submit that the country known to-day as Nigeria is the creation of Britain, and I hope that it has been agreed by all sections, not only in this House but by the whole country, that that memorial to Britain, that creation, Nigeria, is a useful creation, and we must keep it intact, united and strong, not only now but for evermore. (*Hear, hear.*)

Not only has Britain given us a united country in the name of Nigeria, she has also given us our own system of parliamentary democracy. I think this is a great contribution to this country, and it will be one of the lasting memorials to Great Britain.

I need not exhaust the whole catalogue of the benefits that have accrued directly or indirectly as a result of our link with Britain. I refer to the creation of this country as a unit, I refer to the introduction of liberal education on the British pattern, the establishment of law and order, the establishment of modern communication, the furtherance of public health—all these are part of the goodness that has emerged out of British imperialism; what is more, Britain ruled over Nigeria, and it is often said by politicians and by nationalists that Britain has deprived us of our political freedom. While that may be so, Britain has also succeeded in whetting our appetite for freedom and British love of freedom has become infectious, and it is the urge pushing us on to-day, so that we may within the near future find ourselves on the same pedestal as imperialist Britain.

Well, I have given the evils in imperialism, and I have also been able to persuade you, I hope, that there is an element of goodness in imperialism, but much as Britain has done for this country in the name of imperialism, I respectfully submit that the end does not always necessarily justify the means. If Britain uses imperialism as a means of bringing benefit to this country, that result does not necessarily justify imperialism. I therefore respectfully submit that the time has come for us to put an end to imperialism.

How do we put an end to imperialism? Examples have been given in other countries, by attaining a new status, the status of an independent or self-governing country. When we attain that status, it does not mean that we sever our link with Britain. In fact Britain and Nigeria have been so indissolubly welded together that nothing ever can separate us. By putting forth this Motion we are merely trying to forge a new relationship between Nigeria and Britain which would no longer be that of a master and a servant, but which would be based on mutual trust, reciprocal goodwill, and mutual understanding. During that stage we would be masters within our own home. Britain will remain as master within her own home, but we shall still be linked together, joined together as friends and brothers, all in a common allegiance to Her Majesty the Queen at the head of the Commonwealth. (*Hear, hear.*) . . .

And what is left now? In the Council of Ministers we have only three expatriate officers, only three, as against ten Nigerian and Cameroon Ministers. Well that shows that the remaining responsibility to be undertaken would be the responsibility being discharged at the moment by three expatriate Ministers. Could an arrangement not be made between now and next December, for taking over the duties of only three Ministers? . . .

I feel as if I have satisfied the House that we are ready, in this year of grace, 1957, and I will end up by assuring the House that nothing will make for the unity of this country better than attainment of self-government. We can afford the luxury of dissension and we can make a mountain of a molehill at the moment, because we are not masters of ourselves; but immediately the responsibility passes to our hands, you will observe that the North will come nearer the East, the East will come nearer to the West, and all will come nearer to the Cameroons, and we will all admit that this country is our own. Its future is our own, and we can make or mar it, but I am quite sure that it is the desire of every section of this House to make Nigeria, and not to mar it. We are united in spite of occasional lapses which people may observe to-day. We are united, because we believe we have a common destiny. We are united because we believe in our country; we all want to create a new era, in which our children, and children's children, will live as citizens of a common country. In spite of these divisions which we have often heard about, and which newspapers and other critics magnify, I notice that the depth of unity is much greater than is generally realised. The tribes marry and inter-marry in this country, which is not a small achievement. In spite of our divisions, in spite of our dissension, we are united in one thing, we are united in the quest of political freedom, in the quest for independence. Is there anybody who does not want this country to be self-governing? There is none!

And as far as the question of Prime Minister is concerned, I notice that Nigeria is coming closer and closer together, and with the attainment of self-government in 1957 I am quite sure that Nigeria will surprise the whole world. We will surprise the world in creating the impression that we are one, one country, indivisible, and what will make us still more united is the fact that we have a Government which is our own, a Federal Government which belongs to the whole of the people of Nigeria. I am sure that hon. Members here, from every side, will agree with me that Nigeria is to-day yearning for freedom, Nigeria is yearning for independence, and the attainment of self-government by the State of Ghana has given a new impetus to everybody in different parts of this country. Our people will not be satisfied until we establish in this country a Government of the people of Nigeria, by the people of Nigeria, and for the people of Nigeria.

Mr. Speaker, Sir, I beg to move. (*Applause.*)

M. ABUBAKAR TAFAWA BALEWA (*The Minister of Transport*): Mr. Speaker, Sir, right from the start, I want to make clear the position of my Party, the Northern Peoples' Congress, on this most important question of self-government for the Federation of Nigeria on a given date.

I want the Honse to know that the Northern Peoples' Congress, as a Party, has never reached a firm decision on a definite date for the attainment of Nigerian independence. The members of my Party in this House, therefore, are taking part in the discussion of this subject with a view to conveying to our Party the wishes of the Members of the House of Representatives and to seek for their co-operation at the next Constitutional Conference. (*Applause.*) Sir, once this is understood, we see no reason why we of the Congress should refuse to allow the House of Representatives the opportunity to instruct their political delegates to press for the fixing of a date for Nigerian independence in 1959. (*Loud applause.*)

The Northern Peoples' Congress has never been at any time opposed to the idea of self-government. (*Cheers.*) The only difference between us and the other Parties on this subject is the question of fixing a date. We were opposed to the idea of fixing a date for many reasons, and, Sir, I am happy that to-day I have the opportunity to explain those reasons. I do sincerely hope that I shall be able to satisfy our critics and make them see clearly our position so as to appreciate our difficulties.

Sir, in the first place, we say that by accident of history, I mean the fact that the British entered this country from the sea, the areas that we now call the Northern, the Eastern and Western Regions of Nigeria came under the British administration at different times. By virtue of their being geographically situated near the sea coast, the Western and the Eastern Regions came under the British influence much earlier than the Northern Region. For this reason, Mr. Speaker, the rate of progress and development in the Western European civilisation has been uneven with the vast Northern Region dragging behind.

For the purpose of making the position more clearly understood, I will in this speech refer to the Eastern and the Western Regions together as the South. Now, in the field of Western education the South is farther ahead of the North and let us admit that whatever efforts the North may make, it will take some years before we can hope to reach parity with the South in this field. Sir, we have not been idle in exercising our energies to catch up with the South, for if we compare the progress that we in the North have made in the last 50 years of our British connection with the progress made by the South in more than 100 years, we can be satisfied that we have not done badly. (*Hear, hear.*) We should not forget, Sir, that the first elementary school in Northern Nigeria was opened in Kano in 1908. I think that it is to our credit that we are to-day able to speak on equal terms with the South. (*Applause.*) I am happy to say that the North is now wide awake and I hope it will not be long before we overtake the South. (*Cheers.*) However, Mr. Speaker, time is required for this, and we hope that in the interest of us all and for the sake of Nigerian unity, the people of the South should exercise a little patience to give us time to catch up.

We still cherish the plea that the development of a Federal system of government in any country largely depends on the even progress of the units comprising the Federation. (*Hear, hear.*) Man at times, Sir, is by nature suspicious, and it is therefore natural for the people of the North, though greater than the South in numerical strength, to fear domination. (*Some hon. Members: No!*) I am sorry to say, Sir, that those fears still exist and they can only be erased from our minds by the most sincere practical demonstration of goodwill and by the unselfish co-operation of the South. (*Hear, hear.*) By this I mean that the South should have sympathy for our shortcomings and that they should not be too hasty to condemn our actions.

Sir, take the question of staff in our Public Services. The South with its many schools and colleges, is producing hundreds of academically and technically qualified people for the Public Services. The common cry now is Nigerianisation of the Public Services. It is most important in a Federation that the Federal Public Service shall be fully representative of all the units which make up the Federation. Now, what do we find in Nigeria to-day? There are 46,000 men and women in the Federal Public Service. I have not been able to obtain the figures of the number of Northerners in the Service but I very much doubt if they even amount to 1 per cent.

This is, Sir, an intolerable situation and unless some solution is found it will continue to be a cause of dissatisfaction and friction. In the Regional Services we in the North are sincerely grateful to all Southern officers who have served in the North (*Applause.*) and we gladly recognise their services; but I must also say that our Northernisation policy is not an ingratitude; it is a policy now being actively pursued by all the other Regional Governments in the building of their Regional Services.

Mr. Speaker, people often forget that the people of Southern Nigeria came to be associated with the British pattern of legislative assembly about 1922: but we from the North have only come to be associated with such a body in 1947 and a quarter of a century is a very long start in political affairs. I consider it a great achievement that in only ten years in the Legislature the representatives of the North have learnt to hold their own (*Applause.*) and to-day on account of our modest contributions to our country's progress, we are in a position to discuss in our own right this most important subject of Nigerian independence. Surely, Sir, all reasonable people will agree that the Northerners have done very well. (*Applause.*)

It is now about ninety-five years ago since the British administration of Nigeria started. No one will doubt that Nigeria has benefitted immensely in its association with Britain and whatever people may say against colonialism and the so-called imperialism the British people have demonstrated in practical terms that among all colonial powers they are the best administrators. (*Prolonged applause.*) By their grant of independence to the peoples of non-European stock the British have fully demonstrated their sincerity and honesty in the pursuance of their colonial policy. India, Pakistan, Ceylon, and quite recently Ghana, are now all independent. British colonial policy is to grant self-government to all their colonial territories as soon as the people become ripe for it. . . .

In discussing the question of Nigerian self-government one must speak about unity in the country. National unity in a country like Nigeria where the means of easy communication have only been opened in the last fifty years is a thing which cannot be achieved overnight. Both time and patience are required, particularly if one remembers the diverse tribal communities which make up the country. Many parts of Nigeria did not even know of the existence of the other parts as recently as the beginning of this century. The obvious factor which will bring about unity amongst all Nigerian peoples is the economic factor, but time is required to work this out. I have travelled extensively throughout the Federation in the last five years and I must say that I have discovered everywhere that all our communities are happily living together with one another in peace and that in those places where discord is arising it is the politicians and our newspapers who preach disunity for their own ends and thereby foster bitterness. (*Applause.*) For many years before 1945 Nigerian tribes were living happily together in peace because at that time, Mr. Speaker, political parties were not organised.

This brings me to say that as far as the natives are concerned there is no disunity if politicians and newspapers will not go about preaching it. The political parties and newspapers in Nigeria must solely be held responsible if we in this country fail to achieve our national unity. This question of unity in Nigeria is often confused. It may sometimes be difficult to understand what some people really mean by the word "unity." I hope that we are now all agreed that a Federal form of Government is the best for Nigeria and that any attempt to impose a centralised unitary system will just split the country. (*Applause.*) Our diversity must be recognised at the same time as we recognise the importance of keeping our country together if we are not to disappoint the entire African race which looks to us for leadership.

We are the biggest single African state in the world and we should regard it as a duty to bring prestige and recognition to the African wherever he may be in the world: that we can do this I am certain, provided we are careful and become realists in dealing with the situation in our country.

I think I can rightly claim to have had some experience in this House and, during my ten years of unbroken legislative duties (*Applause.*), I have come across many people from the South who are most honest and sincere in their wish for Nigerian unity and I have no doubt that there are thousands of others whom I have not yet met. Sir, let us not play with the destiny of our country. We who are privileged to be Members of the legislature owe it as a duty to our people to bring this country together. Those of us who have travelled through other parts of the world know how important it is for Nigeria to remain one. We can exert great influence in world affairs if we are one—none if we are not. (*Loud applause.*) . . .

It must be recalled, Sir, that anything done in a rush and without careful preparation is bound to break into pieces. Let us, therefore, save Nigeria from breaking into pieces. Furthermore, Sir, certain issues are still at stake, and have not yet been resolved. These are also major issues.

There is still the question of breaking the country into states, which is a controversial matter; the question of boundary, about which some political parties have been making a fuss has not been finally settled. The Lagos and Colony State Movement is still pressing for a separate colony. The Nigerian Currency is not yet in the making, much less can it be said to be on its feet. The Federal Prime Minister, to which all parties have agreed, would mean reshuffling of the Cabinet. And all these things are things to which we must turn our attention for the next two years.

Sir, unless we are able to solve these problems, and unless we have actually been able to solve them, we shall be merely deceiving ourselves if we accept independence for the whole Federation of Nigeria. Over and above all these things, Sir, there are still certain intricacies and technicalities which must be dealt with. The system of revenue allocation, for instance, will have to be revised, and this is a most important issue.

Mr. Speaker, Sir, I must make it clear that with all these problems before us, and with all the intricacies of constitutional technicalities, Nigeria has got the men capable of shouldering all the responsibilities that self-government will bring with it. In any field, Sir, Nigeria will not be found wanting, but to build a house is one thing, and to furnish it ready for human abode is another. At this stage Nigeria has been able to build the house. We only need to furnish it, and we need to have the time and ample opportunity to furnish the house.

Finally, Sir, I wish to make this appeal to all political leaders of Nigeria and the Cameroons, that Nigeria and the Cameroons have come to stay under these political leaders and, therefore, Sir, each one of them should not, and cannot, in fact, do without the other. Let us, therefore, sink our differences, and shape the destiny of a Nigeria in which we may enjoy life more abundant. Let us make it clear, therefore, that if anything goes wrong with Nigeria, all of us will be held responsible.

Mr. Speaker, I beg to support.

11 / FRENCH AFRICA AND THE FRENCH UNION

FÉLIX HOUPHOUET-BOIGNY

Mr. President,

I am happy to be given this opportunity, as an African, and as a Minister of the French Republic, to greet and thank the honorable represent-

From Address by Félix Houphouet-Boigny to the Fourth Committee of the United Nations General Assembly on January 7th, 1957. Reprinted in Ambassade de France, Service de Presse et D'Information, *Speeches and Press Conferences No. 85* (New York, 1957), pp. 2-8.

atives of all the United Nations who propose, by patient and steady efforts, to fulfill the century-old dream of brotherhood among all peoples and all men.

My presence at this rostrum, in a debate like this, may perhaps cause some astonishment.

To the representatives of the peoples which only yesterday were under colonial rule, I may appear to be a man simply charged with defending the Government of which he is a member. That would be showing scant respect for my conscience. I can say to them categorically that I have not come for that reason.

In order, however, that you may clearly understand what I have to say, it is no doubt necessary—with your permission, Mr. President—that I break somewhat with the tradition of this august assembly, and with my own habits as well, by introducing myself.

I can assert, without running the risk of being in any way contradicted, that I have come to this great rostrum of the Nations as a free man, subject only to the dictates of his own conscience.

I am a native of the far-off Ivory Coast and have been a member of the French Parliament for the last ten years. I have the honor of presiding over the largest African political movement, the "African Democratic Rally," which is struggling for the human and social emancipation of Black Africa. I think I have the right to regard myself as the genuine representative of the African populations which, four consecutive times and sometimes under difficult conditions, have elected me to the French National Assembly. As I speak to you, I express the feelings and opinions of millions of African men and women.

And it is because of the increasing influence of the "African Democratic Rally" among the African masses and because of its strength as a popular movement, that one of its members was called upon, for the first time, to be a member of a French Government.

I should have liked to be able to borrow the infallible and serene eloquence of certain orators of Metropolitan France and Africa, an eloquence that is the pride of our Parliament, in order to outline for you, in the course of this debate, the conclusions of my own meditations on the political relations between France and the Overseas Territories and, more especially, on France's relations with Black Africa. But I am only a man of the African soil.

I have always lived among our good farm people. I have shared their joys and their sorrows, I have made their great hope my own. I am an African farmer.

In the absence of persuasive eloquence, I shall try, by appealing to the traditional good sense of all the farmers of the earth and to the conscience of all the doctors of the world, to give you quite simply the thoughts I have derived from a long search.

All the peoples of the earth aspire to independence. Africa cannot in principle escape this universal law of the evolution of peoples. But words are often ambiguous and the United Nations knows better than any one how similar terms often conceal very different realities.

Therefore I hope you will allow a man—who is the leader of a powerful African movement, who until this day has unceasingly denounced abuses and mistakes and tirelessly demanded justice and equality—that you will allow this man to tell you his feelings on African realities, always bearing in mind the present framework of the struggle for emancipation, bearing in mind the interdependence of peoples which has become the golden rule of this century, bearing in mind, finally, the insufficiently known changes in the behavior of Frenchmen in their relations with the peoples formerly under colonial rule and, more especially, with those of Black Africa.

The Atlantic Charter has made the right of peoples to self determination a universal principle. The dependent peoples of Black Africa also must, therefore, move toward the constitution of new nations.

But we Black Africans are just becoming acquainted with political life at a time when the very notion of the absolute independence of nations is undergoing a remarkable development.

In this century, each nation feels more and more cramped within its boundaries. The nations, even the largest, the most powerful or the most prosperous, can no longer complacently enjoy the deceptive luxury of isolation. Thus the world is tending to become organized in large economic and political units.

On the morrow of the last world war, France conceived a very beautiful and grand design: to free and emancipate her former colonies scattered on the five continents of the world and to associate them with her destiny.

She undertook, by the very act of setting up the French Union, to lead the peoples for whom she is responsible toward the freedom to administer their own affairs democratically.

France renounced force as a means of domination: she knows that the same is true of the force of men as of that of nations; it is born, grows and dies. That which endures is work done together in equality and justice; that which endures is brotherhood. She wants to construct a new community, based on confidence and friendship.

"Watch out," we were then advised from various quarters. "Don't let yourselves be taken in by the voice of the Sirens; the association offered you is that of the horse and the horseman."

The conscientious and responsible men of French Black Africa, those who have fought colonialism the hardest and are still fighting colonialism in all its forms, want, while remaining extremely vigilant, to do away with paralyzing distrust, to rise above all feelings of bitterness, even the most legitimate, and to grasp the brotherly hand that is held out to them.

We do not have any complexes. We are a young and proud people. The brothers, sons and grandsons of all those magnificent infantrymen who, during the two world wars when France's independence and the freedom of the world were jeopardized, vied in bravery by the side of the French and of their allies, will know how to give proof of the same courage and the same abnegation, in the peaceful struggle now beginning for their human and social emancipation.

Would France want to deceive us? But her whole tradition of progress, all her generous and emancipating inclinations deny this, as well as her humane ideals and her most obvious self-interest.

She knows that if we need her in order to succeed in our struggle for emancipation, we are indispensable to her if she is to play in the world, and first of all in Europe, that great role of rapprochement between men and peoples which is in her best tradition.

France is a light which must not be extinguished.

Simple justice demands that after having denounced and condemned all the discriminatory laws of French colonialism, we recognize in all honesty the positive side of colonization, colonization which, in itself, is not an isolated fact, peculiar to France, but has been a universal process of history.

France has not exterminated the races placed under her domination; on the contrary, the indigenous populations have grown everywhere.

She has not imposed her regime on those for whom she has assumed responsibility. Here, thrones have been preserved and protected; there, the individual character of the territory and the customs have been respected—all while paving the way for democracy.

Is it not an edifying spectacle to see before you today a Minister of the French Republic, member of a Government under Socialist leadership, an African who follows the customs of matriarchy, a plain middle class African, leader of the largest democratic popular movement in French Black Africa?

Finally, gentlemen, France has never known racial segregation. Who can prove to me the contrary? Certain individuals, in her name, may have shown themselves to be narrow-minded racists, that is true, but the French people as a whole condemn, *de jure* as well as *de facto,* racism in all its forms. The presence of a colored man[1] in one of the highest posts of the State, the presence of African Ministers within the French Government, is not enough, we agree, to constitute the happiness of the peoples overseas. But France may be legitimately proud of the fact that, for the past ten years, continuously re-elected by large majorities, she has had as President of the Senate, the third-ranking position in the State, the remarkable President Monnerville; she has also had as Vice President of her National Assembly, an African, my friend Modibo Keita, native of the Sudan, one of the leaders of the "African Democratic Rally"; as Vice

[1] Gaston Monnerville, a Negro from the French West Indies. [Eds.]

President of the Assembly of the French Union, another Sudanese, our friend Ya Dombia, a Socialist; and finally, under the Third and Fourth Republics, several native Ministers of France Overseas such as Diagne, Candace, Lamine-Gueye, Fily Dabo Sissoko, Conombo, Senghor, Dicko, and, last of all, myself. . . .

What it is therefore essential to determine, and one must express an opinion on this point, is whether—in Black Africa's present state of development, and bearing in mind the twofold fact that the world trend is toward large economic and political units and that Black Africa is not directly affected by the ideological conflict which divides the world —whether Black Africa's interest lies within the framework of absolute independence or within that of a larger unit.

In West Africa and Equatorial Africa, over 60 million Africans—I wish to speak only of those Africans who are the most advanced politically —were divided, by the accident of colonization in the last century, into two groups of different cultures: English culture and French culture.

The first group, English speaking, is moving toward independence within the framework of the Commonwealth, with ties that are more economic than political.

The second is moving toward self-government within a federal community which remains to be defined juridically but whose ties, within the community, are of a sentimental, economic and political nature.

We, Africans of French culture, are following the bold experiment of our English-speaking brothers with much interest and much sympathy.

Yes, Kwame Nkrumah and the leaders of Nigeria and Sierra Leone have our affectionate sympathy.

They wish to show what the black people of Africa can accomplish on their own initiative. We cannot be indifferent to their experiment. We wish them prompt and complete success.

But we wish, in a spirit of healthy emulation, to conduct our own experiment. The future will decide which of our methods is better.

In this venture without precedent in the long history of the peoples of the world, the French and ourselves—a community of men of different races, religions and degrees of civilization, engaged in the same struggle for happiness, with freedom and fraternity—the French and ourselves are going to shoulder heavy responsibilities with regard to Africa.

It would be unforgivable for us, the responsible African statesmen of today, to betray Africa when it places its confidence in us.

We are fully aware of our obligations. And so is France who knows that she would betray, not only her own interests, but also all that which has constituted her greatness, her traditional generosity, her cherished and proud motto: Liberty, Equality, Fraternity.

The community we want to achieve, together with her, will be humane, equalitarian and fraternal or it will not be at all. But we are confident that it will be. . . .

The United Nations Organization will not attain its goal if it is satisfied with merely facilitating the birth of new nations.

It must help to ensure within nations, or groups of nations, peace, justice, rising living standards and the social progress of their citizens. There are no happy men in an unhappy country. There cannot be happy nations in an unhappy world. To live an oppressed and miserable life in a politically independent country does not make man truly independent. To be independent means not only to enjoy political rights and basic freedoms, but beyond that to have the standard of living, health, and education required to exercise fully such rights and freedoms. I have no intention, gentlemen, of inveighing against any particular person or nation. I am only asking you to be fair and to consider the facts. Is there a single country in the world which would offer to an African of my color, race, and stage of civilization, the liberty, equality, and fraternity we can find within the French community?

We must therefore help nations, such as France, which are doing their utmost to make the human element prevail, for, gentlemen, the centuries-old dream of peoples and men is not stupendous technical progress, proud though men may be of such achievements, nor is it the conquest of interstellar space or the disintegration of matter; the great dream of humanity is brotherhood.

Some have said that I am a mystic.

Yes, I am a mystic fervently devoted to brotherhood. And because I believe in brotherhood, I believe in the final triumph of the French-African community, inasmuch as we want it to be humane, equalitarian and fraternal.

12 / THE THEORETICAL FOUNDATIONS OF THE R.D.A.
GABRIEL D'ARBOUSSIER

. . . In Black Africa, the essential objectives are the same for all classes and strata of society.

Moreover, it would not be right to want to impose on the anti-colonialist liberation movement a firm organization and strict discipline.

We are indeed aware of the differences which separate the African milieu from the European milieu. We know that it is not by chance that the proletariat is the class which lends itself *par excellence* to forms of organization, the rigidity of which could not be applied to our masses. Indeed, the way of life of the worker and of the employee of the great industrial centers subject to a strict schedule such as the daily obligation of taking one's train or one's subway to get to work which is manifest in the necessary precision of the movements and of the solidarity which

From Gabriel D'Arboussier, "La situation actuelle du Rassemblement Démocratique Africain," in *Le Rassemblement Démocratique Africain dans la Lutte Anti-Imperialiste* (Paris: Les Impressions Rapides, 1948), pp. 46-53.

links one worker to his companion on the assembly line, creates an awareness of a different necessity from that which a peasant from our African wilds can acquire, since he is submitted to an altogether different rhythm of work.

It will not be by simple orders that we will modify this state of affairs, but rather by the transformation of the social and economic life of our environment. "It is not consciousness which creates the social being, but, quite on the contrary, the social being which creates consciousness," which in turn has a definite influence on our social behavior.

These considerations justify the attainment of the present objectives of the African masses:

a) The organization of the union of all classes, and not of a political party which is the expression of such and such a class;
b) The creation of a very large mass movement which must be the expression of the masses, not an avant-garde political party.
c) The grant of a large measure of autonomy to the diverse territories, regions and local sections, both in the forms of organization and in the movement's orientations and actions.

It is in terms of these fundamental considerations that we have determined the end and the means of the R.D.A.

The goal is precise: *the emancipation of our different countries from the yoke of colonialism through the affirmation of their political, economic, social, and cultural personalities, and the freely agreed union of countries and peoples, founded on the equality of rights and duties.*

Once the goal has been defined, it is necessary to determine the means, and we have not neglected to state them precisely since the time of the origin of our movement:

1. Union at the heart of a large political organization, embracing all ideological conceptions, all ethnic groups, all social strata, and every territory, and based on a program of concrete goals which must be clearly defined.

2. The solidarity of different countries in the fight against a common enemy, imperialism, which *indiscriminately* exploits, although under diverse forms, the people of these countries.

Let us examine, one by one, the necessary and the sufficient conditions for the application of these means:

1. Union. It goes without saying that it cannot be accomplished by an ideology, since our movement must encompass all tendencies; neither can it be accomplished by the defense of particular claims made by one class or by one social stratum, since our movement must encompass all social strata, all ethnic groups, all territories. But, on the other hand, as we have indicated above, there are claims which are common to all these men of different origins and different ideologies, and the first is the struggle for application

a) of the fundamental principle of the right of people to dispose of themselves as they wish, written into article 73 of the Charter of the United Nations, and, as a corollary, the primacy of interests of the people of each territory;

b) of the Constitution of the French Union, founded on the equality of rights and duties, and the solidarity of the nations and peoples who compose it.

Here is how, on September 1, 1947, I answered Senghor, in *La Voix du R.D.A.:*

"France is a country whose people created its unity and its national independence, which lives from an industrialized economy, whose development had led each day to a greater division of society into two main classes: capitalists and workers, who vie with each other for political power and economic control.

"Africa, on the contrary, is made up of diverse countries and peoples, who have as yet won neither their unity nor their national independence, who still live an agrarian economy, and whose society is still divided into extremely diverse layers and classes.

"Whereas in France, the workers, whose class interest coincides with the national interest, are grouping together more closely each day in their fight against capital, in Africa the different peoples, just like the different classes and social strata, are grouping themselves in their fight against the colonial regime, and this, to a certain extent, has made their unity.

"Thus, whereas in France the particular interests of the workers, who constitute the essential class, are found to coincide with the national interest and justify their fight against capitalism, in Africa the particular interest of each class and social stratum is dominated by the common interest of the whole population which is subjected to the colonial regime.

"As Leopold Senghor said in his report, the essential struggle in Africa is the struggle for the extension of democracy, the number one enemy of which is the imperialism of the Trusts, which dominates both French workers and African colonials.

"You will now understand why we have called our movement the *Rassemblement Démocratique Africain.*

"You will understand why we have affirmed, and we still affirm, that there cannot be any one metropolitan party whose cause Africans could today completely espouse, for all metropolitan parties are organized and act according to the fundamental law of the class struggle.

"The position of our movement with regard to these parties has been determined, first of all by the interest of the African masses who are united, of course, with all oppressed masses, but whose interests are not identical.

"As for us . . . we are not a proletarian party, but a democratic organization, which corresponds to the social and economic foundation of Africa, at the heart of which men of all origins, walks of life, and philosophical or religious conceptions have their place, and which has a program of concrete goals."

2. Solidarity of all the peoples of the French Union and of the world-wide democratic forces.

Examining this problem, we wrote in July, 1947, in *La Voix du R.D.A.*: "The R.D.A. claims to have a policy which is derived from the objective study of the African reality, but also from the world-wide reality."

And it is because of this that, while affirming our determination to accomplish the free development of the African people, we affirm the necessity of an alliance between African democratic forces and French democratic forces.

For the entire history of the relations between France and the peoples of the overseas territories is a testament to it. Each time democracy has advanced in France, it has corresponded to a movement of emancipation in the overseas territories, just as each retreat of the democratic cause in France has corresponded to a reinforcement of exploitation and oppression.

On the one hand, we have the decree of rights of citizenship given to us by the Revolution of 1789, the liberation of slaves and the institution of deliberating assemblies given to us by the Revolution of 1848, the suppression of slavery decreed by the Second Republic, the suppression of forced labor, the right of citizenship, public liberties, the democratic assemblies established by the first Constituent Assembly of 1946.

On the other hand, we have the re-establishment of slavery by the *Consulat*, the limitation of the power of local Assemblies by the Second Empire, forced labor and exceptional laws under the Vichy regime, the limitation of power of local Assemblies by the second Constituent Assembly of 1946, and the reactionary politics of these last months.

But the inverse is equally true. And it was only by relying on the democratic progress of the peoples of the overseas territories that the French democratic forces, in forming their union, gained political, economic, and social victories of crucial importance, such as the overthrow of personal power, the nationalizations, the extension of trade union rights.

It is from this parallel and concomitant struggle that the alliance of the elected representatives of the *Rassemblement Démocratique Africain* and the Communist group resulted, which in the constituent Assemblies had never ceased defining the rights of the peoples of the overseas territories and which recent events have really shown to be the veritable avant-garde of French democratic forces.

Our alliance does not stem from a sentimental or other attitude, but from a political necessity, for we could not rock ourselves to sleep with an "isolationist" illusion in a world where interdependence is the rule which determines the lives of people.

We know that, in the entire world and among all peoples, there exist forces of progress and forces of reaction, and that the former are the natural allies of dependent people, for this dependence is only the result of the tentacular development of a regime which subjects, in industrial countries as well, a mass of men we call the working class.

We know that the selfish interests which cause the American working class share of the national revenue to decline while the capital revenue is increasing, which oppose in France the policy of nationalization and the legitimate claims of the Communist, Socialist, and Christian workers, are the same which support Franco in Spain or Tsaldaris in Greece, and which are trying to sabotage the French Union in Indo-China, in Madagascar, or in Africa.

As for us, we ally ourselves with all democratic forces which struggle against these selfish interests, and first of all with French democratic forces who are undergoing assault by the same imperialist forces which are subjugating Africans.

We enter into this alliance, however, with means, methods, and goals fitted to our movement, for we know that the common interest of France and Africa is not made from an identity of goals, but rather from their interdependence born from given political and economic conditions.

Such is the fundamental position of the R.D.A. which we have deemed necessary to review before approaching the present situation of our movement and the problems posed before it.

13 / AFRICAN AWAKENING: A MARXIST VIEW
MAJHEMOUT DIOP

There is one fact that has become undisputable in this second half of the twentieth century: it is that Africa from the Cape to Cairo, from Dakar to Port-Soudan or Mombasa, has definitely awakened from its long torpor. The immense continent is shaking itself, stretching itself, and because of this it is everywhere cracking the edifice of imperialism in Africa. One is witnessing everywhere the preliminary signs of an explosion as grandiose as it will be salutary.

People have started marching toward Liberty!

Among these people one must evidently cite those of Black Africa under "French" domination, whose backwardness only serves to make the awakening more dramatic.

Of course, the fact still remains that we are a backward country, the

From Majhemout Diop, *Contribution a l'étude des Problèmes Politiques en Afrique Noire* (Paris: Éditions Présence Africaine, 1958), pp. 251-259. Reprinted by permission of Éditions Présence Africaine.

inevitable consequence of the conditions of material life of our society, to the exclusion of all other imaginable causes.

When one then analyzes these conditions, the thing which strikes one is that the secondary factors, the geographic environment and the small density of population—due almost exclusively to the Negro slave trade —have ceased being detrimental to us. But the determining factor, the imperialist method of production, still fully exercises its inauspicious action.

From now on, it is evident that it is against imperialism that Africans, anxious for the destinies of their countries, must fight with their utmost energy. For there is no other way to liquidate Africa's backwardness, to start with firm action en route to a new life of progress and happiness.

But in order to fight against the enemy, it is necessary to know them, to know their tricks by heart, to exercise oneself in order to ward off their blows, while at the same time reserving oneself the joy of returning their blows.

What then is imperialism?

In a word, it is monopolistic capitalism . . . . Better still, it is the administrative and governmental system, the bayonets of the colonial powers behind which the pillaging commercial houses take shelter, as well as the vampire banks which are looting the riches of our nation.

Using trickery and violence, merciless looting and killing, the foreign imperialists, in their assault on the peaceful populations of our countries, thus accumulated immense riches. But, and it is our misfortune, the old European imperialists (the British, the French, the Belgians, the Portuguese, the Spanish, etc.) were only leeches as compared to American imperialism which, since World War II, came to the rescue, taking for themselves the lion's share, to the great detriment of our wounded Africa.

However, in the colonies of Africa imperialism does more than despoil and enslave the people forced to submit to its barbarous yoke.

That is only a consequence, the superficial phenomenon, which is directly visible.

More basically, it is implanting capitalism everywhere. In effect, the predominance of commercial capital in Black Africa, the introduction of money thanks to commerce and money taxes, is weakening the foundations of the old precapitalistic economic systems. Everywhere one witnesses, thus, the passage toward capitalism of the primitive village, of slavery, of feudalism; the old methods of production are winding their way toward new modes of production. This is the complex picture of transition to a superior economic regime, relatively civilizing, and which, in any case, brings with it the seeds of a state of affairs where the exploitation of man by man will be unknown.

It is on this foundation that the present society of Africa is being built. The old caste system has everywhere been strongly eroded, and new classes are arising side-by-side with the old classes and their debris. Thus, we see side-by-side with the proletarians, the petty bourgeoisie of capitalist society, the peasants, the artisans, the semi-feudal peoples.

Here are the classes, the social strata, in a word, the men of Africa who must fight against imperialism. They will be the agents of the struggle, the armies of colonized peoples.

From history we learn the lesson which shows that having been conquered by force, it is not excluded that we should also expect our liberation by force of arms.

. . . But that is still not all. In order to gain not only the battle but the entire war against imperialism we also need allies, for the enemy is powerful and continually groups and regroups its forces.

Until the present time, we have only considered the internal resources of Africa, the internal conditions. . . . It is clear that in a war against so universal and so cosmopolitan an enemy as imperialism, it is imperative, if we want victory, to look beyond Africa, to look all over the world to find if, by chance, there do not exist other enemies of imperialism, that is, natural allies in that which concerns us.

And precisely one event of world-wide historic significance, the Great Socialist Revolution of October 1917, has come in time to bring us these allies. Breaking the imperialist front where the chains were weakest, the Russian proletariat established socialism on one-sixth of the terrestrial globe.

Since then, much water has flowed under the bridge. The Second World War has passed! With the crushing of fascism emerged the popular democracies of Europe and Asia, while Chinese troops established popular power for 600 million men.

That was the second step, that is the opening of the second phase of the all-out crisis of capitalism!

The whole world felt the beneficial wave of the rise of democracies and popular forces. Millions of other allies came to our side forming a vast concert of peoples fighting for democracy and peace.

In Africa, even since October 1946, at the Congress of Bamako, an important event was to mark the lives of the black peoples; an organized and disciplined anti-imperialist movement was born, inspired by modern methods of combat and working to arm itself with an avant-garde theory. This movement took the name of *Rassemblement Démocratique Africain*. Rapidly as a powder fuse, the movement spread from the Lake of Guiers to Lake Tchad, from the Fouta Djallon to the Cameroon Mountains, carrying with it millions of enthusiastic men.

The era had conceived a giant; but, unfortunately, the giant was still a child, and the imperialists decided to stifle it in its crib.

It is true that the R.D.A., although it grew quickly, had one weakness: it was born in the post-October era of proletarian revolutions, and, even though it marked the fusion of all classes of African society, from the workers to the property owners, by way of the artisans, the peasants, the bourgeois, and the intellectuals; even though it correctly resolved the system of alliances with the French proletarians and their Communist Party, and more generally with all the world-wide progressive forces; even though it deliberately placed itself on the side of socialism, democracy, and peace, on the side of the Soviet Union and of popular China, it lacked something to augment its resistance and to conquer from the time of its conception. What then was the weakness of the R.D.A. as a general movement of struggle against imperialism? Just as a nursing child dies from lack of milk, so did the R.D.A. lack an inspiring and a directing force, a nourishing home from which it could radiate ceaselessly the beneficial light of an avant-garde theory; it lacked, because it was a movement and not a single front, a party of the proletariat, a Marxist party, exercising hegemony at its heart.

Of course, to create such a party is not an easy matter, for it is never easy to work according to the demands and the principles of science!

Yes! It is true that the proletariat is being organized in Africa; it is true that the "socialist consciousness" is penetrating these organizations; it is true, in a word, that the external conditions, like the internal ones, seem to lean favorably toward the extension of subjective conditions. But that is not yet all. It would still be necessary for the party of the proletariat, faithful to Marxist-Leninist teachings, to know how to adapt itself to the conditions of our countries, how to profit from the experience of its brother parties, while at the same time avoding all mechanical imitations.

It is the absence of such a party, whose creation was not the order of the day; the absence of this party of the workers, and, consequently, the absence of its direction, which was the Achilles' heel of the R.D.A., which was its weakness, and which allowed the imperialists, mixing threats with corruption, to sow confusion in our ranks.

. . . Lacking a scientific party, it was necessary, looking forward to the future, to force science into the other parties. For the history of the revolutionary movements of the whole world teach us that a day arrives when the disaffected masses of the people erupt. Then the well-fed parasites fall crushed into the ashcan of history.

. . . Now this revolutionary party has seen the light of day. This party is the *Parti Africain de l'Indépendence* (P.A.I.), Party of the new kind, a Party armed with the Theory of scientific socialism, a Party of struggle for Independence and for National Sovereignty, a Party for the Construction of an African Socialist Society.

The R.D.A. relinquished intact the flag of the anti-imperialist struggle. The P.A.I. picks it up and each day raises it higher and higher.

The day, so long waited for, has come; the day of the beginning of victory.

14 / RACE AND POLITICS IN KENYA / TOM MBOYA

One cannot have a true picture of Kenya without dealing with the position of the white settlement of approximately 60,000 as compared with 6,000,000 Africans. In addition there is an East Indian population of some 150,000, and an Arab population of some 25,000. The East Indians came to Kenya about 1895, mainly as laborers to help build the Mombasa-Lake Victoria railway.

European Supremacy

The white man came to Kenya and East Africa to better himself and found a new home. Sir Charles Eliot, the British Commissioner in East Africa 1900-1905, declared that the interior of the country must be regarded as "white-man's country," and that it would be hypocritical not to believe that white settlers' interests must be paramount in the event of a clash between those interests and those of the indigenous people. In 1911-12, Lord Delamere, a European settler leader and owner of some 150,000 acres of land, giving evidence to a Commission appointed to investigate the causes of the shortage of labor on European farms and plantations, stated that the reason for the shortage was that the African had enough land of his own. The solution he therefore suggested was to curtail African land units and thereby create a situation in which the African would have to work in order to live.

Today *land* remains the bone of contention in Kenya politics. It is an issue whose mention raises the highest tempers on both sides. Following Lord Delamere, the British Government set aside some 13,000 square miles of land exclusively for white settlers. Under an Order-in-Council, not only are non-Europeans refused ownership of land in this area—commonly known as the "White Highlands"—but they are not even allowed to manage land for or sub-let from the white owners. Here the white settlers own land on 999-year leases, or on freehold. This is the best and most fertile land in the country. The status of the African who goes in to work or live is that of a squatter; never a landowner. Yet of the 60,000 Europeans in Kenya only some 10,000 live and have an interest in the "White Highlands"; the rest live in urban areas, mostly engaged in commerce, industry, or administration. Even today in this area there is vacant land which awaits new European settlers.

Contrast this with the position of the 6,000,000 Africans who must live in reserves or land units—approximately 52,000 square miles, some of which is dry scrub land. Here, on what is known as "Crown land" the African's position remains that of a temporary tenant of the Crown at

From Tom Mboya, *Kenya Faces the Future* (New York: American Committee on Africa, 1959), pp. 8-11, 17-19. Reprinted by permission of the publisher.

will. He can be moved from place to place without notice or without consent, and he has neither legal title nor right. In a report published in 1955 it was found that in some areas there was a density of 700-800 people per square mile. Despite African protests at these injustices the British Government has refused to rectify them, and thus land remains the most sensitive political issue. In 1954 the government introduced a land consolidation scheme to solve the problem of segmentation, to improve agricultural production and ultimately to grant individual title deeds. However, it does not answer the Africans' grievance over the exclusive reservation of land to white settlers, or the existing landlessness among the Africans.

The concept of European supremacy is gradually changing its character, even though most European leaders still believe in European domination. It is true that some of the more outrageous discriminatory legislation and/or administrative practices are gradually disappearing, but a reference to these helps ousiders to understand the background, and indeed the causes, of the outbreak of violence and terrorism in 1952.

Economically, Africans for years were not allowed to grow any export cash crop (coffee, sisal, etc.) and when he raised maize, his produce fetched less than that grown by a neighboring European farmer. He was not allowed to participate in certain trades or to establish a business in certain areas. Credit facilities were, and to some extent remain, denied him by legislation, fixing a credit ceiling of not more than £10 without the written exemption certificate of the Government. In industry, wages and conditions of service were until 1954 based on race and color. Thus an African with the same qualifications and experience of an Asian or European worker received less than the Asian, while the Asian received less than the European. Today some improvements have been made in such discriminatory practices, since the outbreak of Mau Mau violence, which has unfortunately given the impression that violence has paid. However, discrimination is still practiced under the excuse of the inexperience of the African or the tutorial role of the British. Even now the African may only grow 100 trees of coffee initially, and must obtain a permit before he can enlarge his plantation. Denied the right to own land, the African is told that because he lacks security he cannot avail himself of loan and credit facilities.

Socially, the African was discriminated against in public places and generally treated with contempt and ridicule. Today the color bar in hotels, shops and post offices, cinemas and public transport has either completely disappeared or is on its way out. However, the Government still maintains a policy of discrimination in schools and hospitals, and in urban areas in housing and residence. Despite the introduction of non-racial wages, salaries and conditions of employment in the civil service in 1954, there is still discrimination in employment and promotion opportunities, although generally the situation is more hopeful and the future brighter.

Politically, Kenya's development has been largely determined by an extremist European settler community, aided by an often wavering and undecided British Government, attempting to establish a permanent European-dominated government. In 1919 the white settlers obtained direct representation on the Kenya Legislative Council and thus began to gain a real foothold in the government. Following the increasing agitation by Africans over land and the demand by the Asians for equality, in 1923 the British Government issued a statement aimed at establishing the paramountcy of African interests in the event of a clash between the Africans and the immigrant communities. Yet it was not until 1946 that the Africans were given even the token representation of one legislative member nominated by the Governor; in 1948 they were granted a second nominated member. Meanwhile the Asian demand for a common voters' roll with the Europeans was denied, but Asians were granted direct elective representation in the Legislature based on universal adult suffrage. In 1952 the number of African representatives was increased to six, but all were still nominated while Asians and Europeans elected their representatives directly through universal adult franchise. In 1952, whereas 6,000,000 Africans were represented by six nominated members, 60,000 Europeans were represented by 14 directly elected members. 150,000 Asians by 6 directly elected members, and the 25,000 Arabs represented by one elected and one nominated member.

The State of Emergency

This then was the situation on October 20, 1952, when due to Mau Mau violence the government declared a State of Emergency which cost the country close to £60,000,000, over 3,000 lives, and many more wounded. Arrest and detention without trial resulted in the mass deprivation of freedom and liberty for over 400,000 people since 1952, leaving many innocent women and children without support or means of livelihood. The situation has improved considerably. There is no longer any active fighting. Detention camps are almost empty, and the country is reverting to peaceful conditions. But many of us continue to ask whether this costly and destructive emergency was necessary to awaken the British and the settlers to the realities of African growth and aspirations. And we are concerned about the 2,000 Kenyans who are still detained and about the continuation of the state of emergency, with the consequent restrictions on basic freedoms and arbitrary abuse of power by administrative officials.

The Kenya African desired, and still desires, political, social and economic equality, leading eventually to complete political freedom. The Europeans on the other hand were bent on a policy of permanent supremacy; they desired a government and country similar to South

Africa. Between these two objectives there was no meeting ground. A head-on clash was inevitable.

The African Stand

It is unfortunate that information about the African stand on our ultimate objectives for Kenya, as well as our position toward the immigrant communities, has generally come from settler spokesmen or the European press. We, the African elected members, have been called, among other things, obdurate, intransigent, racialists, extremists, and agitators. I have particularly been singled out and made the target for abuse. The most recent form such attacks have taken is that we are inconsistent, and by implication, dishonest, and that I personally speak with two voices—a sweet one in London and an extremist one in Africa.

Such charges would be more amusing if they did not intensify an already tense situation. As for the last charge of inconsistency, any examination of the position of the African members, and of my own, will show, particularly during the last two years, the consistency of the African position and the almost ludicrous inconsistency of the position of the Europeans and the British Government, particularly in reference to the contradictory British policy toward different African countries.

As for our position on ultimate objectives, that has been clear and consistent throughout: the demand for the development of Kenya into a democracy with equal rights and opportunities regardless of race, color or creed. . . .

Our attitude on the "white highlands" is that this is an anachronism which must go. We cannot see any hope of developing happy European-African relations when our people have only to travel by train or bus from an overcrowded and often arid reserve to see vast areas of apparently unoccupied land and to be told that this is exclusively reserved for white settlers. It is politically unsound for an immigrant community—so small in number—to continue to maintain this exclusive reservation and expect that this will not be a source of friction and ill-feeling. In our view this exclusive reservation cannot be defended on moral, political or economic grounds. . . .

15 / WHITE SUPREMACY AND AFRICAN NATIONALISM
NDABANINGI SITHOLE

The average white man in Africa is scared almost out of his senses by the rapidly emerging African nationalism. An African nationalism is regarded not only as potential but as real danger to the present status of the white man in Africa. The question has been often asked: What is

From Ndabaningi Sithole, *African Nationalism* (Cape Town: Oxford University Press, 1959), pp. 19-23, 36-38, 156-159. Reprinted by permission of Oxford University Press.

it that has brought about this strong nationalistic feeling among the otherwise docile peoples of Africa who had, to all appearance, acquiesced in white domination?

It would be idle to single out one factor as causative of this new vigorous African nationalism sweeping the length and breadth of the vast continent of Africa, the home of approximately 140,000,000 blacks, 65,000,000 Arabs, and 5,000,000 whites. Like all movements, African nationalism roots back into history, and without this historical foundation, the seemingly sudden African nationalism becomes inexplicable. There are chain causes which may be traced back to pre-European days of Africa. In our examination of the factors that have given rise to this much-talked-about African nationalism, it is well to bear in mind that all movements of consequence are preceded by ideas.

World War II, as many people have frequently noted, has had a great deal to do with the awakening of the peoples of Africa. During the war the African came in contact with practically all the peoples of the earth. He met them on a life-and-death-struggle basis. He saw the so-called civilized and peaceful and orderly white people mercilessly butchering one another just as his so-called savage ancestors had done in tribal wars. He saw no difference between the primitive and the civilized man. In short, he saw through European pretensions that only Africans were savages. This had a revolutionizing psychological impact on the African.

But more than this, World War II taught the African most powerful ideas. During the war the Allied Powers taught the subject peoples (and millions of them!) that it was not right for Germany to dominate other nations. They taught the subject peoples to fight and die for freedom rather than live and be subjugated by Hitler. The subject peoples learned the lesson well and responded magnificantly, and they fought, and endured hardship, and died, under the magic spell of freedom. . . .

Here then is the paradox of history, that the Allied Powers, by effectively liquidating the threat of Nazi world domination, set in motion those powerful forces which are now liquidating, with equal effectiveness, European domination in Africa. As a Moroccan put it, "Our struggle against France is a carry-over of the same struggle against Hitler." The emergence and the march of African nationalism are in reality a boomerang on the colonial powers. They fired the anti-domination bullet at Nazi Germany, but now the same bullet is being fired at them!

Unfortunately the outside world, that is the Western world, do not seem to see this African nationalism in its right perspective. They think it is an anti-white movement, and therefore they are not sympathetic to it. Many African nationalists have been branded as rebels and subjected to the severest penalties for their nationalist activities.

◇　　◇　　◇

The overall European policy in Africa may be summed up in two words—white supremacy, and this is what the African means when he says, "White people, from Cape to Cairo, are the same." That is, they have a mania to rule Africa. This European policy is a great challenge to Africa, and since it is the nature of human existence to respond to challenge, the African peoples, despite their great geographical, linguistical, and ethnical differences, have been united by this challenge to which they are now responding positively and persistently. The law of "the greater the challenge, the greater the stimulus" is in full operation on the continent of Africa. So long as the challenge remains, it would seem that the African peoples will continue, by every conceivable effort, to devise ways and means of overthrowing white domination without necessarily driving the white man out of Africa. The chances are that the white man, because he is too proud and too greedy to share life on an equal basis with the African, may leave Africa if equality of races becomes an accomplished fact.

If European policy had adopted, right from the beginning, an inclusive rather than an exclusive policy, it seems reasonable to surmise that African nationalism, as it is today, would have been almost unknown. This is pure speculation and we do not pretend to know what would have happened if an inclusive policy had been followed; so that here we shall speak in terms of possibilities rather than actualities.

On examination, the basic ingredients that go to make up the present African nationalism may be enumerated as the African's desire to participate fully in the central government of the country; his desire for economic justice that recognizes fully the principle of "equal pay for equal work" regardless of the colour of the skin; his desire to have full political rights in his own country; his dislike of being treated as a stranger in the land of his birth; his dislike of being treated as means for the white man's end; and his dislike of the laws of the country that prescribe for him a permanent position of inferiority as a human being. It is this exclusive policy of white supremacy that has created a deep dissatisfaction among the African peoples. It is this exclusive policy that has brought to the fore the African's consciousness of kind. It seems reasonable to say that the present African nationalism is, paradoxically, the child of white supremacy, the product of an exclusive policy. . . .

To conclude our survey, we may now say that white supremacy is a stubborn rejection of the African by the white man, and that African nationalism is a reaction to that rejection. The African does not so much resent rejection in foreign countries, but he loathes it in the land of his birth. He wants to feel accepted by his fellow-men as [a] man, and white supremacy is standing in his way, and he is determined to brush it aside. African nationalism is a struggle against white supremacy, and this struggle will continue to go on until white supremacy in Africa has given way to sound common sense—namely, that people, regardless of their colour or race, do not like to be treated as unwanted strangers in the land of their birth. The victory of African nationalism will therefore be the triumph of human personality and dignity.

Africa has been inhabited by a myth, and that myth is now cracking. In some areas it has reached the last point of falling asunder; in others it is showing only very serious cracks without falling apart; and in yet other areas it suffers only insignificant cracks. . . .

The emergent African nationalism, in many ways, represents the degree to which the white man's magic spell, which at the beginning of the nineteenth century had been cast on the African, is wearing off. As long as this myth was thick and impenetrable, the African adjusted himself as well as he could to what he thought were gods, though god that ate corn. As long as the white man was able to hold up his pretensions to the African as real, the African was scared, and never challenged the white man as his national ruler. Alas, the externals have had their day, and reality has taken its place; but few white people in Africa realize this extremely important change. Most of them still have the picture of the African who worships the white man as a god, and they refuse to face the fact that Time and Eternity are beckoning to them to come down from their ivory towers and dwell among their fellow-creatures for their own sake and for that of their fellow-creatures.

There are certain basic facts that these white people, who would like to be regarded by Africans as myth, forget. The generation of Africans who first came into contact with the white man and his wonders were overwhelmed by the novelty of the white man and the new things he had brought to Africa. It was natural therefore to accord the white man a special place in Africa. But a good part of the present African generation, born in modern hospitals, raised in modern towns and cities, educated in modern schools, travelling by land, air, and sea, using the most up-to-date means of conveyance, trained in modern arts and skills, employed in modern factories, mines, and other occupations, rubbing shoulders daily with white people in towns, cities, schools, and on the battlefield, take the white man as a matter of course, just as they take another African in the same way. They know no other environment. The white man can no longer cast his spell over them by the simple trick of showing them the train or an automobile, or reading to them a story book, or cracking his gun, because many an African now knows how to do these things. It pains the white man to realize that the African now regards him as an ordinary human being. To him the new African generation is all degenerate. It has no proper respect for the white man, not so much because he is human but because he is white. Here then is the dilemma of the white man. He fails to draw a distinction between what was and what is, let alone what will be in a matter of a few decades. He fails to grasp what has happened since his coming to Africa.

This aspect raises the question: How much African is the present-day African? There is a world of difference between the African prior to the coming of the white man and the African after Africa was occupied by European powers. There is therefore a sense in which an African is African, and a sense in which he is not African, just as there is a sense in which an American who has spent two-thirds of his life in Africa is and is not American, and is and is not African. While the Westerners may be consciously Westernizing Africa, Africa is also unconsciously Africanizing them. The interaction between the West and Africa is producing a new brand of the African. That is, it is pushing the white-man-worshipping African into the background, and bringing into the foreground the African who does not worship the white man. The proud and arrogant African may think he is 100 per cent African because both his mother and father are African, just as a proud and arrogant white man born in Africa may also think he is 100 per cent European. The truth is that there is no such thing in a multiracial society as 100 per cent this or that race.

Take an African who has been to school. He may think he is 100 per cent African. Externally and physically this may be true. But an examination of the content of his consciousness, even on a superficial level, will disclose that his mathematical thought, his legal training, his theological views, his commercial and industrial understanding, his economic theories, the themes of his conversation, his present aspirations and hopes, to quote only a few, are radically different from those of an African who lived before the advent of European powers. We are not suggesting here that there is a clean break between the present-day African and his forefathers. We recognize fully a sense of historical continuity, and yet, at the same time, we recognize self-evident economic, political, and social discontinuity between the African and his ancestors. The present-day African has new eyes, as it were. He sees new things that he never saw before. He has new ears. He hears new things that he never heard before. He has a new sensibility. He feels things that he never felt before. He does not see what his forefathers saw. He does not hear what his forefathers heard. He does not feel what his forefathers felt. He does not see the white myth his forefathers saw, for the simple reason that he has ceased in many ways to be the African his forefathers used to be. He is not like his forefathers. Why not? His forefathers lived during the period when the pace was set by the wagon; but he lives during the period when electricity sets the pace.

But in what way is the present African really different from his forefathers? The answer is simple. His forefathers were vaguely conscious of the country in which they lived. They were not conscious of the rest of Africa—certainly not of the countries outside Africa. This was specially true of those who lived inland, but not so true of those who lived along the coast. They spent most of their time looking after their livestock, hunting and trapping game. Perhaps to describe their lot negatively may be helpful here. Their eyes never saw the large cities and towns whose buildings now soar to the sky. They never rode bicycles, motor-cars, trains, and they never flew. They never went to school; that is, they never learned how to read and write. They never built themselves modern houses. In short, their period was marked by the widespread absence of modern facilities and conveniences, and hence, from their point of view, the white man was just a myth. This gives us a new angle of vision so that we may rightly say that a myth depends for its existence upon our ignorance. As soon as this ignorance is removed, the myth also is removed.

The modern African, on the other hand, lives in an environment in many instances totally different from that in which his forefathers lived. He is not only conscious of the country in which he lives, but also of Africa as a whole, and of the whole world. International forces play on his conscious being in a way his forefathers never experienced. Unlike his forefathers' environment that hummed with bees, and that was livened with singing birds, disturbed by wild animals, and moved at nature's pace, the modern African now lives in an environment where the mechanical bird has superseded the bird, where automobiles, trains, and tractors have pushed the ox, the donkey, and the horse into the background. He lives in an atmosphere in which his forefathers' myth lived. If the African forefathers should come back to life and behold their own descendants on the modern scene, it is not far-fetched to say they would mistake their own children for the gods.

16 / INDICTMENT OF SOUTH AFRICA / NELSON MANDELA

In the course of this application I am frequently going to refer to the white man and to white people. I want at once to make it clear that I am not a racialist and do not support racialism of any kind, because to me racialism is a barbaric thing whether it comes from a black man or from a white man.

I challenge the right of this court to hear my case on two grounds:

Firstly, I challenge it on the ground that I will not be given a fair and proper trial.

Secondly, I consider myself neither morally nor legally obliged to obey laws made by a parliament in which I am not represented.

In a political trial such as the present one, which involves a clash of the aspirations of the African people and those of whites, the country's

From Statement to Magistrate's Court by Nelson Mandela, reprinted in *The Globe Magazine* (London, December 22, 1962), pp. 10-11.

courts, as presently constituted, cannot be impartial and fair. In such cases, whites are interested parties. A judiciary controlled entirely by whites and enforcing laws enacted by a white parliament in which we have no representation—laws which in most cases are passed in the face of unanimous opposition from Africans—cannot be regarded as an impartial tribunal in a political trial where an African stands as an accused.

It is true that an African, who is charged in a court of law, enjoys on the surface the same rights and privileges as a white accused in so far as the conduct of his trial in concerned. He is governed by the same rules of procedure and evidence as apply to a white accused. But it would be grossly inaccurate to conclude from this fact that an African enjoys equality before the law.

In its proper meaning equality before the law means the right to participate in the making of the laws by which one is governed; a constitution which guarantees democratic rights to all sections of the population, the right to approach the court for protection or relief for the violation of rights guaranteed in the constitution, and the right to take part in the administration of justice as judges, magistrates, attorneys-general, law advisers and similar positions.

The white man makes all the laws; he charges us before his courts and accuses us, and he sits in judgment over us. The real purpose of this rigid color bar is to ensure that the justice dispensed by the courts should conform to the policy of the country, however much that policy might be in conflict with the norms of justice accepted in judiciaries throughout the civilized world.

The existence of genuine democratic values among some of the country's whites in the judiciary, however slender they may be, is welcomed by me. I hate racial discrimination most intensely and in all its manifestations. I have fought it all along my life. I fight it now, and will do so until the end of my days. Even although I now happen to be tried by one whose opinion I hold in high esteem, I detest most violently the set-up that surrounds me here. It makes me feel that I am a black man in a white man's court. This should not be. I should feel perfectly free, at ease and at home with the assurance that I am being tried by a fellow South African who does not regard the white man as a harsh and merciless type of human being whose contempt for our rights, and whose utter indifference to the promotion of our welfare, makes his assurances to us absolutely meaningless and hypocritical.

In order that the court shall understand the frame of mind which leads me to action such as this, it is necessary for me to explain the background to my own political development and to try to make this court aware of the factors that influenced me.

Many years ago, when I was a boy brought up in my village in the Transkei, I listened to the elders of the tribe telling stories about the good old days, before the arrival of the white men. I hoped and vowed then that, among the treasures that life might offer me, would be the opportunity to serve my people and make my own humble contribution to their freedom struggles.

When I reached adult stature, I became a member of the African National Congress. That was in 1944, and I have followed its policy, supported it and believed in its aims and outlook for 18 years. Its policy was one which appealed to my deepest inner convictions. It sought for the unity of all Africans, overriding tribal differences among them. It sought the acquisition of political power for Africans in the land of their birth. The African National Congress further believed that all people, irrespective of the national groups to which they may belong, and irrespective of the color of their skins, all people whose home is South Africa and who believe in the principles of democracy and of equality of men, should be treated as Africans; that all South Africans are entitled to live a free life on the basis of fullest equality of the rights and opportunities in every field, of full democratic rights, with a direct say in the affairs of the government.

Right at the beginning of my career as an attorney I encountered difficulties imposed on me because of the color of my skin and further difficulty surrounding me because of my membership and support of the African National Congress. In the courts where we practiced we were constantly aware that no matter how well, how correctly, how adequately we pursued our career of law, we could not become a prosecutor, or a magistrate, or a judge. We became aware of the fact that as attorneys we often dealt with officials whose competence and attainments were no higher than ours, but whose superior position was maintained and protected by a white skin.

I regarded it as a duty which I owed, not just to my people, but also to my profession, to cry out against this discrimination which is essentially unjust and opposed to the whole basis of the attitude toward justice which is part of the tradition of legal training in this country. I believed that in taking up a stand against this injustice I was upholding the dignity of what should be an honorable profession.

Your worship, I would say that the whole life of any thinking African is this country drives him continuously to a conflict peculiar to this country. The law as it is applied, the law as it has been developed over a long period of history, and especially the law as it is written and designed by the Nationalist Government, is a law which, in our view, is immoral, unjust and intolerable. Our consciences dictate that we must protest against it, that we must oppose it and that we must attempt to alter it.

Always we have been conscious of our obligations as citizens to avoid breaches of the law, where such breaches can be avoided, to prevent clash between the authorities and our people, where such clash can be prevented, but nevertheless we have been driven to speak up for what we believe is right, and work for it and try to bring about changes which will satisfy our human conscience. If I had my time over I would do the same again, so would any man who dares call himself a man.

We have been conditioned to our attitudes by history which is not of our making. We have been conditioned by the history of white government in this country to accept the fact that Africans, when they make their demands strongly and powerfully enough for those demands to have some chance of success, will be met by force and terror on the part of the Government. This is not something we have taught the African people, this is something the African people have learned from their own bitter experience.

Government violence can do only one thing and that is to breed counter-violence. We have warned repeatedly that the Government, by resorting continually to violence, will breed, in this country, counter-violence among the people till ultimately, if there is no dawning of sanity on the part of the Government, the dispute between the Government and my people will finish up by being settled in violence and by force. Already there are indications in this country that people, my people, Africans, are turning to deliberate acts of violence and of force against the Government, in order to persuade the Government in the only language which this Government shows, by its own behavior, that it understands.

Elsewhere in the world, a court would say to me "You should have made representations to the Government." This court, I am confident, will not say so. Representations have been made, by people who have gone before me, time and time again.

Nor will the court, I believe, say that, under the circumstances, my people are condemned forever to say nothing and to do nothing. If the court says that, or believes it, I think it is mistaken and deceiving itself. Men are not capable of doing nothing, of saying nothing, of not reacting to injustice, of not protesting against oppression, of not striving for the good society and the good life in the ways they see it. Nor will they do so in this country.

Perhaps the court will say that despite our human rights to protest, to object, to make ourselves heard, we should stay within the letter of the law. I would say, sir, that it is the Government, its administration of the law, which brings the law into such contempt and disrepute that one is no longer concerned in this country to stay within the letter of the law. I will illustrate this from my own experience. The Government has used the process of law to handicap me, in my personal life, in my career and in my political work in a way which is calculated, in my opinion, to bring a contempt for the law.

I found myself trailed by officers of the security branch of the police force wherever I went. In short, I found myself treated as a criminal, an unconvicted criminal. I was not allowed to pick my company, to frequent the company of men, to participate in their political activities, to join their organizations. I was not free from constant police surveillance any more than a convict in one of our jails is free from surveillance. I was made, by the law, a criminal, not because of what I had done, but of what I stood for, because of what I thought, because of my conscience. Can it be any wonder to anybody that such conditions make a man an outlaw of society? Can it be wondered that such a man, having been outlawed by the Government, should be prepared to lead the life of an outlaw, as I have led for some months, according to the evidence before this court?

It has not been easy for me during the past period to separate myself from my wife and children, to say good-by to the good old days when, at the end of a strenuous day at an office, I could look forward to joining my family at the dinner table, and instead to take up the life of a man hunted continuously by the police, living separated from those who are closest to me, in my own country, facing continually the hazards of detection and of arrest. This has been a life infinitely more difficult than serving a prison sentence. No man in his right senses would voluntarily choose such a life in preference to one of normal family social life which exists in every civilized community.

But there comes a time, as it came in my life, when a man is denied the right to live a normal life, when he can live only the life of an outlaw because the Government has so decreed to use the law to impose a state of outlawry upon him. I was driven to this situation, and I do not regret having taken the decisions that I did take. Other people will be driven in the same way in this country, by this same very force of police persecution and of administrative action by the Government, to follow my course; of that I am certain.

I must place on record my belief that I have been only one in a large army of people, to all of whom the credit for any success of achievement is due. Advance and progress is the result not of my work, alone, but of the collective work of my colleagues and me, both here and abroad.

I do not believe, your worship, that this court, in inflicting penalties, will deter men from the course that they believe is right. History shows that penalties do not deter men when their conscience is aroused, nor will they deter my people or the colleagues with whom I have worked before.

I am prepared to pay the penalty even though I know how bitter and desperate is the situation of an African in the prisons of this country. I have been in these prisons and I know how gross is the discrimination, even behind the prison walls, against Africans, how much worse is the condition of the treatment meted out to African prisoners than that accorded to whites. More powerful than my fear of the dreadful conditions to which I might be subjected in prison is my hatred for the dreadful conditions to which my people are subjected outside prison throughout this country.

I hate the practice of race discrimination, and in doing so, in my hatred, I am sustained by the fact that the overwhelming majority of mankind hates it equally. I hate the systematic inculcation of children with color prejudice and I am sustained in that hatred by the fact that the overwhelming majority of mankind, here and abroad, is with me in that. I hate the racial arrogance which decrees that the good things of life shall be retained as the exclusive right of a minority of the population, and which reduces the majority of the population to subservience and inferiority, and maintains them as voteless chattels to work where they are told and behave as they are told by the ruling minority.

Nothing that this court can do to me will change in any way that hatred in me, which can only be removed by the removal of the injustice and the inhumanity which I have sought to remove from the political, social and economic life of this country.

Whatever sentence your worship sees fit to impose upon me for the crime for which I have been convicted before this court, may it rest assured that when my sentence has been completed I will still be moved, as men are always moved, by their consciences; I will still be moved to dislike of the race discrimination against my people when I come out from serving my sentence, to take up again, as best as I can, the struggle for the removal of those injustices until they are finally abolished once and for all.

17 / MANIFESTO OF THE BELGIAN-CONGOLESE ELITE, 1956

Our National Vocation

In the history of the Congo, the last eighty years have been more important than the millenniums which have preceded them. The next thirty years will be decisive for our future. It would be vain to base our national sentiment on attachment to the past. It is toward the future that we turn our attention.

We believe that the Congo is called upon to become a great nation in the center of the African continent.

Our national vocation: to work in the heart of Africa to establish a new, prosperous, and happy society on the foundations of an ancient clan society which has been vigorously shaken by too rapid an evolution, and which now seeks its new equilibrium.

We will only find this new equilibrium in the synthesis of our African

From "The *Conscience Africaine* Manifesto" in Washington Okumu, *Lumumba's Congo: Roots of Conflict* (New York: Ivan Obolensky, Inc., 1963), Appendix B, pp. 234-248.

character and temperament with the fundamental riches of Western civilization.

Only the Congolese, with the brotherly assistance of the Western people living in the Congo, can realize this synthesis.

In order to speak of a Congolese nation composed of Africans and Europeans, it is necessary that all be filled with the desire to serve the Congo. We have a right to demand of those Europeans who share in our national life to be, above all, Congolese citizens—that is to say, not to pursue only the good of the Belgian community and their own personal interests in the Congo, but to seek, together with us, the good of the great Congolese community.

Unity in Diversity

One principle is essential for us: the color of the skin confers no privilege. Without this principle, union is impossible.

But a fundamental equality does not signify identity: we wish to be civilized Congolese, not "dark-skinned Europeans." We understand well that the Europeans wish to maintain their own way of life.

Progressive but Total Emancipation

Belgium must not consider that there is a feeling of hostility in our desire for emancipation. Quite to the contrary, Belgium should be proud that, unlike nearly all colonized people, our desire is expressed without hatred or resentment. This alone is undeniable proof that the work of the Belgians in this country is not a failure.

If Belgium succeeds in leading the Congo to total emancipation intelligently and peacefully, it will be the first example in history of a colonial venture ending in complete success.

But to achieve that, the Belgians must realize now that their domination of the Congo will not go on forever. We protest strongly against the opinion sometimes expressed in the press that does not make an essential distinction between the *presence* of the Belgians in the Congo and *their domination* of the Congo.

To those who ask: How long before the Belgians must leave the Congo?, we answer: Why do certain Belgians pose the question to either dominate or abandon completely?

To those who pose this question, we would like to propose for the good both of the Congo and of the Belgians in the Congo, that they pack their bags without further delay.

Political Emancipation

We have read that there is a question of a thirty-year plan for the political emancipation of the Congo. Without declaring ourselves on the whole of its component parts, we believe that such a plan has become a necessity if it is the intention to realize emancipation in peace and concord.

This plan should express the sincere will of Belgium to lead the Congo to its complete political emancipation in a period of thirty years. Only an unequivocal declaration on this point will preserve the confidence of the Congolese toward Belgium.

This plan, which would be a compromise between the impatience of one group and the conservatism of the other, must clearly establish the intermediate stages which it will effect in fixed periods of time. It is the only way to avoid having each reform project give way periodically to discussions, bargaining, and tests of force between two antagonistic blocs, which, finally, would become irreconcilable.

As for political emancipation, we think that there is a way to depart from the existing institutions by having them evolve progressively. The direction is twofold. On the one hand, existing institutions must become more and more representative by replacing progressively the present system of nominations with a system in which the population itself will designate its representatives. On the other hand, the councils which are now purely consultative must receive a true power of decision and control in increasingly extended matters in order to arrive finally at a responsible government at the head of our nation.

Not giving genuine responsibilities to the representatives of the people would only multiply the difficulties and prepare the future poorly. Those who never sought to undertake decisions on their own have always tended to assert exaggerated and unrealizable claims. This would lead inevitably to demagogy.

We are not asking only for a plan of political emancipation, but for a full plan of total emancipation.

At each stage of political emancipation there must be a corresponding stage of economic and social emancipation, as well as progress in education and culture. The parallel realization of these steps is an absolute necessity if political emancipation is to be sincere and effective.

We do not wish that external appearances of political independence be in reality only a way of enslaving and exploiting us.

Our Attitude with Regard to Belgium

We are grateful to Belgium, but an artificial patriotism is not asked of us.

To the question of whether we wish to remain united with Belgium later, we answer: "We do not wish in any way to have the Congo integrated into the united Belgian state. We will never allow a Belgo-Congolese Federation to be imposed on us without our free consent, or as a condition of our political emancipation."

We wish that one day such a community might be the fruit of a free collaboration between two independent Nations which are bound by an enduring friendship.

We do not measure this friendship of Belgium by mounting capital investments, but by the attitude of the Belgians in the Congo with regard to the Congolese, and by the sincerity with which Belgium will help us to realize our total political autonomy.

A year ago the Congo reserved a triumphal welcome for King Baudouin. All the Congolese understood that our King loved his people. Our cheering expressed not only our gratitude, but also our hope that the attitudes of the Sovereign would serve as an example to all Belgians in the Congo and in the mother country.

Need for the National Union

We have only one chance to make our cause triumphant: that is to be and to remain united.

United we will be strong, divided we will be weak; it is the future of the nation which is at stake.

National union is necessary because the whole population of the Congo must, before all else, be conscious of its national character and its unity. How will this be possible if the people are wooed by several competing parties?

This leads us to take a position concerning the introduction of Belgium's political parties into the Congo. Our position is clear: These parties are an evil and they are useless.

Political parties do not fulfill any need in the present political and administrative structure of the Congo, since we have neither a Parliament nor elections. Furthermore, the Belgian political divisions do not have significance for the Congo; they have arisen from historical circumstances peculiar to Belgium.

But above all we do not want parties at present because what characterizes parties is conflict, while what we want is union.

If we let ourselves be divided, we will never realize the ideal of a great Congolese nation. Even if certain parties include political emancipation in their program, the mere existence of these parties is a radical obstacle to this emancipation.

Those Congolese who would be tempted to let themselves get drawn into party politics do not realize the old adage adopted by all dominators: "Divide and conquer"— To divide in order to dominate better.

Let our position be understood: We wish to be neither "a party against parties" nor "an unrivalled party."

We are convinced that it is wholly possible for pagans, Catholics, Protestants, Salvationists, Mohammedans to agree on a program of common good which respects those principles of the natural ethic engraved on the soul of every man worthy of the name. The Congolese can realize this program most surely by being united and by having sincere respect for the convictions of each person.

Later, when the political structures of the Congo make it necessary we can group ourselves according to our affinities, our interests, and our political conceptions. It is highly probable that when that time arrives the specifically Congolese parties will not take the Belgian parties as a model.

Appeal to the Congolese

We have full confidence in the future of our country. We have confidence also in the men who must live in it in concord and in happiness.

With all the sincerity and all the enthusiasm of our hearts we cry out: Long live the Congo! Long live Belgium! Long live the King!

III / POLICIES AND METHODS OF AFRICAN POLITICAL PARTIES

INTRODUCTION

The selections included in Part III of this volume are distinguished from those in the preceding sections in several respects. First, they represent a different period in the evolution of African nationalism—the late period of decolonization when African control of political power is virtually secured, and the period after the transfer of power. Secondly, the focus of these selections is thus less the problem of colonial power than that of African power. As such these selections emphasize the practical problems of organizing new institutions which will move toward the goal of modernization or development.

The perceptive selection by Robert K. Gardiner sets the stage for the rest of the selections in Part III. Gardiner, unlike the other personalities represented in this Part, is not strictly an African political leader. His main career has been that of a professional civil servant and his occasional writings reflect the best in African political thought. His sensitivity to the complexity of African political evolution is related here with subtlety and without equivocation. His intellectual caliber and erudition supersede the more superficial appraisal of the prospects of post-colonial African politics apparent among some African thinkers.

Gardiner is realistic in his recognition that despite the noble intentions of the African political elite as expressed in speeches and writings, African politics is basically like all other politics known to man. It is about power and what power brings those who hold it—prestige, wealth, control over human action, and so on. In the context of the socioeconomic backwardness characteristic of the ex-colonial areas of the world, the tendency for such power to be unresponsive to the wider popular will and need is great. Despite his support of African nationalism and its ultimate goals, Gardiner was one of the first prominent African thinkers to underscore this authoritarian side of African political development.

In this connection the two following selections are election manifestoes of African parties before the attainment of independence. Though they provide a good example of the formal aims of African parties and the manner of projecting these to the populace, most of whom were enfranchised during the later stages of decolonization, they contain no explicit forewarning of the fact that the post-colonial period would move quickly toward authoritarian politics. They do, however, indicate the concern of the African political elite about issues that might produce instability in the emergent political systems. Thus the manifesto of the Convention People's Party for the 1954 General Election in Ghana mentioned the problem of tribal, religious, and regional differences among Ghana's population, and underlined these as a possible source of political instability. The manifesto, in fact, rejected all political activity based upon such differences and promised that a CPP government would "make use of every legitimate means to combat it."

It was within the context of the need to overcome such problems as separatist tribalism that the authoritarian single-party system became virtually universal in post-colonial Africa. The next three selections are reports by leaders in single-party states: Julius Nyerere, President of the Tanganyika African National Union; Sékou Touré, President of the *Parti Démocratique de Guinée*; and Ahmadu Ahidjo, President of the *Union Camerounaise*.

It is of interest that none of these leaders describes the single-party regime as authoritarian. Rather the single-party system is considered "democratic" in at least three ways: 1. In parties like the CPP, PDG, and TANU where the structure of party organization is vast (e.g., the PDG consists of some 7,000 party units embracing 1,600,000 out of a population of 3,000,000), the directness of the relationship of the party to the populace is itself conceived as a form of democracy—"direct democracy" or "popular dictatorship," as Touré terms it; 2. Besides the direct relationship between party and populace, the electoral process continues, and its prevalence is viewed as a democratic form, irrespective of the crucial fact that these electoral arrangements do not provide an effective or real choice of candidates and political groups; 3. The two- or multi-party system is considered essentially a Western phenomenon, conforming to the class structure of fully industrialized societies, whereas African societies are considered basically classless (in the sense that modern socio-economic stratification is still little developed), and thus have no need to express their interests in terms of political competition among many parties or organized groups. Moreover, it is claimed that in traditional African society politics reflected the interests of the community as a whole, not that of any given strata therein.

Whatever one may think about these arguments, the crucial fact about the single-party arrangements, widely as they differ among themselves from country to country, is the use of the party as a mechanism of day-today political control throughout the society. The CPP, PDG, PDCI, and UPS have wide organizational control over such typical units of life as trade unions, marketing and producers' co-operatives, youth and women's groups, traditional and modern recreational bodies, churches, and so on. The bureaucracy is given special attention, penetrated at every key point by party organization. In the Ivory Coast "commissions of control" were established throughout the bureaucracy in 1961, and in Ghana branches of the CPP were formed in government departments and ministries early in 1962. Thus, to quibble about how to characterize African single-party systems is perhaps beside the point, though we do not hesitate to describe them as authoritarian.[1] The basic point is that these systems represent a pervasive form of political control at many levels of life, seeking thereby to render the populace's political behavior predictable for purposes of the governing or ruling elites.

As of 1964 only a few African states, including the Congo (Leopoldville), Nigeria, Sierra Leone, Kenya, Uganda, and the Somali Republic have not yet evolved single-party regimes. However, even in Nigeria, which is frequently cited as the model of a democratic African system in which several parties continue to play a significant role, a form of single-party rule has been established at the regional level, based primarily on the predominance in each region of a single tribal complex. Moreover, since 1962 several leading Nigerian political personalities have made public statements on behalf of a united-front type of coalition government (which French-speaking Africans call the *parti unifié*, as against the *parti unique*) which would entail, *inter alia*, a moratorium on contested elections and related forms of open political competition. One of these proposals for a Nigerian *parti unifié*, made by Dr. M. I. Okpara, Premier of the Eastern Region government, in a speech at the University of Nigeria in December 1962, is included here.

18 / CITIZENSHIP AND POLITICAL LIBERALISM / R. K. GARDINER

From the newspapers and pronouncements of Nigerian leaders, one gets the impression that the supreme duty of every Nigerian citizen is to join the fight for Self-Government. This is a noble and worthy aspiration but, nevertheless a commonplace one. I have felt it myself in connection with my own country, the Gold Coast. I have come across it in my study of dependent territories in other parts of Africa, the Caribbean, the Pacific and the Middle East. It is noticeable in the attitude of the small powers which often expresses itself in resentment against domina-

From R. K. Gardiner, *Citizenship in an Emergent Nation: A Lecture Delivered before Members of an Extra-Mural Residential Course at Oshogbo, Nigeria, on January 12th 1953* (Ibadan: Ibadan University Press, 1953), pp. 3-5, 6-9, 11-14.
[1] Cf. Martin Kilson, "Authoritarian and Single-Party Tendencies in African Politics," *World Politics* (January 1963), pp. 293-94.

tion by the great powers. It is inherent in the determination of the great powers to defend their independence and what they vaguely describe as their "way of life." Put in this way, the nationalism of Nigerian citizens becomes part of a world-wide struggle which is legitimate, human and justifiable. It at once strengthens the case of the nationalist and affords a perspective.

Commenting on the Preamble to the constitution of India, Professor Ernest Barker expresses pride that the people of India should begin their independent life by subscribing to the principles which are usually considered western but have become in fact more than western. This is significant because sometimes the desire to get rid of political domination creates the impression that nationalists wish to reject all foreign ideas. World history and recent events show that independence leads to voluntary acceptance of world ideas. If I could trust my own interpretation of the language of Nigerian politics, I should conclude that Nigeria aspires to join the community of nations and to share the ethos of our age.

Citizenship involves the theory and practice of politics. Some schools of thought regard the study of politics as part of moral philosophy. Ancient Greek writers like Plato and Aristotle regarded it as "moral philosophy" applied to the life of the whole community. "Morality," it has been said, "is the very sinews of politics, being in truth nothing more than the conscience of a nation striving to express itself in state action." This definition of politics needs special emphasis in Nigeria to-day, because too often political discussions concentrate on the mechanics of Government to the exclusion of the purposes of Government. We need, in any country, not only to study the Government as it is—but also to look beyond the existing framework towards Government as it might be, as it ought to be—that is, to study Political philosophy. A good constitution only provides an opportunity for the good life; but the realisation of the good life depends on the vision of citizens and their recognition of the ends of Government.

In the struggle for Self-Government it is necessary sometimes to hate oppression. Indeed it has been said that "Nothing great has been accomplished without passion." And yet passion has its dangers. In periods of tension we may adopt methods which may serve immediate ends. An instance of this is seen in the continued persuasion of our followers to believe the worst about our enemies. Such intolerance deliberately fostered against enemies, or in some cases against all aliens, ultimately does harm to the whole community. It destroys sympathy even for our fellow citizens. What we are apt to forget, under such circumstances, is that "hatred, even of the objectively hateful, does not produce that charity and justice on which a Utopian Society must be based."

There is another danger to responsible citizenship which nationalism tends to bring to the fore. All nations old and new should be aware of it and should guard against it. There is a tendency not only to refuse to admit unpleasant truth, but to shut our eyes to inconvenient facts about our country. We have to remind ourselves here about the relation between political theory and moral philosophy. There are people, perhaps even in this course, who have the impression that one has to be clever or cunning to be a successful politician. This is a very short-sighted view and soon many will realise that the easiest way to forfeit the confidence of a community is to deceive it. Even with all the modern instruments of mass communication and propaganda only those nations which have enjoyed the leadership of people endowed with sufficient moral courage to speak frankly and to give full account even of national catastrophes have passed through trials successfully. It is wise to remember, when facing distasteful facts about ourselves or our country that "the truth may sometimes hurt us: it can never harm us."

Sometimes we wonder why seemingly powerful nations appear to resent criticism, and are ready to suppress internal criticism ruthlessly. The dictatorships are sometimes described as if they have a monopoly of this weakness. But the spread of the fear of communism in the non-communist world seems to sap away the confidence of the democracies and to drive them into suspicion and intolerance. In dependent territories, especially during the period of agitation for Self-Government, a similar tendency develops. Those who refuse to accept the over-simplified explanations and solutions offered by popular leaders are considered traitors. Fellow citizens—who refuse to share in fanatical outbursts, are labelled "fifth columnists," "Uncle Toms," "Stooges," etc. In doing this we ignore the warning that "in matters which are really important we must eschew labels as a snare of the devil." The labels may affect those to whom they are applied directly and immediately; but they have more and far-reaching effects on the community as a whole. We may very rightly state that the fear of uncomplimentary labels is the beginning of social cowardice, civic hypocrisy and insincerity. . . .

I hope the time will never come when Nigeria, or any other part of West Africa, will be driven by suspicion to recall its representatives from foreign conferences or to disown its leaders in the midst of serious negotiations, or, again, to consider association with foreigners as a criminal action. These possibilities may seem remote and far-fetched. One may be tempted to state that they will never occur here in Nigeria or any other part of West Africa. But to state such a thing is unreasonable and dangerous. For situations which are conveniently fostered and exploited by politicians sometimes get out of control and engulf innocent victims and those whose guilt may not be noticeable. Indeed, some sentiments which in other respects are virtuous, such as loyalty to one's community, can be misdirected into destructive channels. It is significant that the methods and policies of Gandhi and his colleagues who believed in non-violence frequently contributed to the occurence of communal strife in India. . . .

For a healthy social and political development we need to recognise the idea of "an adversary in good faith." No co-operation is possible, among fellow citizens and between citizens and foreigners so long as each party refuses to admit that the other party can disagree without being treacherous, vicious or wicked. Our most earnest desires for the welfare of our community may be wrong, and especially may our consideration of means or methods be divergent. There is plenty of room for differences of opinion even in nationalist hopes. In other words, nationalism does not render individuals or people omniscient and infallible. When we lose sight of this fact we drift into authoritarianism. . . .

One can trace a rough line of development in connection with most nationalist movements. First there is a period of acquiescence in which dependent peoples seem to accept alien rule. This is followed by a period of doubt during which resentment and criticism grow more vocal. It is during this period that the final liberators are reared. We must not forget this. The men who, in the old legislative Councils of Nigeria, started questioning the absolute rule of Britain, were not only the fore-runners but the moulders of the outlook of the present generation. It is interesting to compare the ages of our ministers with the ages of the leaders of the "young Turks" or with those of the contemporaries of Lenin during the 1917 revolution. If these young men had started the movements themselves they would not have lived long enough to see the final outcome of their efforts. The citizen of to-day ought to remember what he owes to the past and to the elder statesmen of Nigeria.

The next stage in the nationalist movements may be described as a period of transfer of power. This has not always been a peaceful process —but—thanks to the experience of Great Britain in dealing with United States, with Canada, India, Pakistan—we here in West Africa seem to have secured recognition of our rights almost without bloodshed. The pattern of development is also almost identical. Poverty, crop failures, famine, ignorance and disease are all attributed to the deliberate politics or failures of the alien government. The transfer of power is followed by the drawing up of plans for radical changes. It looks as if all new countries need the sobering revelations of a "Bombay plan" to enable them to start a realistic development programme.

Up to this stage it is assumed that transfer of power will mean freedom for all and that local initiative and local responsibility will provide services and amenities which have been considered unobtainable. Any attempt to question the basis of these assumptions is considered undesirable. Fortunately this phase does not last very long. A second or a third budget session challenges the new cabinet. This is the period of disillusionment for those who have believed in the promises of costless, and painless revolutionary changes. This is the time for re-examination of the past, and admission of errors in forecasting. This is also the time when leaders may be tempted to resort to evasive excuses, shifting of blame and the distortion of facts to exonerate the party in power. This is the testing time of responsible citizenship and statesmanship. . . .

In a nation-state "the masses and man become one." Opinions and passions become the targets of vote catchers. Those who seek to attain power do not always appeal to reason but resort to questionable methods. Some men act on the assumption that the memory of the public is so short that if a lie is big enough and repeated often enough, it tends to be accepted by the people as truth. The temptation to abuse power and to cheat, increases when one has to deal with an anonymous body which is easy to sway and has no definite views. It takes a strong character to deal honestly with crowds. . . .

We cannot escape the judgement of history—for we are making history—and already it is not difficult to see some of the issues on which judgement will be passed. In a world dominated by power politics and injustice, the new nations have emerged without military power, liberated by faith in the justice of their cause. In a world bitterly divided by prejudices, especially racial prejudices, we have risen in spite of malicious misconceptions. We, the people of Africa have had all the odds against us. Future generations will wonder whether our group experience made us sensitive to the suffering of others. Our Self-Government or independence will mean nothing to mankind if it does not enable us to set some moral example to the rest of the world. We are the offspring of the abolitionist movement which appealed to the conscience of the world.

19 / FORWARD WITH THE COMMON PEOPLE: ELECTION MANIFESTO, 1954 / CONVENTION PEOPLE'S PARTY

The dynamic C.P.P., under the indomitable leadership of its Life Chairman, Dr. Kwame Nkrumah, has maintained the struggle for the liberation of Ghana since its foundation in 1949, through the hectic days of POSITIVE ACTION and imprisonment and after the assumption of the reins of Government in 1951 under the "bogus and fraudulent" Coussey Constitution which was imposed upon the common people of Ghana against our will.[1]

Today the name of the Convention People's Party and of its great leader Kwame Nkrumah is world famous and is identified everywhere

From Convention People's Party, *Forward to Freedom with the Common People: Manifesto for the General Election, 1954* (Accra: National Executive of the Convention People's Party, 1954), pp. 4-18.
[1] The Coussey Constitution was the Ghana Constitution of 1950 which was based on the recommendations of a constitutional commission chaired by Justice Coussey. [Eds.]

with the heroic struggle of the people of Ghana for FREEDOM. Yea, the names of the C.P.P. and Kwame Nkrumah are words of hope and inspiration everywhere to oppressed peoples fighting for liberation from Colonial domination. The C.P.P. and Kwame Nkrumah are the hope of FREEDOM to all oppressed people of Africa and of African descent everywhere, while on the other hand the slogan "C.P.P.-104 FREEDOM —NKRUMAH" [2] strikes fear, despondency and alarm in the hearts of tribalists, racialists, communalists, imperialists, and other reactionaries —white as well as black.

Throughout the struggle we have been inspired by the pregnant words of our leader, Kwame Nkrumah: "Seek ye first the political kingdom and everything else will be added unto you." This injunction sounds still in our ears, urging us to organise as never before for the final stage in the LIBERATION OF GHANA. "Organisation decides everything," Kwame Nkrumah has oft repeated.

Now the GOAL IS IN SIGHT. It is only Kwame Nkrumah, the tried and experienced Captain, and his C.P.P. crew of 104 that can pilot the mighty ship "GHANA" into the port of FREEDOM. The forthcoming General Election will be the deciding factor whether we attain *Self-Government Now* or languish further under foreign imperialist domination. Therefore, it is up to you, men and women of Ghana, to give Kwame Nkrumah the tools to finish the job.

VOTE for KWAME and his dynamic C.P.P.—*the Fighting Vanguard of the African Liberation Movement.*

FORWARD TO VICTORY! 104—FREEDOM!!

Part I—Political

So Much in so Little Time

From February 1951, when Kwame Nkrumah came out of prison and assumed the reins of Government, it is only three years. But in that short space of time what tremendous changes have taken place even under the "bogus and fraudulent" Constitution which was foisted upon the common people by the British imperialists, with the support of our own African reactionaries.

Besides the unprecedented material progress, there has been a great spiritual transformation. FREEDOM IS IN THE AIR. Our people have become aware of their dignity as citizens and are burning to be free to govern themselves. They prefer *Self-Government with danger to servitude in tranquillity.* They want in full measure the fundamental human freedoms of press, assembly and speech. And above all, they want freedom from the *contempt* of foreign masters.

The C.P.P. pledges itself to guarantee the people of Ghana all these FREEDOMS, and as evidence of good faith brings the testimony of the

---

[2] The number "104" referred to the number of elected seats in the Legislative Assembly. [EDS.]

material changes which have been wrought by Kwame Nkrumah and his Ministers under semi-self-government in the past three years. . . .

In barely three years our standard-bearer Kwame Nkrumah has demonstrated such great powers of leadership that he is acclaimed throughout the world as the outstanding African statesman and champion of Negro Freedom. Yet our opponents, small men eaten up with their own vanity, jealousy and envy, seek by every means to smear his name and drag his reputation into the mud. These men would rather see Ghana become another British Guiana than allow Nkrumah to finish the job.

Politics and Religion

The Party System has come to stay. It is only through the Party System that Parliamentary Democracy can be maintained. But the C.P.P., in accordance with progressive forms of government everywhere, is opposed to the formation of political parties on the basis of racialism, tribalism and religion, and will make use of every legitimate means to combat it. In our country, with its tradition of religious tolerance and respect for all faiths, it is highly undesirable that a religous association or denomination should take on itself the character of a political party. If it does so, the public is liable to associate its religious tenets, be they Christian or Muslim, with its political aims, and to withhold from such a religious movement the tolerance which is given to purely religious sects.

We have seen the tragedy of religious communalism in India and elsewhere. Don't let us give it a chance to take root and flourish in Ghana. VOTE FOR KWAME NKRUMAH AND THE C.P.P.—Champions of Political Freedom, Religious Tolerance and Social Justice. *Down with Pakistanism! Down with politicians who are exploiting religious fanaticism to further their own ambitions!*

VOTE C.P.P. and assure equal rights for all, regardless of Colour, Race or Creed.

Local Government and the Chiefs

It is the intention of the C.P.P. Government when returned to office with full powers to amend the Local Government Ordinance so that in future all Local Urban District and Municipal Councils shall be wholly elected, as a means of eliminating the continual friction which occurs between elected and traditional members. It will also save our chiefs from being dragged into party politics against their dignity and integrity.

Means will be devised which will enable our chiefs to play their part in local and national affairs. It is not the intention of the C.P.P. to destroy chieftainship but rather to adapt it to democratic practices, by clearly defining the functions of the chiefs in our new society.

There has been friction between some Local Councils and their chiefs. It is, however, the duty of the Local Councils to support their chiefs, financially and otherwise, and of the chiefs to support their Councils in the execution of their duly constituted functions. But it is essential for the chiefs to keep aloof from party politics, so that they may retain the allegiance and respect of their subjects, irrespective of religious or political affiliation. It is the intention of the C.P.P. to effect an harmonious relationship between the chiefs and the people.

Bribery and Corruption

The setting of the Commission of Enquiry and other steps taken by the C.P.P. Government regarding allegations of mal-practices in the country are evidence of the earnestness of Kwame Nkrumah and the C.P.P. to rid the country of bribery and corruption. The Party will continue to do everything it can to purge the body politic of all mal-practices of this kind, which are part of the legacy of over a hundred years of the imperialist colonial system, from which our country is just emerging.

VOTE C.P.P. *and strengthen Kwame Nkrumah to purge our country of evil practices!*

The Civil Service

The C.P.P. will take drastic measures to speed up Africanisation, and will give the utmost support to training schemes devised to improve the personnel and the efficiency of the service itself. The Party intends to attract the best brains into the public service, especially the technical branches, such as Agriculture, Forestry, Animal Husbandry, Public Works, and the Engineering Departments.

It is to be observed that since the C.P.P. has come into power, even under the "bogus and fraudulent" Coussey Constitution, more Africans have been promoted to the Senior Service than at any previous period. Three African Directors have already been appointed. This is only the beginning. Many more will follow. On the other hand, the expatriate members of the Service have already been assured by the Prime Minister that their interests will be safeguarded, and they will be encouraged to give of their best to Ghana's public services. *Efficiency and Service* shall be the watchword of all people engaged in Ghana's public services.

Civil Servants—VOTE C.P.P. and be assured of a glorious future.

VOTE 104—FREEDOM

Foreign Policy

The C.P.P. believes in the United Nations as an instrument for the attainment of world peace and economic progress. It will seek the co-operation of the United Nations special agencies. Unesco, the I.L.O., and other international bodies working for the welfare and advancement of under-developed countries. The C.P.P., however, will not allow any organisation subservient to any foreign power to undermine the Government of Ghana. On the other hand, the C.P.P. Government will seek to establish friendly contacts with all countries committed to the promotion of peace and good-neighbourly relations with Ghana. It will do all in its power to promote trade and cultural exchange between Ghana and these countries.

The C.P.P. is the only political organisation in Ghana which is dedicated to the idea of *West African Unity and Freedom for Africans and peoples of African Descent everywhere.* The Party is opposed to national exclusiveness, colonialism and imperialism, as well as racialism and tribal chauvinism.

VOTE C.P.P. *and help forward the Brotherhood of Man and Africa's Redemption.*

Part II—Economic Development

Agriculture

The C.P.P. will pay particular attention to Agriculture, together with Animal Husbandry, Forestry and Fisheries. For Agriculture and allied industries will be the basis of our industrialisation programme. As part of this programme, the welfare of farmers, fishermen and cattlemen will be included, since their advancement will give greater productivity and increase the wealth of our country.

The cocoa industry—the basis of our economy—will be given all the attention and encouragement it requires. Production, distribution and marketing will be improved. The C.C.P. will work towards the elimination of waste and overlapping of administrations in the agricultural services by inducing better co-ordination and collaboration between the different agricultural development agencies.

Every encouragement will be given by the C.P.P. to the timber, livestock and fishing industries. Everything possible will be done to liquidate the indebtedness of farmers, and a greater proportion of the national revenue will be devoted to agriculture, timber, livestock and fisheries, and to strengthening the CO-OPERATIVE MOVEMENT.

Therefore, Farmers, VOTE C.P.P.

VOTE 104—FREEDOM

Industrialisation

The C.P.P. will see to it that, simultaneously with the expansion and development of our Agriculture and systems of communications and transport, a real attempt is made at industrialising the country. Consistent with the interests of the people of Ghana, every facility will be given to foreign firms to operate in the country and a central agency, such as the Industrial Development Corporation, will be financed by the Government to give all new and prospective firms every assistance and encouragement in their operations, such as the provision of sites, buildings and utility services.

The C.P.P. will at the same time insist that some of the top executive posts in all concerns shall be filled by Africans, that racial discrimination shall not be practised by foreign firms, and that Africans shall be trained to fill responsible posts in all these foreign concerns.

The key to industrialisation is power.

The Volta River Project and Electrification

The C.P.P., subject to the wishes of the people of Ghana, endorsed through their parliamentary representatives, intends to proceed with the Volta River project if the Preparatory Commission demonstrates in due course that the scheme is technically sound, economically attractive, and will not have undue social consequences. This intention is also subject to the Government of Ghana being able to negotiate with the other partners contemplated in the British Government's White Paper on the project, an Agreement which will be beneficial to the country.

When the Volta River project materialises there will be a large supply of hydro-electrical power. Much of this power will be earmarked for the aluminium industry, but some of it will be available for distribution to other large consumers. Such distribution will require the construction of a country-wide transmission grid to the big towns and industrial areas, and this objective the C.P.P. intends to pursue vigorously.

At the same time the C.P.P. is determined to embark on a policy of widespread rural electrification. To this end the setting up of small-scale electrical installations for domestic and industrial purposes will be encouraged, and the possibilities of establishing other hydro-electrical plants will be investigated. The electrification of the whole country is one of the objectives of the C.P.P. in the pursuance of the economic and social development of the country.

Under the Development Plan, the C.P.P. will include the building of factories, workshops and repair yards. We shall process food for storage and use; we must manufacture some of the things which we need and use. We shall seek to make Ghana as self-supporting as possible.

Part III—Social Development

It is the aim of the C.P.P. to see that the general standard of living among the people is further raised, and that the various parts of the country are brought more closely together.

Social Welfare Services, Mass Education and Community Development will be given every encouragement, but the next phase will concentrate on extension services to provide for the dissemination of improved methods of Agriculture, Housing, Sanitation, Road Construction, etc., especially in the Rural Areas and the Northern Territories.

Therefore, *if you want to better the social conditions of the people of Ghana*

VOTE C.P.P.

VOTE 104—FREEDOM

Full Employment

The C.P.P. will do its best to provide jobs for all and to induce people to go and work wherever they are needed. When the various development projects—especially the Volta River project—are in full swing, unemployment will be a thing of the past. But it will be a matter of national duty for people to go wherever duty calls.

Free Independent Trade Unionism

The C.P.P. maintains that only one united, well-organised and strong trade union movement, free from external control—either communist or capitalist-imperialist—can cater for the best interests of the workers of Ghana. The C.P.P. will therefore continue to support the Gold Coast Trade Union Congress in its efforts to maintain its free and independent status, and to work for the welfare of all the workers of our country.

The C.P.P. Government will see that a sound machinery for the settlement of industrial disputes is established in the interests of both workers and employers, and will also seek the establishment of a Technical Institute, an Adult Residential College, as well as the proper facilities of the Kumasi College of Technology for technical training of workers, in order to equip them to play their role in the industrial development of the country.

Education and Cultural Activity

The educational aim of the C.P.P. is the consolidation of the foundations which have already been laid, with emphasis on technical education. Provisions will be made for the establishment of a School of Business Administration for the training of managers, accountants, etc., and for the establishment of an Adult Residential College for the general education of workers and the public at large.

The C.P.P. would also like to see the establishment of a Law School, an Academy of Fine and Commercial Art, and a National Theatre with which will be associated an Academy of Drama, Music and Dance.

The C.P.P. intends to make the whole education in Primary and Middle schools free, and also to provide free medical treatment for school children.

The C.P.P. will give every possible support to the University College and help it to grow into a full-fledged University, able to play its full role in the life of the country. It is hoped to establish a MEDICAL SCHOOL there as soon as finances permit.

Part IV—General

Our Women—Fighters for Freedom

The C.P.P. has always prized the women of Ghana and given them an honoured place in its heart. The women of Ghana have moved shoulder to shoulder with their men in the struggle for Self-Government. The C.P.P. wants the women of Ghana to continue to play their prominent part in all things affecting the destiny of the country.

Therefore, it is the aim of the C.P.P. to help the women of Ghana to advance educationally, socially and politically. The Party is anxious to see some women in the next Legislative Assembly, and has therefore nominated some of our outstanding *female fighters for freedom to stand as candidates in the forthcoming General Election.*

The C.P.P. maintains the principle of equal pay for men and women engaged on the same work. It intends to help develop women's organisations so that women may play an even more active and prominent part in the life of the country and in international affairs. As guardians of our nation, the C.P.P. looks to the women of Ghana to make a valuable contribution to the well-being of our country and the peace and progress of the world.

Therefore, *we call upon the women of Ghana to Vote for Kwame Nkrumah and the C.P.P. so as to promote the cause of African Womanhood.*

MOTHERS, WIVES, SISTERS AND DAUGHTERS!
VOTE C.P.P.
VOTE 104—FREEDOM

20 / NORTHERN RHODESIA U.N.I.P. ELECTION MANIFESTO, 1962

Manifesto

The coming General Election is fraught with vital possibilities for the future of our Nation. Northern Rhodesia is faced with the question whether this generation wills it that she is to march into the full sunlight of freedom for all its peoples, irrespective of race, or is to remain in the shadow of a base second-class status perpetually tied to the exploiting star of Southern Rhodesia, an association which has brought and even will bring in its train naught but ill-feeling and disturbances amidst our Nation.

The United National Independence Party, through the policies which follow hereafter, gives all the people of Northern Rhodesia the opportunity of vindicating their honour and pursuing with renewed confidence the path of National Salvation by rallying to the cause of the one and only truly Nationalist Party which rejects colour, race or tribe as foundation stones for a Nation.

As our policies show, U.N.I.P. stands less for a political party than for a Nation, it represents the inalienable right of all the people of Northern Rhodesia to sovereign self-determination, reaffirming the determination of the people of Northern Rhodesia to achieve it, and guar-

From United National Independence Party, *U.N.I.P. Policy* (Lusaka: United National Independence Party, n.d.), pp. 1-2, 7-8, 28, 41-42, 48-50, 58-59.

anteeing within the Nation, equal rights and equal opportunities to all its citizens.

Believing that the time has arrived when Northern Rhodesia's voice for the principle of self-determination should be heard above every interest of Party or class, U.N.I.P. will oppose at the polls every individual candidate who does not accept this principle.

The policies of our opponents (those who have any policies!), stand condemned on any test, whether of principle or expediency. The rights of the people of Northern Rhodesia to sovereign independence outside the Federation rests upon immutable natural law and cannot be made the subject of a compromise on the basis of false economic statistics.

Any attempt to barter away the sacred and inviolate rights of nationhood begins in dishonour and is bound to end in disaster. The exodus of hundreds of European artisans from Northern Rhodesia in recent months due to political instability; the decay of our industrial life; the ever-increasing financial plunder of our country at the hands of the Federalists and finally the contemplated mutilation of our country by partition, are some of the ghastly results of a policy that leads to national ruin.

Those who have endeavoured to harness the people of Northern Rhodesia to the Federation's so-called economic chariot; ignoring the fact that only a freely elected and truly-representative Government in a free Northern Rhodesia has power to decide for Northern Rhodesia the question of "association," have forfeited the right to speak for the people of this country.

U.N.I.P. goes to the polls handicapped by all the arts and contrivances that a powerful and unscrupulous enemy can use against us in Salisbury. U.N.I.P., however, will go to the polls confident that the people of this country will be true to their pledge—"to Vote" for the party, the principles and the men who disdain to whine to the enemy for favours; the men who hold that Northern Rhodesia must be free from the trappings of a Federation which can only be held together by the use of "firepower."

Sincerely believing in the foregoing, we present the policies which follow as the only true path to the creation of a non-racial society in Northern Rhodesia which will lead to the foundation of a strong nation of which all will be truly proud and to which all will owe unswerving loyalty. . . .

The general structure of our economy is that of under-development. The per capita income, savings and investments and labour productivity are very low. The only developed section of the economy is the mining, but it employs only 8% of the total population. Besides, mining is a wasting asset liable to exhaustion anytime and the price of copper is subject to high fluctuations on the international market as 1958 period shows it. The majority of the population are directly on land and most of the industrial sector in terms of employment of labour and other resources as well as the national income is negligible. Yet this is the most important sector in all developed economies. Much of our resources are idle.

To eliminate this unbalanced growth and to achieve a high standard of living for all the people, a policy for a general growth of the economy, as a whole [is needed], unlike the previous succession of sectoral economic plans. Drastic measures for mobilisation, co-ordination and utilisation of these resources shall be the main objective of all the citizens including the Government if the welfare of the society is to be raised. With dedicated hard work, the socio-economic structure of this country can be transformed with[in] the shortest possible span of time.

A conducive climate for private capital shall be created so that both public and private sectors shall support each other in our struggle for a "take off into sustained growth." This can only be attained if the political instability facing this country could be eliminated. . . .

Education

It is our conviction that adequate education of all persons is a prime responsibility of the state and we affirm that education must be:

(a) Compulsory and free.
(b) Independent of, and in no way subject to the individual's creed, colour or sex.

We shall recognise two main types of educational institutions:

(I) Those for which Government is entirely or partly responsible, and
(II) Those which prefer to receive no financial or other assistance from Government.

It is perhaps necessary to stress two points at this stage; we recognise and appreciate the enormous amount and value of the work done by voluntary organisations—notably the missions and, assuming that they continue to qualify as heretofore, intend to continue assistance to them on a scale comparable with that given in the past. Such schools run by voluntary organisations but receiving assistance from the Government will, of course, fall under group (I). The second point we wish to stress is that there may well be bodies which prefer to receive no aid at all from the Government, and which would comprise the institutions of group (II); inspected and only permitted to operate if they satisfy certain minimum conditions.

Education shall in all normal cases be compulsory up to the age of 15 years. This compulsory education shall begin for all races when the child attains the age of five years. The further implications and method of implementation of this decision we shall consider later.

Compulsory education requires, as a corollary, free education up to at least the age limit, set by law, for attendance at school. . . .

Policy on Judiciary

The common law and the English judiciary system have taken root throughout British Africa, with the exception of Southern Rhodesia and the Republic of South Africa, and we intend to preserve the law and the courts which we have inherited from England. In matters relating to the judiciary, we intend following the comparable British practice. The main changes which we intend to introduce in the present courts are at the highest and lowest level, namely the Appellate Court for the Protectorate and the Chief's Courts. The High Court and Resident Magistrates' Courts now functioning in the territory would not be altered.

All judicial officers will be appointed by the Governor and in the case of judges of the Appeal Court and the High Court, the appointment will be made on Her Majesty's instructions, conveyed through a principal Secretary of State. All judges shall be independent in the exercise of their judicial functions. All judicial officers will have security of tenure and judges of the Superior Court shall not be removed from office except for stated misbehaviour or incapacity and then only by the Secretary of State. The remuneration of a judge shall not be reduced during his continuance in office. After the transitionary period, we intend to enshrine in the permanent constitution provision dealing with the independence and freedom of the judiciary. The judges of the Court of Appeal will then be appointed on the advice of the Prime Minister after consultation with the Chief Justice. A Judicial Service Commission will be established which will advise on the appointment, promotion and transfer of other judicial officers.

Courts of Appeal

There shall be a Court for this Protectorate. The Court of Appeal shall, with such exceptions and subject to such regulations as may be prescribed by law, have appellate jurisdiction from such decisions of other courts as may be prescribed by law. The Court would constitute an independent and impartial body to whom bills would be referred by the Governor on questions of violation of the provisions of the constitution dealing with fundamental rights. We consider that the judiciary can protect the individual against excesses by the Executive in a more effective manner than any Council of State.

The judges of the Court shall be three in number, one of whom will be styled Chief Justice and will preside over the Court. The first Chief Justice shall be a person who has held judicial office. One of the members of the Court will be an African.

African Courts

The system of Chief's Courts, administering African law and custom, is a valuable contribution to good Government in the Protectorate. We believe that it should be continued and strengthened. A difficult task is performed by the judicial officers in a stage of society where customary law has to be applied to changing conditions and circumstances. In time, African customary law will be blended with the imported common law and statute and uniform system will emerge. Before this development can even commence, it is necessary that African customary law should become definite uniform and a system of written precedent is established. . . .

Local Government in Urban Areas

As a matter of history, Local Government was instituted and developed by European settlers. The system of administration has been planned and maintained basically to the advantage of the European, with control remaining in his hands. Local authorities play an important part in the government of the country; they are not fully independent of the Central Government. Local Government officials are appointed by the local authorities and are answerable to them. Local authorities shall be elected by all the people living in the area of their jurisdiction, so that important services and matters such as housing, town planning, trade licensing, lighting, public health, and road construction and maintenance, which affect day to day living are the direct concern of the majority of those who use them.

In Central Government, there is a trend to simplify the franchise and to grant all a right to vote. The same trend shall be extended to Local Government and every person resident in the electoral area, who is of full age, shall be eligible to be registered as a local government voter. A rateable or property qualification is outmoded. The liability to pay rates, or the occupation of an expensive house shall not be the test as it tends to make Local Councils more conservative than the Central Government. A councillor shall be answerable to all the residents of his area and not only to those in the higher income groups. . . .

We envisage the African Affairs Department becoming redundant when the African people are regarded as municipal citizens and not as interlopers on the edge of a white municipality. . . .

Civil Service

To ensure stability and orderly Government an efficient Civil Service is necessary. For example, during the era of France's Fourth Republic the country enjoyed comparative peace and orderly Government in spite of changes of Government.

At present this country cannot provide all the personnel required for the efficient running of the Government. Therefore, for some years to come we shall still have to recruit from outside Northern Rhodesia.

Efforts will be made to retain serving officers by ensuring that their salaries are commensurate with their world market value. A country cannot afford to lose technicians and professional officers whose specialist knowledge is required in the implementation of our economic policy, agricultural policy, etc.

It is vital, however, that the civil service should as much as possible be localised and appointments to posts shall be made according to the officer's qualifications and experience. We appreciate the difficulties which may arise as the result of the fact that in the past the availability of educational facilities for Africans left much to be desired. It is, therefore, the task of a representative Government to rectify this situation. A crash programme for the training of officers shall be instituted. . . .

21 / DEMOCRACY AND THE PARTY SYSTEM / JULIUS NYERERE

"The Elders sit under the big tree, and talk until they agree . . ."
—*Guy Clutton-Brock.*

Democracy is often spoken of as if it were something alien to the African, which he must be taught. Quite well-meaning people will ask "Can democracy survive in an independent Africa?"

During the early stages of our struggle to free this continent from colonial rule, the question asked by our critics was "Can these Africans govern themselves?" That question is no longer asked, for it is too obviously absurd. Colonialism is a very recent historical phenomenon as far as Africa is concerned; until the coming of the imperialists in relatively recent times we did govern ourselves, and the partition of Africa was not prompted by any desire on the part of the colonial powers to save us from our failure to do so! Now that there are so many independent African states to demonstrate that we still know very well how to govern ourselves, our critics have been forced (to quote a West Indian singer) to "rephrase the question."

But this question they are now asking is no less absurd than the earlier one—for democracy, in its true sense, is as familiar to the African as the tropical sun. Nevertheless, to those who ask it the question is seen as purely rhetorical; and the answer they assume is a categorical NO. So let us try to find the source of their anxiety. Let us see whether we and our critics have the same thing in mind when we talk about democracy.

Democracy, in Africa or anywhere else, is Government by the People.

From Julius K. Nyerere, *Democracy and the Party System* (Dar es Salaam: Tanganyika Standard, Ltd., n.d.), pp. 1-8, 14-15, 23-26.

Ideally, it is a form of government whereby the people—*all* the people— settle their affairs through free discussion. The appropriate setting for this basic, or pure, democracy is a small community. The City States of Ancient Greece, for example, practised it. And in African society, the traditional method of conducting affairs is by free discussion. Mr. Guy Clutton-Brock, writing about a typical African village community puts it neatly in the sentence I quoted at the beginning: "The Elders sit under the big tree, and talk until they agree. . . ." In larger communities, however, government by the people is possible only in a modified form.

After pure democracy, the next best thing is Government by the People's Representatives. Where it is the affairs of several million people that are to be settled by discussion, it is obviously not possible for all the people to come together and take a direct part in the discussion. So, instead, we have a parliament in which a number of spokesmen, or Representatives, conduct the discussion on their behalf. And if these Representatives are truly to represent the people, they must be freely chosen by the people from amongst themselves. So Free Elections are the essential instruments of Representative Democracy.

The purpose of a General Election, then, is to elect these People's Representatives. But, because of the historical circumstances of the countries in which Representative Democracy has been most highly developed, such elections are usually organised on a Party basis. The electorate is offered a choice between contending Parties. It could be said that the object is not so much to elect Representatives as to elect a Representative Party. The countries where this system works most successfully are those which have two major political parties. . . .

Those whose political thinking has been moulded by the Western parliamentary tradition have now become so used to the Two-Party system that they cannot imagine democracy without it. It is no good telling them that when a group of a hundred people have sat together as equals and talked until they agreed about where they should dig a well, for example, or whether they should build a new school (and "until they agreed" implies that they will have produced many conflicting arguments before they did eventually agree), they have practised democracy. No, the Western parliamentarians will want to know whether the talking was properly organised. They will want to know whether there was an organised group whose duty was to talk FOR the motion, and another organised group whose duty was to talk AGAINST it. They will also want to know whether, at the next debate, the same two groups will remain opposed to each other. In other words they will be asking whether the opposition is organised and therefore automatic, or whether it is free and therefore spontaneous. Only if it is automatic will they concede that here is democracy! The way they generally put it is: "How can you have democracy with a One-Party system?" It may surprise them to know, therefore, that some "heretics" like myself—who also claim to be democrats—are now beginning to ask: "How can you have democracy with a Two-Party system?"

I must confess that, not so long ago, I would have been content to answer the first of those questions. If I had posed the second it would have [been] in jest rather than in earnest. Recently, however, I have found myself questioning the democracy of the Two-Party system very seriously indeed.

Here in Tanganyika, for instance, we have adopted the Westminster type of Representative Democracy. With it, we took over the whole pattern of parliamentary and local government elections designed for a multi-party system. But it soon became clear to us that however ready we leaders might have been to accept the theory that an official Opposition was essential to democratic government, our own people thought otherwise; for the idea did not make sense to them. As a result of the people's choice freely expressed at the polls, we found ourselves with a One-Party system.

Now nobody who knew anything about Tanganyika could deny that, in spite of our having only one party, we were very democratic. But we were more democratic within the Party than we were outside it. When, for instance, we met to elect our party leaders, nothing could have been more democratic. And our members' freedom of expression during our debates at the Party's National Executive meetings left nothing to be desired! But since we had adopted the method of election to Parliament and local government bodies which was designed for a contest between parties, we had to apply the party unity rule. Once we had selected an official TANU candidate, we required all party members to support him. And if any other member disobeyed this rule and stood in opposition to our official candidate, he had to be punished. Invariably his punishment was expulsion from the Party. As there is only one party in Tanganyika, the inevitable result of enforcing this rule was to make a contested election a very rare thing indeed. Most TANU candidates for Parliament and for local government councils are returned unopposed; which means, in effect, that they are elected by a Party committee. Again, when it came to debates in Parliament we "naturally" (according to the Book of Rules of the Two-Party system) had to apply the party unity rule.

Let me try and illustrate what I am talking about by a comparison of our behaviour at a TANU National Executive meeting and at a sitting of the Tanganyika Parliament. Now at the meeting of the National Executive we are speaking amongst ourselves. As individuals within the Party we are free to express our own opinions; to say exactly what we think about the subject under discussion. There is no distinction, at these meetings, between the leaders and the "backbenchers." We are all on an equal footing, and the only thing that counts is the value or otherwise of the opinion expressed—not the relative "importance" or "unimportance" of the person expressing it. And this, surely, is just as it should be in any democratically conducted meeting. But what happens when we take our seats in Parliament? Many of us are the same individuals who were expressing our views so freely in the National Executive; but, the moment we enter the Parliament, we are expected to behave quite differently. In Parliament it is no longer permissible for each Member to express his own personal opinion. There is a Party Line to be followed—the line approved by the Party's leaders, i.e. the Government. And, in order to ensure that it *is* followed, we actually hold a private debate within the TANU Parliamentary Party before each meeting of Parliament.

Again because of the absence of any rival party, the membership of the TANU Parliamentary Party is almost identical with that of the Parliament itself. Yet it is at these private meetings of the T.P.P., and not in the Parliament, that we expect Members to speak their minds freely. Here it is that they learn from their leaders what the "party line" is to be, and just how far they may go in criticising any particular piece of legislation when this comes up for "debate" in Parliament. Fortunately, and I use the word deliberately, this has not so far prevented our Members of Parliament (particularly those who are accustomed to the freedom of speech which is characteristic of the National Executive) from expressing their own opinions in Parliament from time to time with a most "unparliamentary" independence of the party line! Nevertheless, whenever one of them does this, we leaders are rather disconcerted; and we generally feel obliged to rebuke him severely for his lapse from party discipline. . . .

I realise that the political theorists are so attached to the pattern of democracy which depends on the existence of opposing parties, that they are likely to have been shocked by my expressing a doubt as to its being so very democratic after all. I am afraid they may be even more shocked by what I am now going to suggest: that, where there is *one* party, and that party is identified with the *nation* as a whole, the foundations of democracy are firmer than they can ever be where you have two or more parties, each representing only a section of the community!

After all, we do have it on very reliable authority that a house divided against itself cannot stand! So it is surely up to the advocates of the Two-Party system to defend their own case more convincingly. It is not enough for them simply to insist that it *is* more democratic than a One-Party system, and then be horrified when we presume to disagree with them! . . .

Our critics should understand that, in Africa, we have to take our politics a little more seriously. And they should also remember the historical difference between parties in Africa and those in Europe or America. The European and American parties came into being as the result of existing social and economic divisions—the second party being formed to challenge the monopoly of political power by some aristocratic or capitalist group. Our own parties had a very different origin. They were not formed to challenge any ruling group of our own people; they were formed to challenge the *foreigners* who ruled over us. They were not, therefore, political "parties"—i.e. factions—but nationalist movements. And from the outset they represented the interests and aspirations of the whole nation. We, in Tanganyika, for example, did not build TANU to oppose the Conservative Party of England, or to support the Labour Party! The divisions of English politicians meant nothing to us. As far as we were concerned they were all colonialists, and we built up TANU as a national movement to rid ourselves of their colonialism. A Tanganyikan who helped the imperialists was regarded as a traitor to his country, not as a believer in "Two-Party" democracy! . . .

Let me come back, then, to my contention that where there is *one* party—provided it is identified with the nation as a whole—the foundations of democracy can be firmer, and the people can have more opportunity to exercise a real choice, than where you have two or more parties —each representing only a section of the community. In countries which are accustomed to the Two-Party system it might be difficult to make any drastic change in the method of conducting elections. But what about a country like ours, where the electorate has virtually ruled out the possibility of any inter-party contest? Here, surely, we have a splendid opportunity to give our people a chance of exercising their own choice of leadership through the ballot box. Supposing we accept the fact that there is only one party, and stop trying to follow the rules of a multiparty system; then, as long as TANU membership is open to every citizen, we can conduct our elections in a way which is genuinely free and democratic.

I would go further. I would say that we not only have an opportunity to dispense with the disciplines of the Two-Party system but that we would be wrong to retain them. I would say that they are not only unnecessary where you have only one party, but that they are bound, in time, to prove fatal to democracy. We have already seen how severely these disciplines must limit freedom of expression in a Two-Party parliament. This is bad enough, but at least each party can still allow its members to argue freely within their own party meetings. Party loyalty will rally them behind their leaders when they face the rival party in Parliament. (This party loyalty, indeed, is something which feeds on opposition and makes the task of preserving discipline comparatively easy.) In fact, if the only alternative to the Two-Party system were a One-Party system which retained the rules and disciplines of the Two-

Party system, it would be better to have even an artificial opposition party, despite all the inconsistencies and limitations of freedom this would involve. For the task of imposing party discipline, of limiting freedom of expression in Parliament, with no rival party to help, would sooner or later involve us in something far worse than the factionalism of which I have accused the Two-Party enthusiasts. It would become more and more necessary to limit freedom of discussion within the party itself, until eventually it was almost entirely suppressed. Why? Because you cannot limit freedom of expression anywhere without a reason. People are not fools. They might accept the "party unity" rules for a time, but the more intelligent Members of Parliament would soon begin to ask why they must always support the Government in public without argument, since there was no fear of being pushed out of power by a rival party. And what reason could we give them? We should have to convince them, and ourselves, that the "party line" they were compelled to support was so fundamentally right that any deviation from it would be tantamount to a crime against the "people." In other words, we should have to elevate policy decisions to the category of dogma. And once you deal in dogma you cannot allow freedom of opinion. You cannot have dogma without putting contrary ideas on the "index."

This, I believe, is not unlike what has befallen our friends the Communists. They have made their policies a creed, and are finding that dogmatism and freedom of discussion do not easily go together. They are as much afraid of the "other party" as any government in a Two-Party democracy. In their case the "other party" is only a phantom, but a phantom can be even more frightening than a living rival! And their fear of this phantom has blinded them to the truth that, in a One-Party system, party membership must be open to everybody and freedom of expression allowed to every individual. No party which limits its membership to a clique can ever free itself from the fear of overthrow by those it has excluded. It must be constantly on the watch for signs of opposition, and must smother "dangerous" ideas before they have time to spread.

But a National Movement which is open to all—which is identified with the whole nation—has nothing to fear from the discontent of any excluded section of society, for there is then no such section. Those forming the Government will, of course, be replaced from time to time; but this is what elections are for. The leadership of our Movement is constantly changing; there is no reason why the leadership of the Nation should not also be constantly changing. This would have nothing to do with the overthrowing of a party government by a rival party. And, since such a National Movement leaves no room for the growth of discontented elements excluded from its membership, it has nothing to fear from criticism and the free expression of ideas. On the contrary, both the Movement itself and the Nation have everything to gain from a constant injection of new ideas from within the Nation and from outside. It would be both wrong, and certainly unnecessary, to feel we must wait until the leaders are dead before we begin to criticise them!

Any member of the Movement (which, in this context, means any patriotic citizen since it is a National Movement we are talking about) would be free to stand as a candidate if he so wished. And in each constituency the voters themselves would be able to make their choice freely from among these candidates; they would no longer be obliged to consider the party label rather than the individual. Of such elections it could truly be said that they were for the purpose of letting the people choose their own representatives. If that is not democracy, I do not know the meaning of the word!

There would be no need to hold one set of elections within the party, and another set afterwards for the public. All elections would be equally open to everybody. In our case, for example, the present distinction between TANU and the TANU Government—a distinction which, as a matter of fact, our people do not in the least understand—would vanish. We should simply have leaders chosen by the people themselves to do a job. And such leaders could be removed by the people at any time; there would be no need for a statutory period of so many years to elapse before an unsatisfactory leader could be replaced by them. In this way the government of the country would be truly in the hands of the electorate at all times. It would no longer be a mere matter of their casting votes for or against a "party" at intervals of four or five years. And anybody who continued to occupy a position of leadership, under such conditions, would do so because the people were satisfied with him; not because he was protected by a law which made it impossible for them to replace him until the next General Election.

Furthermore, there would be no need to continue with the present artificial distinction between politicians and civil servants—a distinction desirable only in the context of a multi-party system where the continuity of public administration must not be thrown out of gear at every switch from one "party" government to another. For, once you begin to think in terms of a single national movement instead of a number of rival factional parties, it becomes absurd to exclude a whole group of the most intelligent and able members of the community from participation in the discussion of policy simply because they happen to be civil servants. In a political movement which is identified with the nation, participation in political affairs must be recognised as the right of *every* citizen, in no matter what capacity he may have chosen to serve his country.

22 / THE ROLE OF THE PARTY / *SÉKOU TOURÉ*

The peoples of Guinea have consciously chosen the revolutionary way, in order to rapidly and radically end economic and social underdevelopment and human insufficiency which goes with them.

The national and democratic revolution constitutes the ideal frame for the march of our nation towards democratic progress which is founded on the concepts of liberty, equality and justice, without whose respect, a nation would not reach its harmonious revival. By fighting the regime of foreign domination, by denouncing the exploitation of man by man, our people aspired to the full mastering of their own destiny, to bring themselves to the level of exercising their liberty and creative powers.

That is why, since their independence, their action has been oriented towards one aim: human happiness, fraternity, international cooperation and peace and progress for the whole of humanity. The principal idea which guides their activities is based on the equality of all men and the identity of aspirations of all peoples.

Already on the path of history, which is from now on inseparable from the history of their Party and the history of a revolutionary Africa, the people of Guinea have won many important victories over the forces of evil.

From the forces of evil, they have snatched their freedom, they have taken away their men, their economy, their culture from arbitrary domination. They have created for themselves new political, economic, administrative and social structures.

They have defined and organized the framework of their economic and social development, to which they resolutely wish to confer a highly harmonious and well balanced character.

In the field of thought, by benefiting from the immense contribution of the progressive thinkers of the world, our peoples impose upon themselves the necessary efforts to contribute in a qualitative way to the enrichment of the cultural and political values of humanity.

In fact, the original character of their methods of action has implied an objective study of their own realities and a realistic definition of their principles of organization and of struggle.

The Guinean Revolution, thought out, led by, for the people, brings everything forward to the close interest of the working masses and to the dynamic solidarity which binds the future of our country to the future of the democratic forces of the world.

The political preeminence of the people marks the end of the subor-

From Sékou Touré, *The International Policy of the Democratic Party of Guinea* (Conakry: S.O.P. Press, n.d.), pp. 180-184, 189-192, 218-219, 221-222. (Original in English trans.)

dination of popular interest to the imperialist trusts, to the traditional feudalists, financiers and others.

The political preeminence confers, equally, upon the Democratic Party of Guinea, the historic role of national structure, on a democratic and honest basis.

The Democratic Party of Guinea has eloquently proved its high political and moral qualities, by assuming with efficiency the role of vanguard at the head of the anti-colonial front and the socialist edification of our nation.

Through its 4,142 committees which regularly hold one or two general meetings each week, through its 43 sections which every six months hold their regional Conference, through millions of parallel organisations of youth, workers, women, etc. . . . the Democratic Party of Guinea has placed the power of conception, of deliberation and of realisation at the level of the whole people, with no limitation to initiative and good will for all those who wish to bring their contribution to the edification of the Republic of Guinea.

The Democratic Party of Guinea defines the popular objectives and the stages of the evolution of our country [and] through its administration, cooperatives and unions, it controls the realisation of these objectives.

Already, in the field of workers, it has promulgated the democratic Code of labour, a unique frame work of the public Function, of social Security in favour of all the collective and democratic management of the State enterprises. Since January 1st 1962, it proceeded to the reevaluation of the pensions of the category of the disinherited. This reevaluation is based on the principle of continual tightening up of the [structure] of salaries.

The Democratic Party of Guinea has organised the youth of the nation on national bases. It has given to the national movement of youth all the necessary material means for the flourishing of the intellectual and physical faculties of youth. It has proceeded to the Reform of teaching, to make of teaching and education a dynamic sector for the valuable and conscious formation of leaders. By considerably developing the structure itself of teaching, whose number has increased in three years from 42,000 to 125,000, it had put an end to the confessional teaching and has ordered the Africanisation of churches.

In the course of the year 1962, each administrative region of the country will be furnished with the necessary installations for the functioning of professional and second degree teaching. In this programme, the fate of the feminine youth has the particular attention of the Democratic Party of Guinea, which has decided to liquidate as soon as possible the striking difference which still exists between girls and boys.

The emancipation of women studied from the economic, social, political and cultural angle, has already been the object of important resolutions passed by our national conference. The Democratic Party of Guinea uses all possible means to assure to its policy of feminine emancipation a complete and rapid success—already discrimination in the professional field and in salaries is forbidden.

The new code of liberalities and of persons which was the object of the deliberations of all the main committees will very soon be adopted by the National Assembly, and will regulate the conditions and forms of marriage as well as the conditions of divorce and the problems of inheritance.

The Democratic Party of Guinea will continue, with all vigour, its campaign against alcoholism, corruption, theft and opportunism. It invites all its sections all its committees . . . to exercise from now on . . . extreme vigilance against the enemies of the revolution, the traitors of the nation.

The Party invites its administrative and political leaders, to scrupulously respect its principles and faithfully apply its methods of work.

The administrative and political decentralization which has just been decided upon in the last session of the national conference, will considerably increase the powers of management and control of the bodies [at the base]. The success of this decentralization will depend on the honesty and the devotion of the political and administrative frames of the Nation.

. . . The national revolution has become an impetuous movement, going each day towards the conquest of more power and of the well-being of the people. It is because our revolution is a sector of the world revolution, an active part of the democratic forces against imperialism and colonialism, it is because our revolution contributes to the acceleration of the revolution of Africa, to assure the victory of the peoples against their exploiters, that the P.D.G. supports and will always support the revolutionary aims of all the exploited classes and of all the dominated and oppressed peoples.

The P.D.G. hails and encourages the creation of the Pan-African Union, whose revolutionary aims is the improvement of the living conditions of African peoples, which it shares so completely.

It greets the anti-imperialist and anti-colonialist movements of Afro-Asian peoples and always considers the five principles of Bandung as the just basis of an international cooperation. . . .

The Preeminence of the Party

The preeminence of the Party does not imply rashness, and if the party enjoys absolute freedom of decision and holds the greatest part of the power, these are limited by the frames it has imposed upon itself, in conformity with the directing principles. Therefore it is clear that the

Party could not transgress its own rules, and moreover, a man acting in the name of the Party could not distort the preeminence and the authority of the Party so as to put forward his ideas or his preferences, or impose himself on the population through pressure or fear or mystification.

No responsible political man, whatever the authority he represents . . . could substitute himself for the Party. If he emanates from it, if he is its speaker, he can but act as a reflecting instrument, not of his own personality, but of the Party, which alone can express the will, the aspirations, the needs and the hopes of our people. . . .

We have already affirmed, with no mis-understanding, that the Party wanted to apply dictatorship which is by its nature, the logical consequence of a democracy established at the level of [the] people and by the people, and which finds its expression in the application of democratic centralization. This means that the individual whatever his personality, his functions, his responsibilities, his socal rank or his political work may be must withdraw himself for the benefit of the political, human social personality of our people, or at least his own personality may be used as a means of expression [of] the human collectivity which he represents.

Yet, certain leaders have the tendency, in this domain, to impose a formal preeminence contrary to the spirit of the Party. This attitude may lead in short time to many abuses which would naturally distort fundamental orientation of the action of our Party.

We must therefore be vigilant in that domain, so that preeminence be applied, not only in its form, but in its spirit. The Party is not the will of one man or a group of men, the preeminence of the Party is that of the people to realise their own happiness, the organisations of the Party are qualified to defend at all times and in all places the aspirations and the interests of the people. It is to say that only the Party is entrusted with the task of making the people's will respected. The force it uses to impose this preeminence must directly serve the people and not the leaders as individuals.

In this respect, we ask our active members, who are directly responsible for the election of their representatives in the Party itself, not to succumb to easy sentimentalism, to know how to select the men whom they may trust, with no other criterion than that of faithfulness to the Party, but should also ask them to fully exercise their right of control over the behaviour, the action and the attitude of their leaders. No honest and conscientious political leader would escape such a control, by arguing that his responsibilities place him above the control of the masses.

The political leader is not above the active members, he is the instrument of the people and of the Party. Therefore his activities and his behaviour must be a continuous reflection of the activities of the Party and the faithful image of the struggle and the pre-occupations and the aspirations of the popular masses; on the other hand there exists in certain others a lack of ideal, a lack of conviction and as soon as this spirit exists in a section, one is immediately aware of it for it is directly reflected in the life of the section. The lack of ideal drags in the lack of self-confidence, which ends up in the neglect of the political line and an obvious disinterest in its correct implementation. Our ideal, thrown in time and space, is determined by our political line . . . whereas conviction, as a power of admission to the program of the Party, is inside each one of us, it gives each one of us all the amount of trust and faith which is personal, trust and faith in oneself, trust [and] faith in the Party. When trust is lacking, the apparatus of the Party becomes a brake for the revolution and acts implicitly against it. When we study the history of our Party, we realise that it has always lived by its own means, it is a major party, able to establish its own definition and its own line of action in close harmony with the realities, the needs and the aspirations of the Guinean people, in the light of a historic and dynamic evolution, to realize the happiness of society and the widening of the creative powers of man. . . .

It is in order to provide the higher interests of the people with a constant protection against any harm that our Party imposes political preeminence and applies popular dictatorship. Some people, more sensitive to the expression than to the real meaning of thoughts, dislike the use of certain words. For these romantic souls who separate democracy from the power of the people by approving the democratic regime while opposing popular dictatorship, we should reaffirm that the democratic regime of the Republic of Guinea is a people's regime and that it should remain so.

We should stress also that the power of the people of Guinea shall constantly be increased and consolidated, that the preeminence of the party will continuously be imposed, and that the popular dictatorship will be exercised always with more strength in the various organisations of both the Party and the State.

The structures of the Democratic Party of Guinea are in conformity with the principles of our regime and with the efficient exercise of democracy which we could not possibly confuse with any form of democracy of a nature which is not popular.

With its 7,164 first degree committees who assemble twice a week, with its 150 sections each of which holds, with its thousands of leaders from the first degree committees, at least two meetings a year in regional conferences and, lastly, with the two national annual conferences, the Party could not be anything other than the direct and permanent expression of the people's will. The activities of the State are subordinated by the interests of the people, and not the opposite. Such a structure that characterises the popular nature of our regime is bound to be maintained, thanks to the political preeminence that defines, decides, and controls all national activities. This is how the people's dictatorship is exercised and guaranteed. . . .

We urge all militants and leaders to constantly extend the popular nature of our democratic activities so that real revolutionary firmness of the people may be imposed upon all those whose interested liberalism harms the revolutionary action and distorts the democratic expression of popular power established in the Republic of Guinea by the P.D.G.

We call upon all militants, men and women, of the P.D.G., to work constantly towards the consolidation of national unity which is the pride of our people and whose essential bases remain freedom in justice, equality and democracy in solidarity.

Long Live the Revolution!

23 / POLICY REPORT OF THE UNION CAMEROUNAISE
AHMADOU AHIDJO

We have . . . to set ourselves to the task of national development. This job is immense, but it is noble and captivating. It will indeed enrich our spirit and will make us noble before History.

The job of nation-building is inscribed within the framework of a program of political, economic, and social planning. In fact, it merges into our national policy. It is the objective of this policy. It is, however, realizable only through the blossoming of our sovereignty in every sector of the nation's life.

As we all know, and as I have already had the occasion of telling you under other circumstance, definitions are always approximate. They always give reality an over-enlarged or a shrunken image. Nevertheless, in order to express our ideology in the sacred words of the twentieth century, let us say that the theme of all our reflections, of all our political, economic, and social philosophy, is social humanism; or, in other terms, African socialism.

For us Africans, indeed, as my friend Senghor would say, nothing material constitutes an end in itself. Thus, money, merchandise, or technique in all its aspects, are of value to us Negro-Africans only in as much as they have a meaning, a human and social utility. Even when, in whatever way, they give man some satisfaction, they fulfill the mission which we assign to them only if they strengthen and vivify the bonds of affection without which no society can live either physically or spiritually.

Our essential preoccupation must be the constant search for projects

From Ahmadou Ahidjo, *Rapport de Politique Générale du Président Général: Quatrième Congrès du Parti Politique de l'Union Camerounaise* (Ebolowa, Juillet 1962), pp. 7-8, 10-15, 17, 21, 44-48.

capable of spreading African humanist socialism by means of an intro-spective analysis, and with this analysis as a basis, to seek with untiring effort enriching factors and points of conciliation with the other socialisms of the world.

At no moment, whether it be a question of the search for national unity, of the interest we take in the evolution of our traditional institu-tions, of the grouping, the education, and the mobilization of our masses, of the fight against rebellion, or of our diplomatic activities, must we forget the specifically African principles of ideology which explain and justify them.

National Unity

What is the motive force of this policy? Clearly it is you; that is to say, our Party. The goal of our Party, whose very name constitutes a program, has always been and remains the union of all Camerounians, without ex-ception. We have already said that the theme of our policy is national development, which is not possible without dynamism and enthusiasm. And there is no dynamism, there is no enthusiasm without faith. There is no faith without the union of hearts and the union of minds.

Thus, national unity is the essential objective of the day, the mortgage which we must first pay off in order to consider ourselves as sons of the Camerounian Nation. No obstacle, no material, sentimental, or ideo-logical interests, can stop us from setting out on the road to national unity. Does not History teach us that national unity is always incom-patible with personal interests? We must then repulse certain feelings, in order to wage the necessary battle, to make the unity of minds and hearts intervene from the foundation up. The divisions, the hatred, which have arisen and are caused by ambitious speculation must be dis-covered, revealed, and their perpetrators banished from the Nation.

With regard to this, the Party has a role of primary importance. In-deed, the breath of unity must enjoy a special warmth in the units and formations of the Party. The essential mission of the leaders of cells, of the basic committees, of the sub-sections, and of the sections must consist in maintaining a spirit of *camaraderie,* of highly developed fraternity between militants. This preoccupation must have highest priority.

No conflict or difference of opinion among militants must be allowed to grow into spiteful opposition. We sometimes observe that some mili-tants of the Party have a hatred for other militants which they have never manifested against our adversaries, or even against the rebels. We must no longer tolerate such spectacles. Such sentiments constitute a considerable obstacle to the very evolution of the Party. They can give the Party a bad image: a conglomeration of individuals united by no one sentiment, no one ideology. We want to, and we must, convince all

Camerounians of the imperative necessity of national unity. Let us start by giving the example of unity. It is a question of instilling everywhere, and in every possible way, the faith which animates us into the hearts and minds of other countrymen. . . .

In that which concerns us, in our decisions, we exclude all considerations and all factors capable of directly or indirectly affirming or maintaining tribal particularism.

National unity means that there is no place, in the blueprint for national development, for the Ewondo, the Douala, the Bamileke, the Boulou, the Foulbe, or the Bassa, etc. etc., but rather a place everywhere and always for Camerounians.

Camerounian ethnic groups are without a doubt a reality, but a reality of which the leaders of the party or the State must be aware in order to search for the characteristics by which the parts may be grafted on to the whole, in order to integrate them and thus to accelerate the realization of national unity. . . .

Following the same train of thought, the system of instituting tribal units within the Party must cease. It also seems to us that from now on militant Party members must no longer manage the traditional associations which play a political role. Instructions will be given to Party leaders, at all levels, not to tolerate any longer such groups under the Party standard. Party organizations in urban and rural centers must be formed within the framework of housing projects, neighborhood subdivisions, villages, groupings, etc. This set-up will, however, be effective only if it adapts itself to certain social and psychological realities. . . .

African Unity

One must say that our first preoccupation [in foreign policy] has been and remains the creation of working African solidarity, with a view toward African unity, the necessity of which—now unanimously accepted—no longer seems necessary to prove. We have tried, because we are especially aware of the inconveniences of the division in other continents, to work to diminish the ever-recurring impact of imperialisms in Africa and thus consolidate the young independent states. . . .

However, unity requires the total liberation of Africa. One would be dangerously misled to think that it could be accomplished in a satisfactory manner as long as only certain African countries are independent. We are convinced that our liberty is indirectly related to that of all African peoples, and that the slowness of decolonization in certain parts of the continent constitutes a real menace to the security of African States and the peace of the world which we need so much in order to succeed in our national development.

Auto-Decolonization

The behavior of the bureaucrats, who have been by far the principal beneficiaries of decolonization, with respect to the masses gives us the greatest anxiety. The latter, indeed, have the impression that one kind of colonialism has replaced another. This situation is painfully felt by our compatriots. The old colonialism was the enslavement of the black men at the hands of the white man. The new colonialism is the servitude of the African at the hands of his brother. . . .

It is not exaggerated to affirm that, in the eyes of our masses, these élites have replaced the Europeans—not only in their functions and material prerogatives, such as homes, cars, etc., but especially in the habits and customs which they have assumed—habits which were decried but yesterday; the enslavement of citizens today goes well beyond that of colonialism. For this category of Camerounian, independence means the policy of "get out of there so that I can put myself in your place."

And since the masses, we must admit, do not read the *Official Journal,* and since they hardly know the laws and regulations, in their eyes these bureaucrats will incarnate the State and the regime. They know, of course, that there is a head of state and that there are institutions, but they only see the regime's appearance and value through the intermediary of the public agents.

In the presence of certain modes of behavior, one is forced to ask oneself if it is not a question of the deliberate or unconscious sabotage of the institutions of the state by an enemy in disguise.

One must, then, reawaken at the same time the professional awareness and the patriotic sentiment of the public servants.

The Party, which is the avant-garde of the Nation, must play a determining role in this renewal of awareness.

It is not our intention to hand over the bureaucrats to the public's vengeance. We know, when the occasion warrants it, how to honor those among them who are proving their limitless devotion and high awareness in the administration of affairs of state. . . .

Moreover, we do not need to again recall that the *Union Camerounaise* is a democratic party, and that, consequently, the *Union Camerounaise* accepts the confrontation of different tendencies at its center.

The evolution of the Party, its adaptation to contingencies of all kinds, will not be able to be the work of the founding militants of the Party alone.

We place with them, of course—but also on the militants of today and of tomorrow—all our hopes. Our doctrine is of necessity syncretic.

Some people also claim that they have found proof in our thinking of our desire to install, by means of a unified party, a dictatorial regime in Cameroun.

Almost every independent French-speaking African State has adopted the regime of the united national party. Are these States dictatorial because of it? What is meant by this word "dictatorship"? We believe we know that a dictatorship exists when a minority of citizens imposes its will on the majority of citizens. We believe we know that democracy is essentially characterized by the submission of the minority of citizens to the laws and regulations established by the representatives of the majority of citizens, as well as the respect for the legal rights of this minority.

Are we in the majority or in the minority? I think that anyone with normal mental faculties can make the necessary calculation in order to answer this question. . . .

Voluntarily and freely, we have chosen the path of democracy, but the democratic systems of the Occident and of Eastern Europe are not products which are directly exportable to the countries of Africa.

Our European friends must make room in their thinking, and in their conceptions, for the necessary flexibility required to understand that our countries, which are in the process of being developed, must discover their own political formulas in the context of their situations and of their civilizations which are extremely different from those of European or American countries.

The unified national party is the political expression of the African spirit and of our communizing tendencies. Even at the national level, our civilization is one of the family; in other words, a civilization which carries no trace of selfish interest, and no signs of profound individualism.

24 / PROGRESS WITHOUT TEARS / M. I. OKPARA

The clearest single fact which has emerged since our Independence on the first of October, 1960 is the disparity between our standard of living and that of the more advanced nations. We are all aware of the fact that considerable ground has yet to be covered in the social services, the public utilities and production. Nevertheless the basic infrastructure has been laid. Even so we are still a young and developing country. It has been reckoned that a per capita income of about £170 per annum is the dividing line between developing nations and advanced ones. Per capita income in Nigeria on an optimistic estimate is about £30 per annum. When we remember that in America and Canada it is more than twenty times as high as Nigeria we can see how far removed our way of life must be from theirs. An important point to remember is that our per capita income is about one-sixth of the dividing line per capita income

From M. I. Okpara, *Progress Without Tears: Address at the Convocation, University of Nigeria, Nsukka, 17th December 1962* (Enugu: Government Printer, n.d.), pp. 3-5, 10-16.

of £170 per year. In the pre-independence period the importance of this fact was overshadowed by the great exigencies of the day: the winning of national independence with honour and in peace and unity. This has been the experience of other emergent nations. The fight for political autonomy has a way of commanding total attention from nation builders, but as soon as this fight is over, these nationalists begin, if they are capable of making the necessary mental reorientation, to think about the economic welfare of the citizens. *This reorientation, then, is the first major re-thinking that must take place.* It is not, however, an easy change to make, for modes of thought dictated by decades of colonial tutelage are difficult to modify overnight. But there is another reason why it is difficult to make the change: political controversy is far more exciting than the complicated and painful problems of economic development. Up till today, there is not one national daily or weekly devoted to the problems of economic change. The stuff of politics is their sole daily material and fills every column. . . .

Granted then that this change is possible and is indeed made, we are confronted with the primary question of our generation: *How can we pull level with the more advanced nations in the shortest possible time while still retaining our freedom and happiness?*

It amounts to this: that the next one and a half decades in Nigeria must be regarded as a period of economic emergency by the Governments, the citizens, the Universities and all our friends abroad. Some countries eager to liberate themselves from poverty as quickly as possible have selected the quick sure way of totalitarianism or total war, when enormous sacrifices are taken for granted and forced savings made by all; when all land is commandeered by the state for increased production and when political controversy is reduced to a minimum by the system of a one-party state or coalition Government, and when Universities and industries concentrate on science and technology. It is said by some experts that under such a system investment can rise up to 30 per cent. per annum of gross national product. This is the great temptation that is sweeping all over Africa today. Is this the short cut to success? Its inherent danger is in the ease with which the people under such a system, without adequate safeguards and checks, easily lose their freedom. If this danger can be overcome, then there is every reason to mobilise as in total war all the resources of the nation in a general assault on poverty.

How can this delicate operation be done?

Firstly there should be a review of the constitution which should make provision for a united front Government in which all shades of political opinion will be represented, for a period of not more than fifteen years. I use the figure fifteen because I am assuming, as we all did in the development plan, that self-sustaining growth will be achieved after the third or fourth plans. After this period the nation should then return to the luxury of partisan politics. Of course, adequate distribution of powers between the Legislature and the Executive and the Judiciary is an additional safeguard. Inherent in this crash programme is that all land must be mobilised immediately for modern agriculture, crops diversified, and modern implements, machines and fertilisers introduced. All universities must fall into line with this programme and concentrate on the basic essentials for rapid growth. The plan also implies that Nigeria will be manufacturing practically all her needs from aeroplanes to pins by the end of fifteen years. We all know the weaknesses of an ordinary coalition Government. In point of fact I have always opposed the suggestion in the past as it was only designed to lessen political bickering and nothing else. But a United-Front Government as a tool for rapid economic growth such as I have outlined is another matter and should be very closely studied by all. It is quite different from the controversial one-party Government. The advantage of this approach is that we shall not only continue to develop within a framework of democratic government but we shall develop rapidly within such a system. Such a constitution could have written into it safeguards against totalitarianism, thus ensuring the complete return at the end of the emergency of our much beloved partisan politics!

No one who has studied the rate of growth of the totalitarian countries can fail to be impressed by their performance. But this is usually achieved at the cost of human suffering and the loss of a good deal of happiness. I have equally had a very close look at India. This is the one shining example where a deliberate effort is being made, as we are making, to develop within a framework of democratic government. Herein lies the great importance of the Indian Experiment. But such development always relies on massive external aid. Many people in Nigeria wonder whether we shall be so lucky in attracting foreign aid in such massive amounts. They may be right, since the dangers posed by communism next door to India do not exist here, and to that extent the West does not feel the urgency of the Nigerian problem. But a temporary modification of the Indian experiment by us is possible and can be achieved provided we are all agreed and determined to cut the chains that bind Africa to poverty. The formula that I recommended may be summarised under six heads:

(a) Mass assault on poverty through greatly increased agricultural production and maximum use of the land.
(b) Rapid Industrialisation with fixed targets.
(c) Raising the battle cry for, and adequate emphasis on, Science in all Nigerian Universities.
(d) The conscious projection of an African Common Market and other remedies to the ills of the European Common Market.
(e) The establishment of a United Front Government for a period of fifteen years after appropriate Constitutional Review.
(f) The maintenance of the Nation's stability.

It is assumed that we shall, of course, fully use the levers of the Central Bank and the National Economic Council to achieve the first, second, third and fourth objectives.

Perhaps the most controversial suggestion is that of a United-Front Government. This proposal is likely to be of the greatest interest to politicians who would be spared the bitterness of partisan political conflict for at least fifteen years. But I must remind them that this proposal must go along with massive effort in Agriculture, industrialisation, science, the realisation of an African Common Market and the maintenance of the nation's security. Indeed the idea of a United-Front Government is the one proposal that is incapable of standing alone. . . .

Implicit in all my suggestions, of course, is the maintenance of the nation's security and stability. Economic development is impossible without stability; no pains should therefore be spared in order to guard the nation's name and stability jealously. I do not wish to dwell at length on our security. I merely wish to point to the fact that the recent experiences of India show clearly the need for adequate internal security forces to back a policy of non-alignment. In order not to cripple our economy with too large a security force we might take a leaf from Israel where the armed forces are not only for defence but also for production. Indeed, our battalions here are already famous for launching bailey bridges for the villagers. This idea could be extended in suitable cases to productive farming such as in some border *kibutsm*.

No doubt there will be warning voices and fears for our democratic way of life. Let me assure these people that only rapid economic advance will safeguard democracy in this country. And in any case all such fears will be taken care of by the constitutional review which will spell-out all the checks and balances. I have no doubt in my mind however that in the absence of massive external aid this is the only acceptable alternative to slow crawling growth. But its implementation will require the highest forms of statesmanship and patriotism if the people are not to gamble away their freedom as in some one-party states. In a nutshell we must all declare war on poverty and prosecute this war as in an emergency. But in all the campaigns of such a war we must remember that the purpose of the exercise is the welfare and happiness of all the citizens of Nigeria.

All births are painful processes. The emergence of Nigeria from centuries of under-development to an era of technology is a birth. But a midwife can, through guidance, make a birth less painful than usual. As the nation's midwives, the leaders of the country, whether in Government, industry or the Universities, must deliver the baby safely and on time, so that the citizens' vigil may end with a happy reward.

INTRODUCTION

The selections in the last section of this volume concern the complex and difficult problems of the relations among the African states, including the pervasive ideology of Pan-Africanism, and their relations with the world outside Africa. Inter-African relations as a practical matter of finding technical and organizational mechanisms by which African states can mutually assist their development is essentially a question of recent vintage, stemming from the emergence of independent African states since the late 1950s. The doctrine of Pan-Africanism, on the other hand, is of much older date, originating among persons of African descent resident in the Americas.

As far as is known, the term "Pan-Africanism" was first used by H. Sylvester Williams, a British-trained West Indian barrister who initiated the first organizational expression of Pan-Africanism by convening the Pan-African World Conference in London in 1900. Several members of the Negro American intelligentsia of this period were associated with Williams at the 1900 Conference, especially Bishop Alexander Walters of the African Methodist Episcopal Church, and Dr. W. E. B. DuBois, the first Negro American to secure the doctorate degree, which he received at Harvard University in 1895. It was DuBois who, at the close of World War I, spearheaded the mainstream of political Pan-Africanism, an effort which earned him the acclamation of contemporary African leaders like Jomo Kenyatta, Nnamdi Azikiwe, and Kwame Nkrumah as the "Father of Pan-Africanism."

At the beginning of the Peace Conference in Paris in 1919, Dr. DuBois, along with a number of Negro American, West Indian, and African intellectuals, organized the First Pan-African Congress. This First Congress concentrated upon securing fair treatment of African colonies by the Western Powers at the Peace Conference, and it resolved to press for the thoroughgoing humanization and democratization of colonialism in

Africa, with the ultimate goal of African self-government. Dr. DuBois pursued these aims with vigor, intelligence, and self-sacrifice in four additional Pan-African Congresses. The Second Congress was held in London, 1921; the Third in London and Lisbon, 1923 (in the latter city the Negro Brazilian intelligentsia played a leading role); the Fourth in New York, 1927; and the Fifth and last in Manchester (U.K.) in 1945. At the Fifth Congress DuBois's role was mainly that of the grand patron of modern Pan-Africanism, for this Congress saw for the first time the control of Pan-Africanism pass from the hands of the new world Negroes to those of Africans. Among the young African political personalities at the Fifth Congress were Kwame Nkrumah, co-chairman of the Congress along with Dr. DuBois, Jomo Kenyatta, I. T. A. Wallace-Johnson of Sierra Leone, and Peter Abrahams of South Africa.[1]

It was to be expected that with the independence of Ghana in 1957, the center of gravity of political Pan-Africanism would shift to the African continent and, more particularly, to Ghana. In 1958 Nkrumah organized the Conference of Independent African States and the First All-Africa People's Conference. From these meetings the organization of Pan-Africanism was elaborated at many levels, entailing ties between not merely African governments but also trade unions, political parties, and other groups.

The first selection in Part IV is from a speech by Kwame Nkrumah at the first Positive Action Conference for Peace and Security in Africa, which he called into being as one expression of the Pan-African movement. The Conference was composed mainly of representatives of militant political parties, especially those from southern African territories like the Rhodesias, but also militant opposition parties in independent African states. The orientation of the Conference was a radical form of post-colonial Pan-Africanism which Ghana, and particularly Nkrumah himself, came to epitomize.

This bifurcation of political Pan-Africanism along radical and conservative or moderate lines, with certain African governments falling on one or the other side although still preserving a certain fluidity of alignments, is another facet of the organizational elaboration of Pan-Africanism since 1958. A minority of African governments have followed Nkrumah's radical approach, notably Guinea and Mali in West Africa, and Algeria and Egypt, sometimes joined by Morocco, in North Africa. Even these countries, however, have been hesitant to give a working endorsement to Nkrumah's repeated demand for a true political union of all the independent states on the African continent.

The overwhelming majority of African states have made clear their objection to any such proposal for immediate political unification. While no one state has put itself forth as leader of the majority sentiment in

[1] For an account of the Five Pan-African Congresses, see Colin Legum, *Pan-Africanism* (New York: Frederick A. Praeger, Inc., 1962).

favor of limited moves toward Pan-African unity through functional co-operation, Nigeria is widely looked upon as the most effective spokesman for this school of thought. The position it holds is ably and judiciously discussed in the selection in Part IV from Nnamdi Azikiwe, President of Nigeria, though it is to be noted that he is no less committed than the radical group to the essence of Pan-Africanism as the ultimate answer to basic problems not only of Africans but also of peoples of African descent the world over. Thus, the intellectual and emotional features of Pan-Africanism, like the issues of Negro self-identity, or African Personality and Négritude, are integral parts of Azikiwe's view of Pan-Africanism.

The selection from the writings of Léopold Senghor, President of Senegal, equally approaches Pan-Africanism in functional terms, concentrating on limited political links short of full union. He supports limited regional federations of African states wherever possible, assuming that in time such federations, like bricks in the building of a house, will result in an integrated structure.

The next two selections from the writings of Sékou Touré, President of Guinea, and Julius Nyerere, President of Tanganyika, emphasize the question of inter-African relations as they affect the remaining colonial territories in southern Africa—including the independent Republic of South Africa which African leaders view as an anachronistic and intolerable domination of whites over blacks—and the international politics of the Cold War. Kwame Nkrumah of Ghana was in fact the first African leader to emphasize these features of inter-African relations, as indicated in his selection in Part IV. No effective means has yet been found, however, either to fend off the intrusion of the Cold War into Africa or to deal with the problems of the south of the continent. The southern African territories under European control seem extraordinarily resourceful in their defense against pressures from independent African states, and, given the extremely modernized and technically proficient military forces of the Republic of South Africa, this defense would seem secured for the near future.

Moreover, most independent African states are militarily in their infancy, depending upon heavy material and financial support of their military by the former colonial power. In fact, Kenya, Uganda, and Tanganyika required the intervention of the British army to quell a mutiny of their armed forces in 1963, and in Gabon the French army intervened to prevent the Gabonese army from deposing a pro-French regime. As regards the intervention in African affairs of the contending powers in the Cold War, the degree of political instability in post-colonial Africa almost serves to invite such intervention, as the chronic crisis in the ex-Belgian Congo testifies. The best to be hoped for is that African states, through inter-African organization, can at least regulate such intervention, thereby maximizing the gains and minimizing the losses to be derived from foreign intervention.

Some such policy has been arrived at through the machinery of the Organization of African Unity, founded in 1963 in Addis Ababa, Ethiopia, and embracing all independent states on the African continent, including North Africa. Haile Selassie, Emperor of Ethiopia, has played a leading role in the OAU, and the last selection in Part IV is his speech at the founding conference. Ethiopia, though briefly under Italian rule in the 1930s, has been an independent state since the dawn of the Christian era. It has only recently turned inward to Africa as a source of emotional identity and inspiration for its modernization, and the Emperor's speech at the founding OAU Conference is the culmination of this process.

25 / FREEDOM AND UNITY AS AFRICA'S SALVATION
KWAME NKRUMAH

Fellow Africans, you all know that foreign domination in Africa effectively disintegrated the personality of the African people. For centuries during which colonialism held sway over our beloved continent, colonialism imposed on the mind of Africans the idea that their own kith and kin in other parts of Africa were aliens and had little, if anything, in common with Africans elsewhere. It was in the interests of the colonial and settler rulers to perpetuate the subjection of us, the indigenous people, by pursuing a policy not only of "divide and rule," but also of artificial territorial division of Africa. It played upon our tribalistic instincts. It sowed seeds of dissension in order to promote disunity among us.

It is therefore with great pride and happiness that we note how resurgent Africa is witnessing to-day what is by no means a humble beginning of the process of re-integration of the African personality, and forging closer and stronger bonds of unity which are bound to bring us to our ultimate goal: the attainment of a union of African States and Republics which, to my mind, is the only solution to the problems that face us in Africa to-day.

Fellow Africans and friends: there are two threatening swords of Damocles hanging over our continent, and we must remove them. These are nuclear tests in the Sahara by the French Government and the apartheid policy of the Government of the Union of South Africa.

It would be a great mistake to imagine that the achievement of political independence by certain areas in Africa would automatically mean the end of the struggle. It is merely the beginning of the end of the struggle. We must watch out for and expose the various forms of the new imperialism with which we are threatened. Among these, we must men-

From Address by Kwame Nkrumah to the Conference on Positive Action and Security in Africa, Accra, April 1960.

tion nuclear imperialism that dawned upon Africa on a tragic day last February when the French Government exploded an atomic bomb on our soil. . . .

In spite of world protests and condemnation of its first test, the Government of France has actually carried out its intention by exploding the second bomb in the Sahara. This is an act of stubborn and inhuman defiance that not only challenges the very conscience of mankind, but also undermines the United Nations. . . .

The Government of Ghana, as I have said, has already taken action by freezing all French assets until the extent of the damage to the life and health of her people becomes known. Since the explosion of the second bomb, she has also recalled her Ambassador to France. But a critical situation such as this calls for concerted action and it will be for the committees of this conference to discuss what action can be taken to prevent further nuclear outrages in Africa. Another committee will discuss Positive Direct Action to prevent further tests. . . .

Positive action has already achieved remarkable success in the liberation struggle of our continent and I feel sure that it can further save us from the perils of this atomic arrogance. If the direct action that was carried out by the international protest team were to be repeated on a mass scale, or simultaneously from various parts of Africa, the result could be as powerful and as successful as Gandhi's historic Salt March. We salute Mahatma Gandhi and we remember in tribute to him, that it was in South Africa that his method of non-violence and non-co-operation was first practised in the struggle against the vicious race discrimination that still plagues that unhappy country. . . .

But while we consider the new forms of imperialism and colonialism, let us not forget its crude blatant forms that wreak havoc in parts of our continent such as Algeria, Angola, Kenya, Ruanda Urundi, Nyasaland and in South Africa. The passive sympathy of the African masses must be converted into active participation in the struggle for the total emancipation of Africa. Africa is too sacred a land to harbour hypocrites. Sooner or later, but sooner rather than later, our continent will be purged of all forms of colonialism, for the fire of intense nationalism is blazing all over Africa and burning to ashes the last remnants of colonialism. The civilised world stands aghast at the brutal massacre of unarmed Africans in South Africa. Yet this wanton outrage of the Government of South Africa is hardly more terrible than the explosion of French atomic bombs in the Sahara.

It is ironical to think that the rulers of South Africa call themselves Christians. If Christ were to appear in South Africa to-day he would be crucified by them if he dared to oppose the brutal laws of racial segregation. Apartheid and nuclear weapons must shake the conscience of the Christian world. But what are the churches of the world doing about these very contradictions of Christianity? . . .

The cardinal principle upon which the peace and security of this continent depends, is the firm insistence that Africa is not an extension of Europe or of any other continent. A corollary of this principle is the resolution that Africa is not going to become a cockpit of the Cold War, or a marshalling ground for attack on either West or East, nor is it going to be an arena for fighting out the East-West conflict. In this particular sense, we face neither East nor West: we face forward. . . .

There can be no peace or security in Africa without freedom and political unity. So long as one inch of African soil remains under colonial rule there will be strife and conflict. So long as any group on this continent denies the principle of one-man one-vote, and uses its power to maintain its privilege, there will be insecurity for the oppressors and constant resentment and revolt on the part of the oppressed. These are the elementary facts of life in Africa to-day. No man willed this situation and no man can stem the tide or divert the "winds of change." We decry violence and deplore it. We are devoted to non-violent positive action. Experience has shown that when change is too long delayed or stubbornly resisted, violence will erupt here and there—not because men planned it and willed it—but because the accumulated grievances of the past erupt with volcanic fury. . . .

We welcome men of goodwill everywhere to join us, irrespective of their race, religion or nationality. When I speak of Africa for Africans this should be interpreted in the light of my emphatic declaration, that I do not believe in racialism and colonialism. The concept "Africa for Africans" does not mean that other races are excluded from it. No. It only means that Africans, who naturally are in the majority in Africa, shall and must govern themselves in their own countries. The fight is for the future of humanity, and it is a most important fight.

Fellow Africans: Africa is marching forward to freedom and no power on earth can halt her now.

Our salvation and strength and our only way out of these ravages in Africa, lies in political union, and those who doubt the feasibility of such a union appear to have forgotten their history lesson too soon. The vastness of Russia and all the towering obstacles of her beginning did not prevent that country from building its greatness in unity by the union of eighteen different republics. The sprawling spread of America and her original colonial difficulties have not stopped that country from building a union of forty-nine states. If these countries can do this, why cannot Africa? I repeat that nothing but our own groundless fears and doubts can stop us from building a real practical political union. But remember —"Our fears are traitors and make us lose what we might often achieve by fearing to attempt."

So dear is this African unity to our hearts, that in our proposed republican constitution a definite provision has been incorporated by a concrete proposal that Ghana's sovereignty should be surrendered in whole or in part as a contribution toward the attainment of the great objective. Fellow Africans: permit me the liberty of stating in categorical terms that the greatness of this objective so transcends all other purposes and its sublimity is so profound, that it behooves each and everyone in the leadership of this struggle to endeavour to subdue his own little interests, his individual pride and ego and other petty considerations which merely serve to create needless obstacles in our path. The over-riding importance of African unity demands the sacrifice of all personal, tribal and regional objectives and considerations.

26 / PAN-AFRICANISM / NNAMDI AZIKIWE

When we speak of Pan-Africanism, what do we exactly mean? To envisage its future, we must appreciate its meaning. To some people, Pan-Africanism denotes the search for an African personality.

To others, it implies negritude. Whilst to many it connotes a situation which finds the whole continent of Africa free from the shackles of foreign domination with its leaders free to plan for the orderly progress and welfare of its inhabitants. In order not to be misleading, we must also explain what we mean by the term "African." Is he a member of the black race or is he a hybrid of the black and white races inhabiting Africa? It is necessary to say, too, whether an inhabitant of Africa, irrespective of his race and language, qualifies to become an African within the context of the use of this terminology.

I would prefer to be very broad in my use of the words "Africa" and "African." For reasons which will emerge by the time I have finished analysing the problems of Pan-Africanism, it should be obvious that unless we accept a broad definition of terms, there can be no worthy future for Africanism. That being the case, I would like to speak of the peoples of Africa in general terms to include all the races inhabiting that continent and embracing all the linguistic and cultural groups who are domiciled therein.

Human Society

In other words, I am using the term strictly in its political context so that whatever solutions are offered by me would in the final analysis be political. This approach simplifies my problem because it would enable me to formulate policies which can be implemented, bearing in mind the empirical history of human beings in other continents of the earth. It would be useless to define "Pan-Africanism" exclusively in racial or linguistic terms, since the obvious solution would be parochial. And chauvinism, by whatever name it is identified, has always been a disintegrating factor in human society at all known times of human history.

From Nnamdi Azikiwe, *My Plan for Africa* (Enugu: Anno Press, n.d.), pp. 1-5, 14-17, 27-28.

It is true that the roots of Pan-Africanism are, to a large extent, racial, but the evolution of the idea itself took different forms in the last four centuries so that today Africanism cannot be restricted to racial factors. What are these roots? Mainly individual actions and group pressure. Take the individual prophets of Pan-Africanism and it will be found that in all cases they were ethnocentric in their ideas and concepts of Pan-Africanism. For example, Paul Cuffe of Boston was more concerned in the repatriation of freed black slaves to Africa. When Edward Wilmot Blyden of Danish West Indies preached the projection of the African personality, he had at the back of his mind the black inhabitants of Africa. The same may be said of Casely Hayford of Ghana, Marcus Aurelius Garvey of Jamaica, Burghhardt Du Bois of America, Mojola Agbebi of Nigeria, Jomo Kenyatta of Kenya, Javabu of South Africa, George Padmore of Trinidad, Nwafor Orizu of Nigeria, Kwame Nkrumah of Ghana, and Leopold Senghor of Senegal.

But when we consider the role of organisations, as distinct from individuals, no rigid line of distinction on the basis of race appears to be drawn, generally speaking. The Anti-Slavery Society and the American Colonisation Society, for example, were actuated by humanitarian motives to plan for the emigration of freed black slaves from America and the Caribbean to Africa for permanent settlement.

The International Conference on Africa which was held in Berlin in 1885 partitioned that continent without taking into consideration racial, cultural or linguistic factors. The United Native African Church in Nigeria revolted against ecclesiastical control of African churches from outside Africa, but it did not preclude non-Africans from joining its communion and fellowship. The United Negro Improvement Association was ethnocentric in the sense that it preached the doctrine of "Africa for the Africans" on the basis of race. The National Congress of British West Africa sought for political reforms in the former British territories in West Africa without attaching much importance to race or language or culture.

The history of the continent of Africa in ancient, medieval and modern times has followed a pattern which ignores the factor of race in its evolution. Whilst the white races of Assyria, Syria, Phoenicia and Israel developed their civilization, the brown races of Egypt and the black races of Ethiopia proceeded to develop their civilization contemporaneously. In medieval times, the Arab did not distinguish between the black or brown or white Hamitic, Semitic, Sudanic or Bantu-speaking converts of Islam. All that has come down to us shows that the civilizations which flourished in Africa at that time attached little attention, if any, to such an extraneous factor as race.

When the so-called Barbary States flourished in Algeria, Morocco, Tunis, and Tripoli, race was a minor factor in their political evolution. The British West Africa Settlements were originally a sort of concert of territories consisting of Gambia, Sierra Leone, Gold Coast and later Lagos.

In fact, all these countries were governed by one Governor at various times from 1827, 1866, 1874 until 1886. French West and French Equatorial Africa were each governed as a federation until 1958 when the French Community was organised and the right of each member to separate autonomous existence was recognised.

Even the Union of South Africa (much as we hate it) is a federation of various racial, linguistic and cultural groups. The Anglo-Egyptian Sudan was a condominium which held two culturally-opposed groups together until independence was attained by Sudan in 1956. The East Africa High Commission was a quasi-federal instrument which bound Uganda, Kenya, Tanganyika and Zanzibar together, and efforts are being made not to dissolve it with the dawn of the independence of Tanganyika. The High Commission of the Protectorates of South Africa, the Central African Federation, the Federation of Nigeria, the Ghana-Guinea-Mali Union—these are efforts to weld together political entities comprising various races, languages and cultures.

In other words, in spite of racial, linguistic and cultural differences, conscious efforts have been made at all known times of African history to form a political union either on a regional or continental basis. From the evidence at our disposal, it would appear that whilst European nations may be rightly accused of Balkanising Africa in the nineteenth century, yet they have atoned for it by federating many African territories, which are now being Balkanised by African nationalists on the attainment of the independence of their countries. The British West Africa, French West Africa and French Equatorial Africa, are examples of Balkanisation by African nationalists, and the Central African Federation is an example of Balkanisation in process brought about by the racial segregation and discrimination practised by a small minority of European settlers against the African majority who are owners of their countries. . . .

African Unity

First, the inhabitants of the African continent are not racially homogeneous. In North Africa, the majority of the population belongs to the mediterranean group of the Caucasoid race. In Africa South of the Sahara, the majority are Negroid, with the exception of a small minority of European settlers in southern Africa who are either members of the Alpine or Nordic groups of the Caucasoids. The co-existence of these racial groups has created a social problem in Africa as the apartheid and mau mau have shown.

Secondly, the existence of various linguistic groups in Africa has intensified the problem of communication and human understanding. Whilst those who live on the fringe of the Mediterranean are Hamitic-speaking, the Africans of the West are mainly Sudanic-speaking. The indigenous central and southern Africans are Bantu-speaking. The inhabitants of eastern Africa are partially Sudanic, Bantu, Hamitic and Semitic. The small European elements in south Africa speak either English or Afrikaans. Emerging out of this milieu is the fact that to millions of Africans either English or Arabic or Swahili or Hausa is the lingua franca, whilst the rest have to manage as best they could.

Thirdly, the impact of various cultures on African society has created basic problems of social unity. One example is the activities of the Pan-Arab League which seeks to unite under one fold all the Arab-speaking peoples not only of Africa but also of the Middle East. Another example is the attempt being made in certain quarters to create an Islamic Confederation which will cut across racial, linguistic and cultural lines. Then there is the move to interpret Pan-Africanism purely in terms of race and to restrict its membership and activities to the Negroids and thereby exclude other races who live in Africa who are not black.

These three problems are real. The practice of racial segregation and discrimination is a disturbing factor in society, as the examples of the United States, the Union of South Africa and the Central African Federation have shown. The official use or recognition of any particular language to the detriment of others has not made for harmonious human relations and the experiences of India, Pakistan, Ceylon, and the U.S.S.R. are a great lesson. My conclusion is that parochialism in the realms of race, language, culture or religion has often led to social distintegration. Therefore, it constitutes a social and psychological barrier which must be hurdled if Pan-Africanism is to become a reality.

If the anthropological problems are basic, then the sociological are complex since they affect the economic, political and constitutional aspects of the lives of those concerned. Economically, the existence of tariff walls and barriers has tended to alienate rather than draw closer the relations of those who would be good neighbours. High competitive markets have led to cut-throat methods of bargaining and distribution. The use of separate currencies as legal tender has accentuated social differences. With separate road, railway, aviation and communications systems, Africans have become estranged to one another.

The political issues are even confounding. Granted that political union is desirable, the question arises whether it should be in the form of a federation or a confederation. If the former, should it be a tight or a loose one? In any case sovereignty must be surrendered in part or in whole, in which case, it will be desirable to know whether it is intended to surrender internal or external sovereignty or both? . . .

Implications

An African federation or confederation, either on a regional or continental basis, has many blessings for the continent of Africa and its inhabitants. Politically, it will raise the prestige of African States in the councils of the world; it will make Africa a bastion of democracy, and it will revive the stature of man by guaranteeing to African citizens the fundamental rights of man. From a miiltary point of view, such a concert of States will protect the people of Africa not only from external aggression and internal commotion, but also it would safeguard the whole of Africa by a system of collective security.

Economically, by abrogating discriminatory tariffs, we create a free trade area over the entire continent and thereby expand the economy of all African countries involved, thereby raising living standards and ensuring economic security for African workers.

Socially, it will restore the dignity of the human being in Africa.

In conclusion, it is my firm belief that an African leviathan must emerge ultimately; it may be in the form of an association of African States or in the form of a concert of African States; but my main point is that so long as the form of government is clearly understood and an efficient machinery for organisation and administration is devised, backed by multi-lateral conventions which would enhance the standard of living of Africans, safeguard their existence by collective security, and guarantee to them freedom under the law in addition to the fundamental human rights, the dream of Pan-Africanism is destined to come true.

Finally, one of the leading Africanists of all times, Edward Wilmot Blyden, said: "It is really high time that a unity of spirit should pervade the people of the world for the regeneration of a continent so long despoiled by the unity or consent of these same people. Thinking Negroes should ask themselves what part they will take in this magnificent work of reclaiming a continent—their own continent. In what way will they illustrate their participation in the unity of spirit which pervades the people for their fatherland?"

That was Dr. Blyden preaching Pan-Africanism in the nineteenth century. On our part, what shall we do? History will chronicle the choice made by us in the twentieth century.

27 / NATION, STATE, AND FEDERATION
LÉOPOLD SEDAR SENGHOR

At this point it is appropriate to distinguish between Nation and State. First we shall note the difference between Nation and *Fatherland*. The idea of Nation, in the modern sense of the term, was developed in France during the seventeenth and eighteenth centuries. It found its purest expression during the 1789 Revolution. As M. Denis de Rougemont pertinently observes in an article entitled "Fédéralisme et Nationalisme" the French soldiers at Valmy did not shout: "Long live France! nor "Long

From Léopold Sedar Senghor, *Nationhood and the African Road to Socialism* (Paris: Présence Africaine, 1962; New York: Frederick A. Praeger, Inc.), pp. 22-31. Reprinted by permission of Frederick A. Praeger, Inc.

live the Fatherland!" but "Long live the Nation!" What does this mean? The Fatherland is the heritage handed down to us by our ancestors: a land, blood, a language or at least a dialect, mores, customs, folklore, art, in one word, a culture rooted in a native soil and expressed by a race. In old France the Fatherland was identified with the province. It was what the Girondins, who were federalists, wished to maintain. In Africa, the Fatherland is the *Sérère* country, the *Malinké* country, the *Songhay* country, the *Mossi*, the *Baoulé* or the *Fon*.

The Nation groups fatherlands in order to transcend them. Unlike the Fatherland, it is not a natural determination and therefore an expression of the milieu, but a determination to construct or to reconstruct. . . . Far from rejecting the realities of the Fatherland, the Nation will lean on them, or more precisely, will lean on their virtues, their realistic character, and therefore on their emotional strength. It will unite the virtues of the fatherlands or most often will choose those virtues which, by reason of climate, history or race, have a common denominator or a universal value. Once realised, the Nation forges a harmonious ensemble from its different provinces: a single country for a single people, animated by the same faith and striving toward the same goal. In the words of Hegel, the theoretician of the Nation-State: "It isn't the natural limits of the Nation that form its character, but rather its national spirit."

As can be inferred, the Nation is superior to the Fatherland on the level of humanity, and even of efficiency. It distils the values of the latter, sublimates them by transcending them. In this respect it is *humanisation*. For the proper characteristic of Man is to snatch himself from the earth, to rise above his roots to blossom in the sun, to escape, in an act of *freedom*, from his "natural determinations." It is liberty by which man, conquering nature, reconstructs it on a universal scale: thus man realises himself as a God, which is freedom.

If the Nation is a conscious determination to reconstruct, the State is its major means. The State is to the Nation what the contractor is to the architect. It is incarnate in the institutions: government, parliament, public services. The government officials are its workers. It is the State which fulfils the Nation's will and ensures its permanence. In domestic affairs, it mingles the fatherlands and kneads the individuals in the mould of the prototype. In external affairs, it defends the Nation's integrity that it preserves from foreign intrigues. The two temptations of the State are assimilation and imperialism, for it is by nature a conqueror.

The Federation

The delegates to the Constituent Assembly of January 17, 1959, were wise to proceed by stages. A nation is not realised in a day; like fruit, it needs an inner ripening. The building of a state resembles that of a cathedral in the Middle Ages. It is a long-term enterprise, requiring centuries of effort and patience. France took nearly 2,000 years—up to Napoleon's time—to become a nation-state, and she was the first in Europe to do so.

We were wise to begin at the beginning with the foundation, with a federation of states, the Mali Federation. The latter did not suppress the federal Republics; it simply coordinated their policies by transferring to the federal authorities general prerogatives, strictly defined and limited. We must await the adhesion of the other States of the former French West Africa to see in what direction and how far we shall go. We must also test, by experience, the results of the first phase. The fact remains that the Mali Federation is a State with a government, parliament, justice, and its own services. It has authority to sign certain agreements with other member States of the Community with the exception of the French Republic. Mali provides the basis for a Negro-African Nation, with a flag, an anthem, and a motto.

I personally do not believe that it will ever be necessary to form a unitary State. The most powerful nations today are federal States: the U.S.A., USSR, China, India, Canada, Brazil. The weakness of France comes perhaps from her excessive centralisation. The most clear-sighted Frenchmen are beginning to recognise this. All that could be done would be to effect a redistribution, a new cutting up of federated States. You can imagine what psychological difficulties we would encounter, because of the crystallisations—routines and prejudices—already existing. Men cannot be handled like piles of dead wood. Above all else, we shall take care not to succumb to one of the temptations of the nation-state: the uniformisation of people across fatherlands. The archetype is the impoverishing of persons, their reduction to the status of robot-individuals, a loss of vitality and sap.

Wealth springs from the diversities of countries and persons, from the fact that they complement each other. We shall always remember a truth often expressed by Father Teilhard de Chardin: races are not equal but complementary, which is a superior form of equality. So it is with countries and men. Whence the superiority of the federal over the unitary State. I shall go even further. There is but one way to reduce the tyranny of the State, to avert its weakness, as the socialist Proudhon said, and that way is through federalism; in other words, the decentralisation and deconcentration of its institutions, economic as well as political.

We can regret that Dahomey did not join the Mali Federation and that Upper Volta did not remain a member. On second thought, this is fortunate from both the political and the economic point of view. Contrasting with their constituents, the Prime Ministers of those two States were never federalists by conviction. In the Federation of Mali they would have caused dissension. At the very least, they would have strained the federal links.

We have made a good start in Mali by uniting populations whose natural characteristics—climate, soil and blood, language and customs, art and literature—are similar. Senegal and the Sudan constitute, moreover, a rather homogeneous and relatively rich economic ensemble. In the old A.O.F. these two territories alone furnished almost half the revenue of the group. With the best harbour (Dakar), the most powerful industrial set-up, and a market of 7 million consumers, we have important advantages. I note, in passing, that many African government employees and technicians in our upper cadres are not originally from Mali. Thus the freedom enjoyed here represents another advantage.

And yet, in the interest of Black Africa and of France, our aim must be to unite, within the Mali Federation, all the States of the old A.O.F. and to sign, in the meantime, economic and cultural pacts with the other States, including the Republic of Guinea. By so doing, we shall only be following the French example.

The principal and permanent objective of the kings of France was, for nearly a thousand years, to make a nation out of diverse races and to extend their kingdom to the natural frontiers of ancient Gaul. These frontiers were natural, however, only in the geographical and economic sense; for the Basque, to the anthropologist, differs more from the Fleming or the Breton than the Wolof differs from the Baoulé or the Fon. The aim was to reduce progressively the provincial fatherlands and assimilate them into the Ile de France, which imposed its dialect as a national language. In West Africa, if we may limit ourselves to this example, France borrowed, for her own use, the great design of the emperors of Mali and Songhay: to link Senegal to the Hausa country and the Sahara oases to the Gulf of Benin in order to group the "Sudanese" races into an economically and politically viable entity. Our intention is not different. Why should what was good for France and Black Africa in the first half of the twentieth century no longer be so in the second half? Could logic have ceased to be French, and common sense Negro-African?

The reconstruction of the old French West African federation on new bases is in the political interest of the Africans; this is clearly in line with our concept of "Nation." The Upper Volta and Niger are grassland, prairie countries, like Senegal and the Sudan. The fact that the Ivory Coast and Dahomey are composed mostly of forests offers an additional reason for not separating them from the other countries. They are *complementary* to the others, necessary to the others, as the others are necessary to them.

The reconstruction of the old federation is in the political interest of France; this is obvious to anyone who follows the extension of the Cold War to Black Africa. Guinea provides a typical example, as does—we dare say—the Ghana-Guinea Union. The Cold War is being waged not only between East and West, but also secretly between the members of NATO. (We know that the British Foreign Office did not look with disfavor on the birth of this union.) We can be sure that, troubled by domestic difficulties, the French-speaking States run the risk of swinging, one by one, in the direction of the Commonwealth or of the popular democracies. What can Dahomey do, situated between Nigeria and Ghana? How can the people of the Niger, poverty-stricken and crushed under a feudal regime, resist the attraction of a rich and democratic Nigeria, inhabited, moreover, by 35 millions?

The reconstruction of the old federation is finally in the interest of the French Community. As I have often said: the association of the earthenware pot and the iron pot is contrary to nature. Based on unequal strength. it causes trouble, engenders weakness. However, the strength of each of the partners is moral as well as material, political as well as economic. The French Community will be solid only to the extent that the States—I mean their populations—feel that they are morally equal partners and have a real share in the decisions of the Executive Council. How could this be achieved if they came to it disunited, while the metropolitan French ministers of the Community always formed a cohesive bloc? How could this be achieved if th y get the discouraging impression that their progress depends not on their united organisational effort, but rather on the pleasure of metropolitan France?

More than the consciousness of their poverty, it was such a feeling of frustration, their inferiority complex, that pushed the peoples of Bandung toward revolt against the privileged nations, against the West. We fear that the *balkanisation* of Black Africa, unless remedied, may prepare a new Bandung for the French Community. And we know that the most formidable revolts are not those of armed men, but of men whose arms are folded in passive resistance.

The Federation offers an economic as well as a political advantage. Economists have claimed repeatedly that development requires, in addition to the accumulation of capital, the extension of the domestic market. This is basically where the material power of the Big Two lies. For example, the foreign trade of the United States equals only one tenth of its domestic commerce. This obvious truth also explains the creation of the European Common Market. In Europe, the largest nations involved have populations of from 45 to 60 millions and an annual per capita income twice that of the former A.O.F. inhabited by only about 20 millions. How, then, can one believe that the erection of eight customs barriers would aid our development? Our industrialists have admitted that, if the balkanisation of French-speaking Black Africa is maintained, they will be compelled to close their factories. For the first quarter of 1959, customs and fiscal income on imports was already down 12%. No lyricism, no sentimentality can refute these facts. . . .

There is the disguised federation that is being formed to oppose Mali. Its weakness will lie in not being a "federation in the strict sense" but an instrument at the service of a State. As we are warned, the new regrouping will be effected "under the leadership of the Ivory Coast." I have nothing against Ivory Coast—we must avoid any bitterness against her and consider her a sister State. I do not under-estimate her agricultural potentialities; I affirm that she is the greatest Negro-African art centre. But I simply state one additional fact: as the richest State, the Ivory Coast will seize not only political hegemony, but also the lion's share in the economic sector. She will gain, at little expense, an important market for her industries. For she will retain for herself the major portion of the customs receipts and fiscal taxes on imports, leaving France the task of meeting the budgetary deficit of the poor States. The other weakness of the *Entente* will be to rely more on French generosity, on a policy of facility, than on a policy of rigor and austerity. A nation, and a State even less, is not built on a policy of facility but by the labour, the conscious effort of all its citizens. In any event, one is not advancing the cause of African unity by making, with the help of certain politicians in Paris, Dahomey and the Upper Volta leave the Mali Federation in order to create another regrouping to oppose the latter.

As you know, the Mali Federation rests on quite different bases, first of all, on honesty. The Union "will not insist," M. Decraene announces, "as the promoters of the Mali Federation are now doing, on the theme of eventual independence." That we are doing so is the first proof of our frankness. We do not have one language for Europeans and another for Africans. We do not say to the former: "There is no longer any political problem between France and Africa; we renounce independence forever." And to the latter: "Let us ask France for massive aid and, when we are ready, we shall take our independence." Let us say that, even in politics, honesty is the best policy. The greatest cleverness often consists in not being clever at all.

In the Federation of Mali, however, the important thing is that there is no leader-State, but complete solidarity among the member States. In other words, the only leadership belongs to the Federation, to the general interest. Customs receipts and taxes on imports go first to the federal services. The balance is shared by the federated States according to their needs, it being understood that the fiscal effort and the austerity effort will be everywhere the same. . . .

Our conclusion concerning the Federation is that it will serve the best interests of the whole French Community. The British and the Belgians, who are realists, have understood the problem more clearly, I regret to say. It is true that the Africans themselves are primarily responsible for the balkanisation. The British accepted Nigerian independence only on condition that the Federation be safeguarded. As for the Belgians, a recent speech by Mr. Van Hemelrijck, minister to the Congo and Ruanda-Urundi, leaves no doubt as to their intentions: to lead the Congo gradually to independence, but in unity. At any rate, balkanisation will be avoided even against the will of the Congolese. Both the British and Belgians intend to fulfil, to the end, their duties as guardians and not allow their wards to dissipate the family heritage.

28 / AFRICAN INDEPENDENCE AS AN INTERNATIONAL ISSUE
SÉKOU TOURÉ

Africa, emerging on the world scene, approaches the rest of the world not as an antagonistic element, but, on the contrary, in a complete spirit of co-operation, with a constant and conscious concern to be a contributing factor of which the world could not be deprived without compromising its chances and its resources.

This is why it is irrelevant to accuse the African patriots and nationalists of being rebels or terrorists, and call the nationalist and patriotic movements of Africa subversive or dangerous, because for these men and movements of rebellion it is a question of the right of free determination against colonial monopoly. The natural and legal right can at no moment of its expression be considered as a subversive or dangerous act. Beyond the modifications which are implied in the exercise of the right of each people to self-determination, and beyond the political progress which this produces, there exists in fact a natural right of peoples, be they large or small: this is the right to liberty. And is not this right one of the essential bases of the Charter of the United Nations, so that no argument may pervert its legal and legitimate character?

The Fundamental Problem

Thus, the independent States of Africa were totally justified, in the exercise of their sovereignty, to concentrate their interest on the prospects of a free and united Africa. They will not, under any pretext, ignore the fundamental problem: that of the national independence of colonized peoples who are trying to elude the colonial Powers by more or less fortunate and just transformations of the legal ties which these Powers have imposed upon their victims.

And it can surprise nobody if the African States inscribe in their programme of action, as a priority, the implacable struggle against any form of paternalism and against any complex inculcated by the oppression which not only degrades man but renders him unfit for any progress.

For a long time the nations which had arrogated to themselves the leading role in Africa thought that they could act in the name of our peoples. The failure with which they met is well known. Often the same Powers which dominated our continent proclaimed to the world that their presence in our lands was morally explained and justified by the need to bring us their civilization, as if Africa did not have its own past, its own highly developed civilizations whose contact with imperialism could only

From Sékou Touré, *The International Policy of the Democratic Party of Guinea* (Conakry: S.O.P. Press, n.d.), pp. 32-36, 41-44. (Original in English.)

result in their alienation, even their disappearance. Today, no one will deny the impossibility of imposing a foreign civilization upon a people, above all by force and at the same time when such pretended humanitarian preoccupations are accompanied by a systematic exploitation.

The determination of Guinea to see the realization of unity in the independence of Africa, is notably, as regards the means of development, the determination to see Africa itself participate in the development of its own wealth in the primordial interest of its populations.

The Failure of the Colonial Concept

The failure of the colonial concept stems precisely from the fact that the colonial Powers, holding the means for the development of this wealth, did not use these means to resolve the disequilibrium existing between the standard of living of the colonized peoples and that of sovereign peoples, but on the contrary they accentuated this disequilibrium by the systematic exploitation of the goods and raw materials, maintaining the populations in the most degrading poverty and dependence. There is no longer any need to conduct the trial of colonialism in so much as events and history have clearly pronounced themselves for its complete disappearance. One could add, moreover, that even had the balance-sheet been different, even that would not have permitted that the will of the colonized peoples for independence and their legitimate right of self-determination be defied.

It is in this view that we wish ardently to see colonialism cut short, once and for all. It is in this spirit that we call upon each nation to pronounce itself—not upon the right to self-determination, a right already recognized and acquired—but upon its real application, without trickery or manoeuvres, without illusionary facades or false reserves. This affects, of course, the interest of Africa, but it is even more in the interest of the world which cannot deliberately deprive itself of the creative contribution of 200 million men and women or play with the destiny of our peoples in order to safeguard the material interests of the colonial Powers.

The safety and the survival of the independent countries of Africa are tied to the social, economic, cultural and political unity of Africa. And we see clearly that the independent countries of Africa cannot be islands of good fortune in a continent of misery.

Too long excluded from free human enterprises, too long held on the sidelines of history, Africa—fully aware of the needs of its future—refuses from now on to remain on the back lines of history, it refuses to allow the unlimited sacrifice of generations of its peoples.

Paternalism Condemned to Failure

It is clear that paternalism, or any desire of intervention in Africa beyond the authentically African will and aspirations will be condemned to failure. We wish to alert the United Nations against operations still under way designed to impose upon our continent ideas or principles foreign to its own will. It has often been noted that, to succeed in their endeavours, certain governments assure themselves of the co-operation of African men or organizations at their service, and who act only in line with these governments' wishes. This is a policy of puppets which, moreover, will succeed less and less in Africa, because the peoples are more and more organized and determined to fight against all forms of domination, even that by the intermediary of African groups or powers.

For centuries, our continent has known paternalism, one might even say, various shades of paternalism, depending upon the temperament of the colonizer. But this long practice of paternalism brought no valid progress to Africa. On the contrary, this paternalism has taken from certain African leaders their sense of dignity and responsibility, that is, it has rendered them less fit to translate the original virtues of their civilization. For such creatures, corrupted by the colonial Powers, is it not shameful to be used in these decisive hours against the most legitimate aspirations of their peoples?

Unknown until yesterday, or rather, known only through the humiliating prism of the colonial system, Africa today is expressing itself clearly and will not admit that those who had taken control of Africa's children and resources may still speak in its name and against its own will. It is thus evident that today more than ever, while Africa needs help to liberrate itself completely and to rebuild itself, it will not tolerate any form of paternalism. We have absolutely no need for anyone to bring us ready-made civilizations, since it is [only] through ignorance of our civilizations by the imperialists during several centuries that these civilizations can be said not to exist. . . .

Colonialists Plan to Divide Africa

The colonialists are ready to "finance" as much independence as one wants; they are ready to flatter the African Governments and to wax enthusiastic before the 3 million free Guineans, before the 30 million Nigerians, etc. But their Machiavellian plan still aims at dividing the Africans in order to remain the masters of the continent. In this, too, they will be disappointed, for the progress achieved by our populations no longer makes it possible for them to be opposed one against the other or for them to be led into a war or competition against one another. What counts for the Africans is not to know if Sékou Touré or Nkrumah have more prestige than Tubman or Bourguiba, far less to know whether the regime in Ghana will be more democratic than that in Nigeria.

Having affirmed during the referendum organized by France that Guinea prefers liberty in poverty to opulence in slavery, we consider it another duty to declare before the representatives of the United Nations that, in the perspectives of a swift and democratic evolution of Africa, we, the national leaders of the Republic of Guinea, would prefer to be the last in a united Africa rather than the first in a divided Africa.

In effect, that which counts is the sum of liberty regained throughout the continent to the detriment of those who oppress or exploit Africa. Yes it is certain that those who dream of guiding the independence of Governments of Africa by remote control will suffer bitter disappointments. Africa is ripe for its real independence, that is, for the end of supremacy of foreign Powers, for the effective exercise of its own sovereignty, for the control of its wealth and the development of all its faculties, not only for the development of its own personality but also for the enrichment of the world's heritage. . . .

Africa's Future Shaped by Africans

We know that for the imperialists, Africa is a minor continent whose only interest is as a coveted object more or less open to this or that foreign propaganda. This view is an error which I feel it my duty to emphasize before it is too late for certain nations who risk alienating friendship in Africa if they continue to judge events in Africa without regard for the concrete realities of our continent. For some, there are but two cardinal points; East and West. They submit that Africa will fall under the influence either of Europe or of the USSR and that, as a result, Africa will live within the framework of the concepts and civilization of the East or West. They willingly forget that the world did not begin with the colonial system or with its division into two hostile blocs. They willingly forget that one hundred years ago no people knew that the United States of America and the USSR would become the two biggest nations in the world. They willingly forget that life is an uninterrupted flow and that the future of Africa will be first of all what the African people will want, despite all the obstacles which may be placed in the path of their history.

In remaining faithful to the anti-colonialistic spirit of the Conference of Bandung, Cairo, Accra and Sanniquellie, we clearly declare that the Afro-Asian action which we undertake in the conviction of acting for the acceleration of the total liberation of peoples and the end of racial discrimination in all parts of the world in no way prevents us from concerning ourselves with world peace. In this respect, it is not Africa which should be asked whether it belongs to one camp or another; it is rather to the two camps, to the East as to the West, that we must put the question which we consider as fundamental and of paramount importance: Yes or no, are you for the liberation of Africa?

29 / THE SECOND SCRAMBLE / JULIUS NYERERE

I am a firm advocate of African Unity. I am convinced that, just as unity was necessary for the achievement of independence in Tanganyika, or in any other nation, unity is equally necessary for the whole of Africa to achieve and maintain her independence.

I believe that, left to ourselves, we can achieve unity on the African Continent. But I don't believe that we are going to be left to ourselves! I believe that the phase from which we are now emerging successfully is the phase of the First Scramble for Africa, and Africa's reaction to it. We are now entering a new phase—the phase of the Second Scramble for Africa. And just as, in the First Scramble for Africa, one tribe was divided against another tribe to make the division of Africa easier, in the Second Scramble for Africa one nation is going to be divided against another nation to make it easier to control Africa by making her weak and divided against herself.

It is for this reason, therefore, that before we can talk complacently about "African Unity" we should examine carefully the external ideas which are likely to be imposed upon us—imposed not for the purpose of uniting us, but for the purpose of dividing us!

Now today the world is divided into two blocs; what one might call the "Capitalist Bloc" and the "Socialist Bloc." They are generally referred to as the "Western Bloc" and the "Eastern Bloc"; I have said "Capitalist Bloc" and "Socialist Bloc" for a good reason: it makes it easier to understand the forces behind these divisions.

What is wrong with capitalism? To my mind, capitalism went wrong when it divorced Wealth from its true purpose. The true purpose of Wealth is to satisfy very simple needs: the need for food, the need for shelter, the need for education and so on. In other words, the end of Wealth is the banishment of Poverty; and Wealth is to Poverty what Light is to Darkness. There is enough Wealth in every state for every individual to satisfy these basic needs. But the moment individuals in any single state begin to use Wealth, not for the satisfaction of those needs, not for the abolition of poverty, but for the purpose of acquiring power and prestige, then there is no longer enough. Then Wealth tolerates Poverty; then Wealth is no longer to Poverty what Light is to Darkness. There is not enough Wealth in any nation to satisfy the desire for power and prestige of every individual, so what happens? There is then ruthless competition between individuals—not to get Wealth to feed themselves, or to clothe themselves, or to house themselves—but to seize enough Wealth to give themselves more power, more prestige than their fellows. That is, Wealth which exceeds their real need and which will enable them to

From Julius K. Nyerere, *The Second Scramble* (Dar es Salaam: Tanganyika Standard, Ltd., n.d.), pp. 1-6.

dominate other individuals. When that stage is reached, one millionaire is prepared to spend millions simply in order to destroy another millionaire.

I believe that the purpose of Socialism was to correct this sin of Capitalism, and to return Wealth to its original use—the satisfaction of simple human needs. I think it would be hypocrisy on the part of the Capitalist countries (the so-called "Western" countries) not to recognize the fact that this *is* happening in the Socialist countries; that *within* those countries personal wealth is not a symbol of power or prestige, and Wealth *is* used to banish poverty. But I believe that the Socialist countries themselves, considered as "individuals" in the larger society of nations, are now committing the same crime as was committed by the Capitalists before. I believe that, on the international level, they are now beginning to use Wealth for the purpose of acquiring power and prestige! It would be equally hypocritical on the part of the Socialist countries to deny this. Internationally they are engaged in using Wealth in exactly the same way, now, as the Capitalist countries have always used it—for power and prestige. And Socialist countries, no less than Capitalist countries, are prepared to behave like the millionaire: to use millions to destroy another "millionaire";—and it need not necessarily be a Capitalist "millionaire"; it is just as likely to be a Socialist "millionaire." In other words, Socialist Wealth now tolerates Poverty—which is an even more unforgiveable crime.

I believe that no under-developed country can afford to be anything but "socialist." I believe, therefore, that we in Africa are bound to organise ourselves on a socialist pattern. But let us at least provide another corrective to Socialism, and prevent the Wealth we are beginning to build in our own countries from being used for the purpose of acquiring national power or prestige. Let us make sure that it is used solely for raising the standards of our people. Let us not allow the Wealth that we are creating to live side by side with Poverty and tolerate that Poverty.

We, in Africa, must beware of being hypnotised by the lure of old slogans. I have said already that Socialism arose to remedy the mistakes which Capitalism had made. Karl Marx felt there was an inevitable clash between the rich of one society and the poor of that society. In that, I believe, Karl Marx was right. But today it is the international scene which is going to have a greater impact on the lives of individuals than what is happening within Tanganyika, or within Kenya, or within Uganda. And when you look at the international scene, you must admit that the world is still divided between the "Haves" and the "Have-nots." This division is not a division between Capitalists and Socialists, nor between Capitalists and Communists; this is a division between the poor countries of the world and the rich countries of the world. I believe, therefore, that the poor countries of the world should be very careful not to allow themselves to be used as the "tools" of any of the rich countries—however much the rich countries may seek to fool them that they are on their side! And don't forget that the rich countries of the world today may be found on both sides of the division between "Capitalist" and "Socialist" countries.

All this may not seem to have much to do with African Unity, but in fact it has a great deal to do with it. I believe the danger to African Unity is going to come from these external forces and slogans; slogans which bear no relation to the facts of the world today; and from the fact that today the rich countries of the world—both Capitalist and Socialist—are using their Wealth to dominate the poor countries. And they are trying to divide and weaken the poor countries for that purpose of domination. That is why I said at the beginning that if we, in Africa, were left on our own we would achieve Unity on our Continent, but that I do not believe we are going to be left alone. I have explained why I think we are not going to be left alone.

But there is no need for fear. All we need to do is to use our intellect; to know what is good for us. We need to listen to the outside world; to accept from them what we believe is in the best interests of Africa and of African Unity, and to reject (and reject in no uncertain terms) what we believe is *not* in the best interests of Africa and of African Unity. And that includes all those attractive, but misleading, slogans about "democracy," "socialism," and so on, which are too often used to cloak the real designs of the power-hungry. These slogans bear little relation to what Africa is doing, and they are generally used by those whose purpose is to divide Africa into opposing camps.

At the beginning I used the phrase "The Second Scramble for Africa." It may sound far-fetched, in the context of Africa in the Nineteen Sixties, to talk about a Second Scramble for Africa. But anybody who thinks this is far-fetched has been completely blind to what is happening on the African Continent. Take the example of the Congo. There were obvious weaknesses in the Congo situation, but those weaknesses were deliberately *used* in a scramble for the control of the Congo. There are obvious weaknesses on the African continent; we have artificial "nations" carved out at the Berlin Conference in 1884, and today we are struggling to build these nations into stable units of human society. These weaknesses, too, are being exploited. We are being reminded daily of them. We are told that tribalism will not allow us to build nations; but when we try to take measures to deal with tribalism we are accused of "dictatorship." Whenever we try to talk in terms of larger units on the African Continent, we are told " it can't be done"; we are told the units that we would so create would be "artificial"—as if they could be any more artificial than the "national" boundaries within which we are already building successfully! Some of the people who say this are merely pointing, quite sincerely, to a difficulty; but I believe many of them are deliberately emphasising the difficulties on our continent for the express purpose of maintaining them and sabotaging any move to unite Africa!

The technique is very simple. One power bloc labels a move for unity "A Communist Plot"; not because it *is* Communist, but because they don't like it. Another power bloc labels another move for unity "An Imperialist Plot"; not because it is so, but because they don't like it.

What annoys me is not the use of these labels and slogans by power-hungry nations; that, after all, is something we expect. But what does infuriate me is their expecting us to allow ourselves to be treated as if we were a bunch of idiots!

So I believe that the Second Scramble for Africa has already begun in real earnest. And it is going to be a much more dangerous scramble than the first one. For what happened in the First Scramble? One imperialist power fought another imperialist power for the booty. But what do you think is going to happen in the Second Scramble? No imperialist power is going to fight another imperialist power for the control of Africa today; that would be too crude a method for the Nineteen Sixties. This time, one imperialist power is going to arm one African nation, and another imperialist power is going to arm another African nation; and African brother is going to slaughter African brother—not in the interests of Africa, but in the interests of the imperialists both old and new! . . .

Africa is a young continent. It is young in two respects. Internationally, its nations are young nations; but Africa is also young in another sense—it is governed by young people. I think one of the troubles in the modern world is that nuclear power is being handled by people who were born in the Nineteenth Century and educated in the Nineteenth Century; people with a Victorian turn of mind, who have been overtaken by the achievements of science and by modern ideas about human society. They have not been able to adjust themselves; and while they repeat some of the slogans which sound very "modern" (I have already said that many of the slogans they shout are not, in fact, modern at all!) their actions are those of the past. They talk "peace" and they arm. They talk "unity" and they divide. One advantage of youth is that it doesn't have this dichotomy. The young have had an education which is a present-day education; their ideas are present-day ideas. We in Africa, then, who have not inherited the prejudices of the Nineteenth Century, should be able to put into practice the ideas which modern society demands—but to which the slogan-shouters do little more than pay lip-service.

The role of African Nationalism is different—or should be different—from the nationalism of the past. We must use the African national states as an instrument for the unification of Africa, and not allow our enemies to use them as tools for dividing Africa. African Nationalism is meaningless, is anachronistic, and is dangerous, if it is not at the same time Pan-Africanism.

30 / AFRICA MUST SHAPE ITS OWN FUTURE / HAILE SELASSIE

We welcome to Ethiopia, in Our name and in the name of the Ethiopian Government and people, the Heads of States and Governments of independent African nations who are today assembled in solemn conclave in Ethiopia's capital city. This Conference, without parallel in history, is an impressive testimonial to the devotion and dedication of which we all partake in the cause of our mother continent and that of her sons and daughters. This is indeed a momentous and historic day for Africa and for all Africans.

We stand today on the stage of world affairs, before the audience of world opinion. We have come together to assert our role in the direction of world affairs and to discharge our duty to the great continent whose two hundred and fifty million people we lead. Africa is today at midcourse, in transition from the Africa of Yesterday to the Africa of Tomorrow. Even as we stand here, we move from the past into the future. The task on which we have embarked, the making of Africa, will not wait. We must act to shape and mold the future and leave our imprint on events as they slip past into history.

We seek, at this meeting, to determine whither we are going and to chart the course of our destiny. It is no less important that we know whence we came. An awareness of our past is essential to the establishment of our personality and our identity as Africans.

This world was not created piecemeal. Africa was born no later and no earlier than any other geographical area on this globe. Africans, no more and no less than other men, possess all human attributes, talents and deficiencies, virtues and faults. Thousands of years ago, civilizations flourished in Africa which suffer not at all by comparison with those of other continents. In those centuries, Africans were politically free and economically independent. Their social patterns were their own and their cultures truly indigenous.

The obscurity which enshrouds the centuries which elapsed between those earliest days and the rediscovery of Africa are being gradually dispersed. What is certain is that during those long years Africans were born, lived and died. Men on other parts of this earth occupied themselves with their own concerns and, in their conceit, proclaimed that the world began and ended at their horizons. All unknown to them, Africa developed in its own pattern, growing in its own life and, in the Nineteenth Century, finally re-emerged into the world's consciousness.

The events of the past hundred and fifty years require no extended recitation from us. The period of colonialism into which we were plunged culminated with our continent fettered and bound; with our

From *Proceedings of the Summit Conference of Independent African States*, Vol. I, Section 2 (Addis Ababa, May 1963), pp. 1-3, 5, 10-11.

once proud and free peoples reduced to humiliation and slavery; with Africa's terrain cross-hatched and checker-boarded by artificial and arbitrary boundaries. Many of us, during those bitter years, were overwhelmed in battle, and those who escaped conquest did so at the cost of desperate resistance and bloodshed. Others were sold into bondage as the price extracted by the colonialists for the "protection" which they extended and the possessions of which they disposed. Africa was a physical resource to be exploited and Africans were chattels to be purchased bodily or, at best, peoples to be reduced to vasselage and lackeyhood. Africa was the market for the produce of other nations and the source of raw materials with which their factories were fed.

Today, Africa has emerged from this dark passage. Our Armageddon is past. Africa has been reborn as a free continent and Africans have been reborn as free men. The blood that was shed and the sufferings that were endured are today Africa's advocates for freedom and unity. Those men who held unswervingly through the darkest hours to a vision of an Africa emancipated from political, economic and spiritual domination, will be remembered and revered wherever Africans meet. Many of them never set foot on this continent. Others were born and died here. What we may utter today can add little to the heroic struggle of those who, by their example, have shown us how precious are freedom and human dignity and of how little value is life without them. Their deeds are written in history.

Africa's victory, although proclaimed, is not yet total, and areas of resistance still remain. Today, we name as our first great task the final liberating of those Africans still dominated by foreign exploitation and control. With the goal in sight, and unqualified triumph within our grasp, let us not now falter or lag or relax. We must make one final supreme effort; now, when the struggle grows weary, when so much has been won that the thrilling sense of achievement has brought us near satiation. Our liberty is meaningless unless all Africans are free. Our brothers in the Rhodesias, in Mozambique, in Angola, in South Africa cry out in anguish for our support and assistance. We must urge on their behalf their peaceful accession to independence. We must align and identify ourselves with all aspects of their struggle. It would be betrayal were we to pay only lip service to the cause of their liberation and fail to back our words with action. To them we say, your pleas shall not go unheeded. The resources of Africa and of all freedom-loving nations are marshalled in your service. Be of good heart, for your deliverance is at hand. . . .

What we still lack, despite the efforts of past years, is the mechanism which will enable us to speak with one voice when we wish to do so and take and implement decisions on African problems when we are so minded. The commentators of 1963 speak, in discussing Africa, of the

Monrovia States, the Brazzaville Group, the Casablanca Powers, of these and many more. Let us put an end to these terms. What we require is a single African organisation through which Africa's single voice may be heard, within which Africa's problems may be studied and resolved. We need an organisation which will facilitate acceptable solutions to disputes among Africans and promote the study and adoption of measures for common defence and programmes for co-operation in the economic and social fields. Let us, at this Conference, create a single institution to which we will all belong, based on principles to which we all subscribe, confident that in its councils our voices will carry their proper weight, secure in the knowledge that the decisions there will be dictated by Africans and only by Africans and that they will take full account of all vital African considerations.

A century hence, when future generations study the pages of history, seeking to follow and fathom the growth and development of the African continent, what will they find of this Conference? Will it be remembered as an occasion on which the leaders of a liberated Africa, acting boldly and with determination, bent events to their will and shaped the future destinies of the African peoples? Will this meeting be memorialised for its solid achievements, for the intelligence and maturity which marked the decisions taken here? Or will it be recalled for its failures, for the inability of Africa's leaders to transcend local prejudice and individual differences, for the disappointment and disillusionment which followed in its train?

These questions give us all pause. The answers are within our power to dictate. The challenges and opportunities which open before us today are greater than those presented at any time in Africa's millennia of history. The risks and dangers which confront us are no less great. The immense responsibilities which history and circumstance have thrust upon us demand balanced and sober reflection. If we succeed in the tasks which lie before us, our names will be remembered and our deeds recalled by those who follow us. If we fail, history will puzzle at our failure and mourn what was lost. We approach the days ahead with the prayer that we [who] have assembled here may be granted the wisdom, the judgment and the inspiration which will enable us to maintain our faith with the peoples and the nations which have entrusted their fate to our hands.

BIOGRAPHICAL NOTES

AHMADU AHIDJO: born in 1922 in Cameroon; member of the Fulani tribe and son of a chief; educated in government schools and at Roman Catholic missionary schools; entered politics in 1940s as leader of Muslim youth group known as *Jeunes Musulmans;* elected to the Territorial Assembly in 1947 and to the Assembly of the French Union in Paris in 1953; a leading member of the major nationalist party, the *Bloc Démocratique Camerounais,* he became Minister of the Interior and Vice-Premier when the first African government was formed in 1957; broke with the BDC in 1958 to form the *Union Camerounaise* and was elected President of the Republic of Cameroons in 1960.

SAMUEL LADOKE AKINTOLA: born in 1910 in Western Nigeria; member of the Yoruba tribe and son of a petty merchant; educated in missionary schools and London; qualified in law in 1950 and entered politics upon his return to Nigeria in that year; chosen legal adviser of the Action Group and elected to the Western Region House of Assembly in 1951 and then to the Federal House of Representatives; served as Minister of Labor in the Federal government, 1951-1953, and later Minister of Health; elected Deputy Leader of the Action Group in 1957; became Premier of the Western Region Government in 1959; broke with the Action Group in 1962 and formed a new party called the Nigerian National Democratic Party which now controls the Western Region Government.

OBAFEMI AWOLOWO: born in 1909 in Western Nigeria; member of the Yoruba tribe and son of a peasant farmer; educated at missionary schools; pursued higher education in law in London; qualified as a lawyer in 1947; entered politics first in 1950 as Secretary of the Ibadan Branch of the Nigerian Youth Movement; founded a Yoruba tribal society, the *Egbe Omo Oduduwa,* while still a law student in London in 1944; returned to Nigeria in 1947 and organized the *Egbe Omo Oduduwa* into a political group; elected General Secretary of the *Egbe* in 1948 and in 1950-1951 used the tribal society to launch a full fledged nationalist party, the Action Group; elected to the Western Region House of Assembly in 1951 as leader of the Action Group; chosen by the colonial authorities as Premier of Western Nigeria in 1954 and held this post until 1959; elected to the Federal House of Representatives in 1959 and became Leader of

169

the Opposition; imprisoned in 1962 by the Federal Government on a charge of treasonable felony and is presently serving a fifteen year sentence.

BENJAMIN NNAMDI AZIKIWE: born in 1904 in Northern Nigeria where his father, an Ibo from Eastern Nigeria, was a clerk in the Nigerian Regiment; educated at missionary schools, pursued higher education in the United States at several Negro colleges; received his B.A. degree from Lincoln University, Pennsylvania, and did graduate studies in history and political science at the University of Pennsylvania; returned to West Africa in 1934 and spent three years in Ghana as editor of the *African Morning Post;* returned to Nigeria in 1937 and established a chain of newspapers, the most important and prominent of which was the *West African Pilot;* entered banking and became the largest African banker in Nigeria; entered politics in 1937 as an Executive Member of the Nigerian Youth Movement; left the Movement in 1941 and three years later founded the Nigerian National Council which, in 1945, became the National Council of Nigeria and the Cameroons; elected President of the NCNC in 1946 and was a leading nationalist participant in all the postwar constitutional negotiations with the British colonial authorities; elected to the House of Assembly in Western Nigeria in 1951 and was Leader of Opposition in the Assembly until 1952; in 1952 he was elected to the Eastern Region House of Assembly and chosen by the colonial government as Chief Minister and later as Premier; he headed all successive governments in Eastern Nigeria until 1960 when, through a coalition government of the NCNC and the Northern People's Congress at the Federal Level, he was chosen Governor-General of Nigeria; Nigeria became a Republic in 1963 and Azikiwe was chosen President of the Republic.

ALHAJI SIR ABUBAKAR TAFAWA BALEWA: born in 1912 in Northern Nigeria; a Hausa and son of a Muslim District Head; educated in Muslim schools and in colonial government schools; pursued teacher training at government Katsina College, Northern Nigeria; taught in secondary schools and served as a Native Authority Education Officer; entered politics in 1948 when appointed to the Northern Region House of Assembly and then elected by it to the Nigerian Legislative Council; was a founding member of the Northern People's Congress in 1951 and chosen its first Vice President; elected to the Federal House of Representatives in 1951 and held several Federal Ministerial portfolios; became Chief Minister in the Federal Government in 1957 and Prime Minister in 1959.

EDWARD WILMOT BLYDEN: born in St. Thomas, the Danish West Indies; left the West Indies at the age of seventeen for the United States and then traveled to Liberia which had been founded in 1821 by the American Colonization Society as a haven for freed Negro American slaves; completed his formal education at American missionary schools in Liberia, but the rest of his superior learning was self-acquired; appointed to professorship at the newly founded College of Liberia in 1862, and held this post until 1871; studied Arabic and Islamic culture during the 1860s and became a recognized authority on African Islam; published several books including *Liberia's Offering* (New York, 1862), *Our Origin, Dangers and Duties* (New York, 1865), and *Christianity, Islam and the Negro Race* (London, 1887); appointed Secretary of State of Liberia, 1862-1864, and Minister Plenipotentiary to London, 1877; held membership in several learned societies: a Fellow of the American Philological Association,

1880, Corresponding and Honorary Member of the Society of Science and Letters of Bengal, India, 1882; elected Vice President of the American Colonization Society in 1884; appointed President of the University of Liberia in 1901; died in 1912.

JOSEPH BOAKYE DANQUAH: born in 1895 in Eastern Ghana; the son of a traditional ruling family, the Akyem-Abuakwa in Kibi, and member of the Akan-speaking people; educated in local schools; pursued higher education at the University of London; qualified in law at the Inner Temple, London, 1927, and later received a doctorate in jurisprudence; founded a nationalist newspaper in 1930, *The Times of West Africa;* helped organize the Gold Coast Youth Conference in the late 1930s and served at its Secretary-General from 1937-1947; founded the United Gold Coast Convention in 1947 and served as its Secretary-General until 1949; elected by the Joint Provincial Council, a quasi-legislative body of chiefs, to the Gold Coast Legislative Council in 1947-1951; re-elected to the Legislative Council in 1951-1954; was an Executive Committee member of the Ghana Congress Party, founded in 1952 as a conservative rump of the UGCC; joined the United Party in 1957 and was its candidate against Kwame Nkrumah in the Presidential Elections in 1960; has been imprisoned for political activities by the Ghana Government in recent years, and died in a detention camp early in 1965; he was the author of many political pamphlets and of several scholarly volumes on the Akon traditional society.

GABRIEL D'ARBOUSSIER: born in 1908 in the French Sudan, son of Henri d'Arboussier, a distinguished French Colonial administrator, and a Sudanese mother; was educated in France and qualified in law; entered politics in 1946 when elected as representative of French Equatorial Africa to the French Parliament; was a founding member of the *Rassemblement Démocratique Africain* in 1946 and chosen one of its Vice Presidents; elected General Secretary of the RDA in 1949 but broke with it in 1952; returned to a leading position in the RDA in 1957 and became Minister of Justice in Senegal, 1960.

MAJHEMOUT DIOP: born and educated in Senegal; pursued higher education in France and holds university degree; formed the orthodox Marxist *Parti African de l'Indépendance* in 1957; imprisoned in 1961 when the PAI was outlawed by the Senegal government.

FÉLIX EBOUÉ: born in 1884 at Cayenne, French Guiana; educated in local colonial schools; pursued secondary and higher education in Bordeaux and Paris where he graduated from the École Coloniale; held position of Administrator in French Ubangi-Chari, Equatorial Africa, 1909; Secretary-General of Martinique, French West Indies, 1931; Governor of French Sudan (now Mali), 1935; Governor of Guadeloupe, French West Indies, 1937; Governor of Tchad, Equatorial Africa, 1938; Governor-General of French Equatorial Africa, 1940-1944; appointed member of *L'Ordre de la Libération;* died in 1944 in Cairo, Egypt.

ROBERT K. GARDINER: born in Ghana; educated at Adeisadel Boys School, Cape Coast, Ghana; received higher education at Fourah Bay College, Sierra Leone, and at Cambridge University, England; Director of Extra-mural Studies, University College, Ibadan, 1950-1953; Senior Civil Servant in Ministry of Social

Welfare, Ghana, 1954-1957; member of Secretariat of UN Economic Commission for Africa, Addis Ababa, Ethiopia, 1959.

JOSEPH EPHRAIM CASELY-HAYFORD: born in Ghana in 1866; educated in missionary schools and government schools; studied law in London and qualified for the English Bar; a founder of the Aborigines Rights Protection Society in 1897, and acted as one of its legal advisers; founder and President of the National Congress of British West Africa, 1920; an occasional member of the Gold Coast Legislative Council; author of many books and pamphlets including *Gold Coast Native Institutions* (1903), *Ethiopia Unbound* (1911), and *The Truth About the West African Land Question* (1913); died in 1930.

FÉLIX HOUPHOUET-BOIGNY: born in 1905 in central Ivory Coast; a member of the Baoulé tribe and son of a wealthy planter; educated in local government schools; pursued higher education at the Government Medical School at Dakar, Senegal, and qualified as a Medical Assistant in 1925; practiced medicine in government service for fifteen years; became a canton chief (*chef de canton*) in 1940 and also a planter growing coffee and other cash-crops; founded and became President of the *Syndicate Agricole de la Côte d'Ivoire* in 1944, a business association of African planters; entered politics in 1945 as leader of the first major nationalist party in Ivory Coast, the *Parti Démocratique de la Côte d'Ivoire* (PDCI); elected as representative of Ivory Coast and Upper Volta to the French Constituent Assemblies in November 1945 and June 1946; founder and first President of the *Rassemblement Démocratique Africain,* the inter-territorial nationalist party in French West and Equatorial Africa, 1946: re-elected to the French National Assembly in 1951, and again in 1956; a Minister in the French Government, 1956-1959; he has been the president of the Republic of the Ivory Coast since it achieved independence in 1960.

NELSON ROLIHLAHLA MANDELA: born in 1918 in the Union of South Africa; member of the Zulu tribe and son of a chief; educated in government schools; studied law at the University of South Africa; qualified in law in 1942 and in 1952 entered legal practice; elected President of the African National Congress Youth League, 1951-1952; held position of National Volunteer-in-chief of the ANC's Defiance Campaign in 1952; since then has been tried and acquitted of subversive acts against the South African government, and in 1964 was convicted of treason.

TOM MBOYA: born in 1930 in Central Kenya; member of the Luo tribe and son of an unskilled farm laborer on a sisal plantation; educated at Roman Catholic mission schools; trained as a sanitary inspector by the Kenya government and worked as such for the Nairobi Municipal Council; elected Treasurer of the Kenya African Union in 1953 and also chosen General Secretary of the Kenya Local Government Workers Union and the Kenya Federation of Labor; elected to the Kenya Legislative Council in 1957; founder of the Kenya African National Union in 1960 and elected its General Secretary; he was Minister of Justice and Constitutional Affairs in Kenya's first independent government, and then Minister of Planning and Economic Development.

FRANCIS NWIA KOFIE (KWAME) NKRUMAH: born in 1909 in Ghana (then the Gold Coast); member of the Nzima tribe and the son of a village goldsmith;

educated at Roman Catholic mission schools; in 1926 went to the Government Training College in Accra, Ghana, from which he received a teaching diploma; pursued higher education in the United States at Lincoln University (Pennsylvania), a Negro college, from which he received the B.A. degree in 1939; received the M.A. degree from the University of Pennsylvania; participated in the Fifth Pan-African Congress in London in 1945 and returned to Ghana as General Secretary of the United Gold Coast Convention (UGCC) in 1947; organized a breakaway-group from the UGCC in 1949 called the Convention People's Party (CPP); led by the CPP in its first election victory in 1951 and was appointed Leader of Government Business by the colonial government the same year; became Prime Minister in 1952, and achieved independence from British rule for Ghana five years later; led Ghana as it became a Republic in 1960, and assumed his present title of President of Ghana, commonly referred to as Osagyefo, an Akan word meaning divine leader.

JULIUS NYERERE: born in 1921 in Tanganyika; member of the Zanaki tribe and son of a chief; educated at government schools; pursued higher education at Makerere College, Uganda; taught at Roman Catholic missionary schools and is himself a Catholic; entered politics in 1953 when elected President of the Tanganyika African Association, a quasi-political association; founded the Tanganyika African National Union in 1954 and was elected its President; nominated by the government to the legislative Council in 1955 and led TANU to victory in the 1958 General Election; chosen Chief Minister of the Tanganyika government in 1960 and Prime Minister in 1961 when Tanganyika became independent; was elected President of the Republic of Tanganyika in 1962.

MICHAEL IHEONUKARA OKPARA: born in 1920 in Eastern Nigeria; member of the Ibo tribe and son of skilled laborer; educated in local schools; qualified as a doctor at the Nigerian School of Medicine; entered politics in 1949 as member of the National Council of Nigeria and the Cameroons; elected to the Eastern Region House of Assembly in 1953 and joined the NCNC Cabinet; became leader of the NCNC in 1959-1960 when Nnamdi Azikiwe became President of the Senate and then Governor-General of Nigeria; chosen Premier of Eastern Region government in 1960.

HAILE SELASSIE: born in 1892 in Ethiopia; son of H. H. Ras Makonnen, relative of the Emperor Menelik II; educated in Amharic schools and in the Coptic Christian faith; appointed Governor of Gara Huleta, Harar Province of Ethiopia, 1906; became King of Ethiopia in 1928 and Emperor in 1930; went into exile from Italian-controlled Ethiopia in 1936-1941; active in modernizing Ethiopia in postwar era, and in Pan-African affairs since 1960, when he invited the Conference of Independent African States to convene in Addis Ababa.

LÉOPOLD SENGHOR: born in 1906 in Senegal; member of the Serer tribe and son of a well-to-do family; educated at Roman Catholic mission schools and at the government Lycée in Dakar; pursued higher education in France and gained university degrees; joined the French Army during World War II and was imprisoned by the Nazis; entered Senegal politics in 1945 and was elected one of Senegal's Deputies in the French Constituent Assembly; founded the *Bloc Démocratique Sénégalais* in 1948 and his party gained Senegal's seats in the French Chamber of Deputies in 1951; founded the *Bloc Progrèssiste Sénégalais* in 1956 which later became the *Union Progrèssiste Sénégalaise* in 1958; as head of the Senegal government, helped found the Federation of Senegal and Mali in 1959; became President of Senegal when the Federation failed in 1960; a poet of consequence, Senghor has been a leading figure in the literary renaissance in West Africa.

NDABANINGI SITHOLE: born in 1920 in Southern Rhodesia; member of the Matabele tribe and son of a contractor; educated at missionary schools; gained a B.A. degree through correspondence course from the University of South Africa; attended the Newton Theological School, Andover, Massachusetts, for three years and was ordained in the Congregationalist Church; entered politics in 1959 as President of the African Teachers Association; joined the National Democratic Party of Southern Rhodesia in 1960 and was elected its Treasurer; founded a new political party in 1963—the Zimbabwe African National Union —at a time of growing governmental repression of African political activity.

SÉKOU TOURÉ: born in 1922 in Guinea; member of the Soussou tribe and son of a peasant farmer; educated at Muslim schools and at government schools but gained no higher education; entered politics in 1945 as Secretary-General of the Post and Telegraph Workers Union and helped organize the Federation of Workers' Union of Guinea; was a founding member of the RDA in 1946 and in 1952 became Secretary-General of the Guinea territorial branch, the *Parti Démocratique de Guinée;* elected Deputy in French National Assembly in 1956 by Guinea, and Mayor of Conakry, capital of Guinea; formed the inter-territorial General Union of African Workers in 1957 and exerted wide influence through it in French West Africa; refused to accept de Gaulle's arrangement for self-government in French West Africa in 1958, choosing independence instead; became President of Guinea in 1958.

FURTHER READINGS

Awolowo, Obafemi, Awo. New York: Cambridge University Press, 1960.

Azikiwe, Nnamdi, Zik: A Selection from the Speeches of Nnamdi Azikiwe. New York: Cambridge University Press, 1962.

Bello, Alhaji Sir Ahmadu, My Life. New York: Cambridge University Press, 1962.

Bohannan, Paul, Africa and Africans. Garden City, N.Y.: Doubleday & Company, Inc., 1964

Busia, K. A., The Challenge of Africa. New York: Frederick A. Praeger, Inc., 1962.

Davidson, Basil, The African Past: Chronicles from Antiquity to Modern Times. Boston: Little, Brown & Co., 1964.

Dia, Mamadou, The African Nations and World Solidarity. New York: Frederick A. Praeger, Inc., 1961.

Hodgkin, Thomas Lionel, Nigerian Perspectives. New York: Oxford University Press, Inc., 1960.

Kaunda, Kenneth, Zambia Shall Be Free. New York: Frederick A. Praeger, Inc., 1963.

Legum, Colin, Pan-Africanism. New York: Frederick A. Praeger, Inc., 1962.

McKay, Vernon, Africa in World Politics. New York: Harper & Row, Publishers, 1963.

Nkrumah, Kwame, I Speak of Freedom. New York: Frederick A. Praeger, Inc., 1961.

Oliver, Roland and J. D. Fage, A Short History of Africa. Baltimore: Penguin Books, Inc., 1962.

Quaison-Sackey, Alex, Africa Unbound. New York: Frederick A. Praeger, Inc., 1963.

Quigg, Philip W., Africa: A foreign Affairs Reader. New York: Frederick A. Praeger, Inc., 1964.

Wallerstein, Emanuel, Africa: The Politics of Independence. New York: Random House, Inc. (Vintage), 1961.